Learner Autonomy across Cultures

Learner Autonomy across Cultures

Language Education Perspectives

Edited by

David Palfreyman

and

Richard C. Smith

First published 2003 by
PALGRAVE MACMILLAN
Houndmills, Basingstoke, Hampshire RG21 6XS and
175 Fifth Avenue, New York, N.Y. 10010
Companies and representatives throughout the world

PALGRAVE MACMILLAN is the global academic imprint of the Palgrave Macmillan division of St. Martin's Press, LLC and of Palgrave Macmillan Ltd. Macmillan® is a registered trademark in the United States, United Kingdom and other countries. Palgrave is a registered trademark in the European Union and other countries.

ISBN 1–4039–0354–9 hardback

This book is printed on paper suitable for recycling and made from fully managed and sustained forest sources.

A catalogue record for this book is available from the British Library.

Library of Congress Cataloging-in-Publication Data

Learner autonomy across cultures: language education perspectives/edited by David Palfreyman and Richard C. Smith.
      p. cm.
   Includes bibliographical references and index.
   ISBN 1–4039–0354–9
      1. Language and languages—Study and teaching. 2. Autonomy.
3. Multicultural education. I. Palfreyman, David, 1964-
II. Smith, Richard C., 1961-

P53.L377 2003
418'.0071—dc21   2003046940

10 9 8 7 6 5 4 3 2 1
12 11 10 09 08 07 06 05 04 03

Printed and bound in Great Britain by
Antony Rowe Ltd, Chippenham and Eastbourne

Contents

List of Tables and Figures

Tables

Figures

Preface

One of the wonders of modern communication for us is that we have only ever met each other once, briefly, at the IATEFL conference in Dublin in 2000. An idea shared between us then has grown into this book, a labour of love for both of us during 2002 and the early part of 2003. In our e-mail negotiations across time-zones and, latterly, whizzing to one another across continents of developing versions of this book, we've both learned a lot from the process of collaborating, and have much to thank one another for. David is grateful to Richard for being such a stimulating, supportive, painstaking and polite collaborator (24 hours a day, to judge by the timing of some of his e-mails!); and Richard is grateful for David's up-to-date appreciation of the diverse meanings of culture, his enviable respect for deadlines, and his overall technical wizardry (especially impressed by his e-mail message from the back of a car in a sand-storm!). But we've learned even more from the contributions of the chapter authors, with whom we unfortunately have just as little day-to-day face-to-face contact. It says a lot for the power of a concept like 'autonomy' that it means so much to and can unite people from such a variety of contexts, and we sincerely appreciate the commitment of all the contributors to this project. We thank them for writing with such vision and honesty, for reading and commenting on each other's chapters, and for being willing to refine and re-refine their own chapters on the basis of feedback. Finally, on a more personal note, David would particularly like to thank Aslı and Aithy for their great patience and support; Richard especially thanks Dilek for her support and encouragement.

As we finished editing this book Iraq was invaded, despite popular protests world-wide. Autonomy across cultures, for us, became still more important to understand, support and strive for.

DAVID PALFREYMAN
RICHARD C. SMITH
April 2003

Notes on the Contributors

Naoko Aoki is an Associate Professor in the Graduate School of Letters at Osaka University, Japan, and works with in-service and pre-service teachers of Japanese as a second language. Her pedagogical and research interests include learner autonomy, teacher autonomy and life stories of second language teachers.

Phil Benson is an Assistant Professor at the English Centre, University of Hong Kong, where he teaches English and Applied Linguistics. His research interests include autonomy and language learning biography.

Alice Chik teaches English literature and English language in a Hong Kong secondary school. She is a doctoral student at the University of Hong Kong, where she is researching language learning biographies.

María de los Angeles Clemente is a Lecturer and Tutor at the Universidad Autónoma Benito Juárez de Oaxaca, Mexico, where she directs the MA programme in Applied Linguistics. She has carried out and published research into theoretical and practical issues connected with autonomy and self-direction, and teacher education and beliefs.

E.A. Gamini Fonseka is Senior Lecturer in English and Chair of Languages at the General Sir John Kotelawala Defence Academy, Sri Lanka. He has published song-based course books in English, companions to poetry, drama, prose, and fiction for young learners and teachers of literature, and a recent novel.

Xuesong Gao recently gained his MA from the University of Warwick, UK, and is now doing a complementary degree in Social and Cultural Anthropology at the Katholieke Universiteit Leuven, Belgium. He looks forward to integrating his anthropological training into his future ELT research in China.

Adrian Holliday is a Reader in Applied Linguistics at Canterbury Christ Church University College, UK. He directs the PhD programme in the Department of Language Studies, and is the Director of Research Degrees Training in the Graduate School. His and his students' research concerns social and cultural issues in TESOL.

Hye-Yeon Lim is a PhD candidate in Foreign Language Education at the University of Texas at Austin, USA. Her research interests focus on second/foreign language acquisition in the areas of cognition, emotion, teacher education, and computer-assisted language learning.

Bonny Norton is Associate Professor in the Department of Language and Literacy Education at the University of British Columbia, Canada. She has published widely in the areas of identity, language learning, and social change.

Rebecca L. Oxford is a Professor at the University of Maryland, USA, and the author of a number of books on language learning strategies, motivation, and instructional methodology. She has written over eighty articles and book chapters and has presented keynote addresses around the world.

David Palfreyman is based at Zayed University, Dubai, contributing to ESOL-related programmes in the English Language Centre and educational development in the Centre for Teaching, Learning and Assessment. His research interests include the roles of sociocultural context in language education, vocabulary curriculum development, and the use of information and communication technology.

Philip Riley is Professor of Ethnolinguistics at the University of Nancy 2, France, and Director of the CRAPEL (Centre de Recherches et d'Applications Pédagogiques en Langues). His main areas of interest include language didactics, bilingualism and inter-cultural communication.

Klaus Schwienhorst lectures in Applied Linguistics at the Centre for Language and Communication Studies, Trinity College Dublin, Ireland. His main research interests are learner autonomy, computer-assisted language learning, and the design, implementation, and evaluation of virtual environments for language learning.

Richard C. Smith is a Lecturer in ELT/Applied Linguistics in the Centre for English Language Teacher Education, University of Warwick, UK. Previously he taught for 13 years in Japan. His main research interests are in the fields of learner autonomy, teacher education, cultural studies in ELT and history of language teaching.

Kelleen Toohey is Professor of Education at Simon Fraser University in British Columbia, Canada. She is interested in sociocultural theory, second language learning and the education of minority language speakers.

Flávia Vieira is Assistant Professor at the Institute of Education and Psychology, University of Minho, Braga, Portugal. Her main research areas are pedagogy for autonomy in the foreign language classroom, reflective teacher development and pedagogical supervision.

Transcription Conventions

...	pause
[...]	omitted material
[ ]	added material
( )	non-verbal material

Introduction: Culture and Learner Autonomy

David Palfreyman

In one of the earliest works referring to 'learner autonomy', Holec (1981: 3) describes it as "the ability to take charge of one's own learning". The concept of learner autonomy, promoted by Holec and others in the context of language education in Europe, has in the last twenty years become influential as a goal in many parts of the world (Pemberton et al., 1996; Benson and Voller, 1997b; Cotterall and Crabbe, 1999; Sinclair et al., 2000; Little et al., 2000; Benson, 2001). Several arguments may be used in favour of developing autonomy in language learners: for example, that autonomy is a human right (e.g. Benson, 2000); that autonomous learning is more effective than other approaches to learning (e.g. Naiman et al., 1978); and that learners need to take charge of their own learning in order to make the most of available resources, especially outside the classroom (e.g. Waite, 1994).

On the other hand, the practical details of promoting learner autonomy in different contexts have been the subject of some debate (Benson and Voller, 1997b); and ideas about culture have an important part in these debates. A common way of interpreting 'culture' is to refer to national/ethnic cultures such as 'Chinese culture' or 'Western culture'. The idea of learner autonomy has been promoted largely by Western teachers and academics, and when attempts to implement it further afield have encountered difficulties, these are often seen as due to cultural differences between 'the West' and other communities. One important question is therefore whether the idea of learner autonomy is ethnocentric.

Another interpretation of 'culture' refers to values and customary ways of behaving in different kinds of community: for example, the culture of a classroom, or of a school. Learner autonomy has often been associated with particular kinds of *place*, especially self-access

1

centres; but Benson and Voller (1997b: 12) suggest that it would be better to focus on "the content of learning and relationships between students, teachers and institutions": aspects of education which relate to the *'cultures'* of particular kinds of learning environment.

A third use of the concept of culture relates to the learner in sociocultural context as opposed to the learner in isolation. Autonomy has sometimes been associated with a focus on the individual learner, with cultural context seen as either restricting individual freedom, or as irrelevant to it; and yet sociocultural context and collaboration with others are important features of education, and of our lives.

Learner Autonomy across Cultures examines these three issues in interrelation with each other, studying the ways in which culture and autonomy interact in a range of learning contexts. This collection brings together the focus on sociocultural context which has become influential in applied linguistics (Lantolf, 2000; Breen, 2001a) with global perspectives focusing on ethnic and other cultures (Coleman, 1996a; Oxford, 1996a; Canagarajah, 1999; Block and Cameron, 2002). The contributions to this book link current theory, data and practice in language education to address the following overall questions:

1. What might 'learner autonomy' mean in the context of particular cultures?
2. Is autonomy (in the sense that it has been interpreted in language education) an appropriate educational goal across cultures?
3. If so, how can autonomy be enhanced in a variety of cultural contexts?

This book encompasses autonomous learning activities in educational, work and other settings in Canada, Hong Kong, Japan, Korea, Mexico, Portugal, Sri Lanka, Turkey, the United Kingdom and the United States. However, in an era of increasing globalization cultural context cannot be defined only by location: the activities described additionally involve learners and educators of Chinese, German, Irish and Polish backgrounds; while one chapter studies a virtual environment which could not be said to exist in a single location. Furthermore, as described below, any national or ethnic cultures interact in all these contexts with the cultures of organizations, professions and even particular classrooms.

This introduction will discuss first the concept of 'learner autonomy' and how it has been interpreted in the literature on language education; and then current conceptions of culture and how they relate to learner autonomy. It will then relate the chapters in the book to this conceptual background, and conclude by considering the transferability of ideas from this volume to other contexts.

Learner autonomy in language education

Learner autonomy in language education is interpreted in various ways in the literature on the topic, and various terms ('learner autonomy', 'learner independence', 'self-direction', 'autonomous learning', 'independent learning') have been used to refer to similar concepts. Benson (1997) distinguishes three broad ways of talking about learner autonomy in language education:

- a 'technical' perspective, emphasizing skills or strategies for unsupervised learning: specific kinds of activity or process such as the 'metacognitive', 'cognitive', 'social' and other strategies identified by Oxford, 1990;
- a 'psychological' perspective, emphasizing broader attitudes and cognitive abilities which enable the learner to take responsibility for his/her own learning;
- a 'political' perspective, emphasizing empowerment or emancipation of learners by giving them control over the content and processes of their learning.

As well as these different views as to what constitutes learner autonomy, there are different interpretations of its scope. Some writers are concerned with the independent *use* of language; others focus on independent language *learning*; while others interpret learner autonomy more generally, in terms of being a fulfilled and/or effective *citizen* in a democratic society. Candlin (1997: xiii), for example, refers to "autonomy in language, learning, and, above all else, in living".

The variety in these views of autonomy is reflected in the range of possible approaches to fostering autonomy in learners – approaches which are often linked to broader ideas of learner-centred education (Tudor, 1997; Breen and Littlejohn, 2000). A technical perspective on autonomy may emphasize the development of strategies for effective learning: this approach is often referred to as 'learner training' (Oxford, 1990; Wenden, 1991). A psychological perspective suggests fostering more general mental dispositions and capacities (Holec, 1981; Karlsson et al., 1997); while a 'political' perspective highlights ways in which the learning context can be made more empowering for the learner (Little,

1996b; Benson, 1997). In addition, approaches to fostering autonomy may focus on technology or other resources; on the learner him/herself; and/or on decision-making in the learning context (Benson, 2001). Oxford's chapter in this book offers one way of reinterpreting and extending Benson's (1997) model, presenting an overall framework to facilitate comparison.

Independence from a teacher is often taken as an observable sign of autonomy, indeed the term 'independence' is often used as a synonym for autonomy. However, the individualistic connotations of this term have led some writers (e.g. Boud, 1981; Brookfield, 1986) to emphasize the value of *inter*dependence: the ability of learners to work together for mutual benefit, and to take shared responsibility for their learning. This is in accord with recent sociocultural theories in psychology (inspired by Vygotsky, 1978) and in the study of second language acquisition (Lantolf, 2000), whereby learning occurs through interaction between people and with 'mediating objects' such as learning materials, which 'scaffold' learning (Bruner, 1979). Although working with a teacher, for example, is sometimes seen as compromising autonomy, collabora- tion has come to be seen in a more positive light, as an important component of learner autonomy (cf. Dam, 1995): indeed, Boud (1981) sees interdependence as a more developed stage of autonomy than independence.

In the elaboration of concepts of autonomy in language education there has been a diffusion of ideas between work on teacher develop- ment and on learner autonomy. For example, the term 'learner develop- ment' (e.g. Smith, 1994; Benson, 2001; Wenden, 2002) (by analogy with 'teacher development') has been used as a catch-all term to refer to approaches for encouraging learner autonomy. On the other hand, teachers have started to be seen not only as having an important role in encouraging student autonomy, but also more explicitly as potentially autonomous learners and practitioners themselves (McGrath, 2000; Smith, 2000; Barfield et al., 2001; Vieira's and Aoki's chapters in this book).

While it is useful to distinguish the different perspectives mentioned above, studies included in this volume also highlight the fact that in real educational situations such perspectives are not black-and-white alter- natives, but may combine (or conflict) in various ways (Palfreyman, this volume). For example, attempts to train learners to use technological resources may be underwritten by more philosophical claims about empowering learners as citizens, or about the rights and responsibilities of the individual (cf. Holec, 1981). Candy (1991: 424) draws together some of the different aspects involved in the concept of 'self-direction', which he describes as

> at once a social and psychological construct, a philosophical ideal, and a literal impossibility; an external manifestation and an internal tendency; both the beginning and the end of lifelong learning; the foundation stone and the keystone of the learning society; a supplement to and a substitute for the formal education system; simultaneously process and product, a precondition and a purpose.

As Breen and Mann (1997) point out, this variety of interpretations may make the concept of autonomy more flexible and so more useful for theorizing pedagogy (cf. Oxford, Schwienhorst, this volume); and it is with respect to these multiple perspectives on autonomy that the place of cultural context and variation should be considered.

Culture and autonomy

Culture is important for language learning and education because these take place *within* a culture (or cultures), which influences their *form* (cf. contributions to Coleman, 1996a); and because culture is inextricable from language, and so constitutes part of the *content* of language learning and education (cf. Roberts et al., 2001). Like autonomy, 'culture' is a multifaceted and much-debated concept; indeed, it has been rejected entirely by some writers, partly because of its association with national stereotypes (Atkinson, 1999). Perspectives on culture parallel in some ways the perspectives on autonomy mentioned above. For example, Roberts et al. (ibid.) distinguish between behaviourist views of culture which focus on patterns of observable behaviour, cognitive views which see culture as located in the minds of individuals, symbolic views which see culture as a social system of signs, and ideological views which see culture as shaped by power. The chapters in *Learner Autonomy across Cultures* draw on concepts from a corresponding range of disciplines, including linguistics, psychology, anthropology and cultural studies, as well as language teaching and adult education.

One preliminary definition of culture is:

> the total shared way of life of a given people, comprising their modes of thinking, acting, and feeling, which are expressed, for instance, in religion, law, language, art, and custom, as well as in material products such as houses, clothes, and tools. (Kneller, 1965: 4)

This definition highlights some key aspects of the study of culture: an abstract *"way of life"*; a *community* ("a given people") who share this way of life; cultural *practices* and *institutions* (religion, language, etc.); and cultural *artifacts* (houses, clothes, etc.). Clearly, 'culture' in this definition refers to everyday life, not specifically to literature or music, for example. When these everyday practices, institutions and artifacts are related to learning, we can speak of a "culture of learning" (Cortazzi and Jin, 1998: 100), and even, more specifically, a "culture of learning language" (ibid.). Cortazzi and Jin focus on classroom-based schemata – "culturally based ideas about teaching and learning, about appropriate ways of participating in class, about whether and how much to ask questions" (ibid.); but the concept of a culture of learning can be applied also to learning outside the classroom, whether in a self-access centre (cf. Jones, 1995) or in more informal situations (cf. Diouf et al., 2000).

According to Kneller's definition of culture (above), a particular culture of learning would involve the following elements: a community which shares the culture (e.g. a society, or a classroom); learning practices which are recognized in this community (e.g. going to lessons, or practising language by talking to tourists), with their associated roles (e.g. teachers, learners, learning counsellors); institutions within this community which structure learning (e.g. schools, self-access centres or families); and tools and products which play some part in the community's learning practices (e.g. computers, textbooks or students' essays). We should recall, too, that culture consists not simply of behaviour, but of values and interpretations ("modes of thinking [...] and feeling") which underlie behaviour: we need to look beyond observable words and actions to the interpretations and values of the learners and teachers involved.

One issue in the study of culture is the *size*, or *range* of the culture to be examined. In work on learner autonomy, 'culture' has often been interpreted as national/ethnic culture. In the rest of this section, I will first examine how this view has influenced perspectives on autonomy; then outline some alternative interpretations of 'culture' and their implications for autonomy; and finally comment on the issue of how to research cultural aspects of autonomy.

National/ethnic culture

For educators, one major question is whether autonomy is appropriate as a universal goal, or whether it is less valid, less relevant or less effective in particular *national/ethnic cultures* (such as 'Japanese culture' or

'Arab culture'). On the one hand, Little and Dam (1998) describe a desire for autonomy as "one of the defining characteristics of humanity"; on the other, Riley's (1988) sketch of an "ethnography of autonomy" is more ambivalent: he discusses some prototypical single-nationality learner groups including Vietnamese and Danes, highlighting culturally related factors such as gregariousness, attitudes to authority and individual initiative, which seem to make the development of autonomy more or less successful.

The national cultural background of learners has often been viewed by teachers as a *hindrance* in promoting autonomy. Ho and Crookall (1995: 235), for example, refer to "[Chinese] cultural traits [...] that may be an obstacle to the promotion of autonomy". More recently, writers have suggested that the concept of autonomy itself may be ethnocentric and culturally inappropriate to non-Western cultures. Thus Jones (1995) talks in practical terms of a "retreat from autonomy" by Western educators in the face of authoritarian tendencies in Cambodian culture; while Pennycook (1997) criticizes learner autonomy on ideological grounds, as a neo-imperialist construct: "yet another version of the free, enlightened, liberal West bringing one more form of supposed emancipation to the unenlightened, traditional, backward and authoritarian classrooms of the world" (p. 43).

This issue is part of a wider concern in language education with national/ethnic cultures of learning, and with culturally appropriate methodology versus the inappropriate 'export' of language teaching and learning concepts from Western settings (Holliday, 1994; Canagarajah, 1999; Smith, this volume). Candlin (1997: xiii) distinguishes between the diversity of approaches to promoting learner autonomy on the one hand, and the universal validity of autonomy as a goal on the other: "the how [of autonomy] is locally constructable; the why inalienable". In constructing local approaches to autonomy, the "interpretation of the particular cultural, social, political and educational context in which [autonomy] is located" (Sinclair, 2000: 6) is crucial. Dickinson (1996) and Sinclair (1997) suggest that different interpretations of autonomy are appropriate in different cultural contexts. In terms of methodology, Little (1999a) gives the specific example of Tharp and Gallimore (1988), who identified ways in which adults praise child behaviour in Hawai'ian society, and used this knowledge to reinforce teaching methods to encourage autonomy. These issues are taken up in different ways by Holliday, Smith and Fonseka in this book.

'Culture' may be seen as an abstract feature of a large community (and so at odds with the notion of individual autonomy); but culture is also realized in the conduct of individual people. In an effort to link these two aspects of culture, one significant body of research on culture and autonomy has looked for correlations between individual learners' national/ethnic cultural background and individual variables which are related to autonomy – such as learning strategies, learning styles, beliefs about learning and motivation.

Oxford (1990) developed the Strategy Inventory for Language Learning (SILL), a questionnaire with which individual language learners can rate their own use of behavioural and cognitive strategies. Bedell and Oxford (1996) review a number of studies in a variety of contexts, using the SILL and other means, which suggest that learners from different cultural backgrounds may adopt different learning styles and strategies: for example, that compensation strategies such as guessing are used more by students in Mainland China than by students in Egypt or Puerto Rico. Other papers in Oxford (1996a) consider the effects of strategy training in different cultural contexts; Gao's chapter in this book provides a complementary perspective on these issues, since it investigates how living and studying in a foreign country can itself lead to changes in learning strategies.

It should, however, be remembered that learning strategies are only one aspect of learner autonomy, and the connection between strategy use and other aspects of autonomy tends to be indirect (Press, 1996). Studying underlying learner attitudes and beliefs is an alternative way to investigate links between culture and autonomy, with certain learner beliefs often being seen as more supportive than others to autonomy (Cotterall, 1995; Broady, 1996). Cotterall (1995), for example, analyses individual learners' reported beliefs about the role of the teacher (authoritative or facilitating); the role of feedback (valuing teacher feedback or self-monitoring); risk-taking; and self-confidence. She then interprets these beliefs in terms of "readiness for autonomy": for example, a student who states a belief that the teacher should be authoritative is taken to be less ready to be autonomous than one who expresses a preference for a facilitating teacher.

There is some evidence that such beliefs differ among societies. Hofstede (1986, 1990) categorizes countries according to social-psychological dimensions (based on individual beliefs expressed in questionnaires from IBM employees throughout the world). These dimensions include "individualism/collectivism"; "high/low power distance" (distinguishing hierarchical societies from egalitarian ones); and "high/low uncertainty avoidance" (distinguishing individuals/societies which try to minimize ambiguity as much as possible from those more tolerant of flexibility in interpretation). Hofstede uses these dimensions to analyse prototypical work and learning/teaching patterns in different societies; and they may also be linked to the development of autonomy.

Individualism involves loose ties between individuals and an emphasis on individual self-determination, and is often assumed to be more typically associated with autonomy (Dickinson, 1996; Esch, 1996); while collectivism, characterized by tight, regulating social networks of mutual obligation, is often seen as an obstacle to autonomy. On the other hand, collectivism may be seen as conducive to interdependent, group-based versions of autonomy (Littlewood, 1996a; Aoki and Smith, 1999; Sinclair, 2000) – although Sullivan (2000) points out that Western conceptions of groupwork can still be based on individualist assumptions.

With regard to power distance, Ho and Crookall (1995) cite respect for authority (that is, the teacher's) as a cultural obstacle to developing learner autonomy; and such an attitude is often seen as leading to 'passivity' (Pierson, 1996) in learners. Jones (1995) quotes Chandler's (1983: 88) description of teachers' and students' roles in Cambodia: "The teacher, like the parents, bestows, transmits and commands. The student, like the child, receives, accepts and obeys." Similarly, regarding uncertainty avoidance, Ho and Crookall (1995) emphasize the way Chinese students and teachers maintain face by avoiding any display of ignorance or doubt, especially on the part of the teacher, again using this as an example of a cultural obstacle to autonomy.

In terms of overall cultural values, Triandis (1995) contrasts hierarchical collectivism (seen by Helgesen (1998) as characteristic of Korean society), with more egalitarian collectivism (associated with Japanese society). Similarly, he contrasts the competitive individualism of which the USA is seen as prototypical with more egalitarian varieties of individualism, which are said to emphasize uniqueness. This last type of value system is particularly interesting in connection with autonomy, since it is seen as characteristic of Scandinavian countries, which have produced some seminal learner autonomy projects (e.g. Dam and Gabrielsen, 1988; Karlsson, Kjisik and Nordlund, 1997), and are often seen as particularly supportive of autonomy (Riley, 1988; cf. Brockett and Hiemstra (1991: 184–5) for adult education).

Another psychological variable sometimes linked to both autonomy and culture is motivation. Autonomy tends to be associated with intrinsic motivation (Dickinson, 1995; Ushioda, 1996; van Lier, 1996); but motivation in general is framed by culture, since what is motivating for an individual learner is partly a function of what is valued in his/her society (e.g. marriageability for young Jordanian women – Kaylani,

1996). Watkins (1996) uses the concept of 'locus of control' (who or what learners see as controlling their learning) to analyse the motivation and performance of Chinese learners in Western education systems; similarly, Littlewood (1996a) sees the 'Confucian' emphasis on effort and the collective (rather than on talent and individual gain) as supporting learner autonomy in language learning.

As Smith (1997) points out, the literature described above has tended to assume that culture is national and monolithic, leading to generalizations which may not be easy to apply in particular learning situations. One example of this is the issue of 'what culture' a particular learner comes from, which is more complex than it may seem. For instance, Press (1996), in her study of ethnicity and learner autonomy among British learners of various foreign languages, asked respondents to describe their own ethnicity. This open question elicited an unexpected variety of responses such as 'London Irish' or 'none'; and Press states that for statistical purposes she was obliged to collapse the elicited descriptions under general terms such as 'Asian' (including students of Chinese, Indian, Japanese and Pakistani backgrounds). In contrast to this kind of aggregation, the contributions in this volume tend to take a more particularist approach to cultural background.

Indeed, the kind of generalizations suggested by aggregate studies tend to become less black-and-white under closer examination. To take one example, Dore and Sako (1989: 7–8), discussing the Japanese education system – often represented in the West as producing passive students – describe the typical role of the Japanese university student as a "receptacle into which knowledge and ideas have to be poured" (a standard 'teacher-dependent' metaphor). However, they then add that "a lot of the pouring has to be done by the student himself, sitting down with his books in private study: self-reliance and initiative are required". This suggests that 'Japanese-ness' is not a single quality: Japanese students in the homework situation seem more autonomous than Japanese students in the classroom situation (cf. Holliday, this volume).

There are other reasons why generalizations about cultural groups can be misleading. Stereotypes about particular groups (including stereotypes with positive connotations, and including people's idealized conception of their own traditions) may not correspond to the actual modern 'vernacular' culture (Watkins and Biggs, 1996); and people's behaviour, in turn, may not match in a straightforward way their beliefs. For example, Littlewood (2000) discusses students' stated beliefs elicited by a questionnaire, which seem to contradict common stereotypes (and observations) of East Asian students as passive and dependent on authority.

Cultures of learning may also be misinterpreted by outside commentators – an issue explored by Holliday in this book. For various reasons, East Asian learners have been a focus of attention in the study of international language education, and one example of this is the "paradox of the Chinese learner" (Watkins and Biggs, 1996: 2): that students of Chinese background seem to use learning approaches (such as memorization) which are frowned upon in progressive Western circles, and yet achieve higher than average academic success. However, Watkins and Biggs suggest that this paradox is actually produced by commentators imposing their own understanding of these students' strategies; and that memorization in Chinese culture should be understood as an effective learning strategy rather than as a sign of unthinking repetition.

Non-ethnic cultures

Generalizations about national/ethnic groups, although useful as heuristics, are insufficient, and the conception of culture described above needs to be expanded. The notion of 'subcultures' is one way to refine the concept. For example, Horwitz (1999) notes that in studies of learner beliefs using the Beliefs About Language Learning Inventory (BALLI), American learners of Japanese showed a different pattern of responses from American learners of other languages such as French: that is, beliefs about learning are linked not simply to a particular national group, but to subgroups within it. This may indicate that learners with certain kinds of belief about language learning are attracted to studying certain languages, and/or that the way each language is taught encourages a certain set of beliefs.

The particular circumstances of language learning may be as important as more general cultural features of a society. Pierson (1996) claims that it is Hong Kong's post-colonial education system, rather than innate 'Chinese' qualities, which militate against learner autonomy in schools there (cf. Littlewood, 2000) – a point developed by Benson, Chik and Lim in this book. On a more positive note, Legutke and Thomas (1991) point out that the flexibility allowed to teachers in Danish educational institutions is one of the facilitating factors in Dam's pioneering work on learner autonomy.

Thus, one of the major contributions of this book to the study of autonomy and culture is that it unpicks the traditional tie between culture and nation: 'culture' is used more generally to refer to a value system current in a particular group or setting. It is in this sense that one can speak of the culture of a classroom (Breen, 1985), or the culture of a school. These 'small cultures' (Holliday, 1999a) may be influenced by national/ethnic value systems, but are not simply an extension of them; and they have their own implications for autonomy.

Breen (2001b) discusses the context of language learning in terms of the interactional context, the classroom context and wider communities; while Tudor (1997) uses a similar model to analyse the context for learner-centred language education. The kinds of culture likely to influence autonomous learning include some larger and relatively fixed ones, such as:

- educational and academic cultures (Coleman, 1987; Benson, 1994; contributions to Coleman, 1996a; Benson, Chik and Lim, and Vieira, this volume);
- professional cultures of language teaching (Holliday, 1994; Pennycook, 1994; Canagarajah, 1999; Holliday, this volume).
- organizational cultures (Wright, 1994; Palfreyman, this volume).
- Social class- or gender-associated cultures (Willis, 1977; Gilligan, 1986; Aoki, this volume).

Cultures at the smaller end of the scale, on the other hand, seem more amenable to change, and such change may be taken as an educational goal by teachers, learning counsellors or whole institutions. Several of the chapters in this book (particularly Smith's, Fonseka's and Vieira's) involve more or less explicit attempts to develop a learning environment with a new kind of 'culture' (cf. Dam, 1995; Breen and Mann, 1997).

Although Breen (2001b) uses an 'onion-skin' model for these different features of context, with each nested within the next, Holliday (1994) notes that cultures may also cut across each other. For example, a Japanese and an Algerian teacher of English may share some elements of a professional culture, but not a national/ethnic one. Cultural values interact (without necessarily conflicting) within any given learning context, and even within individuals – for example in work and personal life (Kağıtçıbaşı, 1988); and the chapter by Benson, Chik and Lim in this volume illustrates how learners can negotiate between these various aspects of their identity in pursuit of autonomy.

In anthropology, the kind of consensus implied by Kneller's definition of culture cited above has given way to an understanding that cultural meanings are by no means necessarily shared by all members of a society. In analysing whether 'a culture' appears to support or hinder autonomy in a group of learners, Cowan's (1990: 11) questions are pertinent: "Is [the culture] actually shared? To what extent? By whom? How does it come to be shared?" (cf. also Toohey and Norton, this volume). This leads us to the third interpretation of culture used in this book, which relates to specific situations and processes in which cultural meanings are negotiated.

Sociocultural context

The concept of 'culture' has recently appeared in debates on language learning in sociocultural and cultural-historical approaches to second language acquisition theory (e.g. Lantolf, 2000; Norton, 2000). The appreciation of 'sociocultural context' in these approaches is linked to developments in psychology (e.g. Vygotsky, 1978) and the idea of situated learning (Lave and Wenger, 1991). From this point of view, "culture and context are indivisible" (Breen, 2001c: 177), and *all* learning is 'cultural', since it involves interacting with one's context (including objects, as well as other people and their words and ideas) in order to develop meanings. This interpretation of culture in relation to autonomy problematizes the notion of any learner being 'independent' in the sense of *doing without* others (Schwienhorst, this volume). It also tends to focus on universal social-psychological processes rather than on particular national, ethnic or other group characteristics (Oxford, this volume); although Riley's chapter in this book explores how some ethnic cultural features (notably different conceptions of the person) might influence interaction between learners and educators wishing to promote autonomy.

Sociocultural approaches provide valuable concepts for understanding how the behaviour, attitudes and motivation of individuals interact with cultural meanings and social interests in particular learning situations. Roebuck (2000), for example, highlights the difference between the potential offered by the 'objective' context (e.g. a self-access environment or a classroom task), and the ways in which this context is interpreted by different individuals in terms of their background experience. One implication of this is that learners may *find* or *construct* opportunities for autonomy in unlikely places.

A national/ethnic or other culture provides *orientation points* for such processes of interpretation. Swidler (1986) conceptualizes culture as a resource: a 'toolkit' of symbols, stories, rituals and worldviews used to deal with situations and organize everyday life. Geertz (1973) interprets cultural contact not as a clash of systems, but as a shift in the ways in which the 'toolkit' is used – as "something which happens when [cultural] forms are pressed by unusual situations or unusual intentions to operate in unusual ways" (p. 28) – as, for example, in Coleman's (1987) successful use of the local 'festival' genre to stimulate autonomy in traditionally teacher-centred classrooms.

The 'toolkit' metaphor implies that the cultural meanings available to an individual learner or teacher are constrained by their background; but at the same time that the individual has leeway in how s/he uses these cultural resources in particular situations. Derné (1994), for example, discussing motivation in different societies, shows how individuals may draw on apparently opposing cultural values in order to support their own behaviour or intentions. Individual agency is often assumed in the literature on autonomy to be at odds with cultural background; but sociocultural perspectives, as illustrated in this book, show how the two can work together as individuals use or reject the opportunities (or 'affordances') offered by their learning context, to negotiate their identity vis-à-vis the real, virtual or 'imagined' communities to which they belong and/or wish to belong (cf. Toohey and Norton, this volume). This is a two-way process: Gao (this volume) discusses how a change of context may affect learners' beliefs about learning, while the chapter by Benson, Chik and Lim examines how beliefs may lead to a change in context.

Critical perspectives

Anthropological conceptualizations of culture in recent years (e.g. Said, 1978; Asad, 1979; Wright, 1994), as well as critical work in linguistics (e.g. Chouliaraki and Fairclough, 1999) and education (e.g. Giroux, 1983) have tended to highlight issues of power, access and ideology. The meanings surrounding learning, autonomy and culture are shaped by the interests of those involved and by power relations, whether at the societal or the classroom level. To take one classroom example, Chick (1996) shows how teacher and students in a Black South African classroom appear to collude in concealing how little learning is going on. Brookfield (1993) and Littlejohn (1997) point out that practices which seem to foster autonomy may be controlling at a deeper level.

Benson (1997) proposes a critical, 'political' version of autonomy in language learning, more congruent with the concept of autonomy in adult education: helping students "to view knowledge and truth as contextual, to see value frameworks as cultural constructs, and to appreciate that they can act on their world individually or collectively and that they can transform it" (Brookfield, 1985: 10). This version of autonomy emphasizes both awareness of the sociocultural context and transformation of the context; and it gives a more central position to culture than other versions. Pennycook (1997) sees awareness of cultural alternatives as central to autonomy, while Lamb (2000) focuses on the steps by which alienated learners can be encouraged to engage with learning in a sociocultural context, by developing a 'voice' with respect to that context.

This approach to learner autonomy in language education has so far been largely programmatic rather than empirically based; and as with other approaches to autonomy there are reservations about its appropriacy across contexts, lest it be seen as impractical and/or patronizing (Breen and Mann, 1997; cf. Jay and Graff's (1995) critique of critical pedagogy in general). However, Vieira's and Aoki's chapters in this book illustrate how a critical approach can be applied (in both cases, note, by relative cultural 'insiders') to teacher autonomy; while the chapter by Benson, Chik and Lim shows the potential for critical exploration of language learners' personal histories.

A critical approach to culture is also apparent in recent discussion of research in language education: Breen (2001b), for example, questions the cultural basis of constructs which are used by researchers to analyse learning, and in the following section I will review this issue.

Methods of research and analysis

Effective survey methods, as used in the SILL studies in Oxford (1996a), can produce substantial quantities of data which are amenable to statistical analysis. On the other hand, as noted earlier in relation to Press's (1996) study, questionnaires may not capture significant features of context. Becker (1998) notes how the same informants may give systematically different responses to the same questions, depending on whether they complete the questionnaire at work or at home; indeed, the apparent objectivity of questionnaire data may give the impression that research questions have been answered when they are in fact only just beginning to be conceptualized.

Horwitz (1999) reviews a number of studies using the BALLI questionnaire, to try and identify confirmed hypotheses about the beliefs of particular groups who share a 'cultural background' (i.e. nationality or parent nationality). She states that although there are visible tendencies, "even after examining BALLI responses of several groups of learners on a large sample of items, clear-cut conclusions do not seem possible" (p. 574). She notes that aggregating questionnaire responses obscures individual variation: in the studies reviewed there were often quite significant numbers of respondents who differed in their expressed beliefs from the most common response in their ethnic group. She also notes that BALLI, like any closed-response questionnaire, relies on concepts which are inputted by the questionnaire writers; although in the case of the BALLI these writers came from various ethnic backgrounds, the questionnaire is designed to elicit commonly held beliefs rather than ones which are particular to certain informants or groups.

Some chapters in this book (e.g. Clemente's) refer to quantitative data, but this is linked with qualitative data concerning the interpretations of individual learners and educators. Several chapters (e.g. those by Benson, Chik and Lim, and Palfreyman) attempt to provide "thick descriptions" (Geertz, 1973) of individual cases of autonomy, relating observable data to the meanings which these have for participants in the social setting. This approach aims primarily to *interpret* social life rather than to *predict*: Geertz (p. 14) warns that

> Culture is not a power, something to which social events, behaviours, institutions or processes can be causally attributed; it is a context, something within which they can be intelligibly [...] described.

This tentative approach contrasts with the claims to predictive validity which are sometimes implicit in writing on learner autonomy and culture.

Most of the chapters focus in depth on particular cases (on particular individuals, or particular classrooms); but in each case they examine how the wider cultural context is critical in offering various kinds of constraints or opportunities for learner autonomy. Running through the book there is a concern to avoid taking for granted the researcher's or practitioner's own cultural background and values, and to develop a 'sociological imagination' (Holliday, 1996a): an understanding of connections between people's individual experiences and actions, and the sociocultural contexts which frame them. In adopting this perspective, the authors often use their position *between* cultures to interpret how autonomy fits into cultural settings where they are both insiders and outsiders (Atkinson, 1999).

The chapters in this book

The ordering of the chapters in this book deliberately reflects the editors' beliefs that theory about culture and autonomy should be grounded in "thick description" (Geertz, 1973), and that the experiences of learners are an appropriate starting point for such theorizing – beliefs supported by contributions to a recent international symposium on learner autonomy (Benson, 2002; Shaw, 2002), which emphasized the need to balance teachers' perspectives with those of learners.

The first three chapters deal with particular learners and particular settings, examining from different viewpoints how learners exercise their autonomy in responding to the contexts within which they learn. Benson, Chik and Lim use retrospective autobiographical accounts to challenge stereotypes of 'dependent' Asian learners. They analyse the sociocultural contexts within which two of the authors learned English, and the ways in which they actively reinterpreted and even physically changed context, in order to achieve learning goals. These goals were developed through ongoing reflection on experience in relation to both individual and cultural factors. Gao's chapter examines in detail how learning strategies may change in another situation where learners enter a culturally different setting, in this case Chinese students moving to the United Kingdom for university studies. He discusses learner and contextual factors, and the effects which these seem to have had on the learners' strategies. Toohey and Norton then develop this focus on learners' interaction with their environment, examining in detail specific learning contexts in and around a workplace and a kindergarten. Using interview and observation data, they contrast the ways in which two effective learners were "empowered or depowered [*sic*], motivated or demotivated to maximize their learning strategies within particular contexts" (Pollard and Filer, 1999: 158); and they highlight the importance of both individual agency and community norms in supporting or thwarting language learning.

The three chapters which follow offer theoretical contributions to debates on culture and autonomy. Oxford extends Benson's (1997) model of learner autonomy to include sociocultural perspectives of the type proposed by Toohey and Norton; and she discusses the role accorded by different perspectives to the key concepts of context, agency, motivation and learning strategies. She suggests that a combination of these different perspectives is the most fruitful way forward for research on culture and autonomy. Riley examines the social construction of individual identity, reviewing relevant concepts from anthropology and linguistics and the possible implications of these for learner autonomy and for self-access counselling in particular. Holliday, on the other hand, considers the ideological implications of the way learner autonomy and culture are constructed in TESOL discourse – including in critical interpretations of autonomy. He suggests a more radical perspective on culture and autonomy, based in learners' social reality, and on an expectation that autonomy in some form is potentially present in all situations.

Following this section are three chapters which deal with particular pedagogical interventions aiming to make use of the opportunities for autonomy available in particular contexts. Smith describes the development of an English course in a Japanese university, in which students were involved in a process of classroom culture change, building on a cycle of group activity and reflection. As in Holliday's chapter, the assumption is that students need to be enabled in appropriate ways to exercise and develop an autonomy which they already possess, rather than being 'trained' into a new way of learning. Fonseka discusses a learning context quite different from others described in this book, in that the resources available (both material and cultural) do not appear to support autonomy as normally envisaged. However, he shows how available means and a blend of new and familiar genres can be used to promote collaborative autonomy in such an environment. The context described by Schwienhorst is also unique in this book, consisting of a collaborative, bilingual learning project in a virtual environment (MOO) where learners can develop autonomy at the individual and social level, but also crucially at an exploratory experimental level. In this chapter culture is taken as an aspect of content, as learners take advantage of the opportunities and navigate the constraints of the online medium to explore each other's language and culture.

The final section of the book shifts the focus from learners and classrooms to teachers and organizational contexts. Palfreyman's chapter, like Holliday's, examines the construction of autonomy by TESOL professionals. He uses interviews with curriculum planners and others in positions of organizational responsibility, together with official documents relating to autonomy, to trace how autonomy is represented in different ways within a single organization, and how these representations are influenced by the interests of the organization. Clemente analyses specific interactions between self-access counsellors and learners in a Mexican university self-access centre, in terms both of discourse and of participants' post-session commentaries on the interaction. She highlights the social aspects of the counselling session, contrasting participants' contributions and interpretations, and linking these also to the wider context of the self-access centre and the university. The final two chapters share a concern with developing autonomy in teachers, as well as sharing a critical-emancipatory interpretation of autonomy.

Vieira describes a teacher development initiative in Portugal which uses reflection and action research to link learner and teacher autonomy, while working with the constraints of an education system in which such aims have not previously been prominent. Aoki, like Benson, Chik and Lim, focuses on the development of an individual learner: a teacher of Japanese as a foreign language. She draws on feminist theory to deconstruct gendered representations of teachers and their knowledge, and to illustrate a process by which she and the teacher attempted to redefine and exercise the teacher's own autonomy vis-à-vis her professional development.

As noted earlier, most of the chapters in this book study particular local contexts and particular cases, which may resemble to varying degrees situations familiar to the reader. Our hope is that readers will be able to relate insights from these chapters to their own learning or teaching settings; and the contributors have tried to facilitate this by relating specific cases to their wider context, and by describing the context explicitly enough to help readers make connections with their own situations. Another means for supporting this is the inclusion of reflection/discussion questions at the end of each chapter. These are intended for individuals or groups of readers to use as a stimulus for reflection on their own experiences and their own situations.

We hope that this book will contribute to further research and practice relating to learner autonomy in language education. The contributors to this book re-examine assumptions and definitions in the field which are often taken for granted, clarify concepts which are still developing, and raise issues for future exploration in the light of work in other disciplines. Most of all, they lay the groundwork for the development of locally appropriate practices to foster learner autonomy, informed both by local knowledge and by the challenge of new experiences and understandings.

Acknowledgement

I am grateful to Naoko Aoki, Stephen Bax, Jay Bidal, Gökçe Kaşıkçı, Jo Mynard and Richard Smith for their comments on previous drafts of this introduction.

Part I
Autonomous Learners

1

Becoming Autonomous in an Asian Context: Autonomy as a Sociocultural Process

Phil Benson, Alice Chik and Hye-Yeon Lim

Introduction

Since the publication of Riley's (1988) seminal paper on the "ethnography of autonomy", the discussion on autonomy and culture has tended to focus on the relevance of the 'Western' idea of autonomy to learners from 'non-Western' cultural backgrounds. Discussion of this question has in turn been dominated by what Smith (2001: 70) has called "an ongoing debate regarding the validity of learner autonomy in Asian settings". In the course of this debate, a particular image of the Asian learner has emerged – that of an individual whose learning styles and preferences are largely conditioned by values of collectivism, conformity and respect for authority inculcated through early experiences at school and in the family. In the light of this image of the Asian learner, contributors to the debate have questioned the cultural appropriateness of the emphasis on *individual* development in the Western idea of autonomy in Asian settings, leading to proposals for approaches to autonomy based more upon the idea of 'autonomous interdependence'.

The debate on autonomy in Asia has thus been motivated by a concern for cultural sensitivity in the implementation of an educational idea originally developed in a Western cultural context. In our view, however, this concern may be problematic to the extent that it involves a view of the Asian learner developed in the same Western cultural context. As Ram (2002: 35) points out, "the contrast between the Western 'individual' and the non-Western 'collectivity' is just one of the many forms of the opposition between the modern and non-modern which underlie the basis of social theory's constructions of difference". In the context of this opposition, she argues, "quests for individual autonomy" in non-Western settings are easily redefined as instances of an illegitimate "Western consciousness" (p. 36). In other words, the fact that Western social theory has captured the notion of individuality for itself may lead us towards the paradoxical view that Asian learners who succeed in developing individual autonomy are deviating from the norm, or not really 'Asian' at all.

The Western view of Asian culture as 'collectivist' also implies a conception of membership based on conformity and respect for authority, from which the idea of individuality is excluded almost by definition. Asian learners are, therefore, often unjustifiably viewed as *products* of their cultural backgrounds in a way that learners from more 'individualist' Western cultures are not. From this perspective, both the sense in which language learners "actively engage in constructing the terms and conditions of their own learning" (Lantolf and Pavlenko, 2001: 145) and the sense in which language learning involves the construction of new, and often highly individual, cultural identities through the medium of the target language tend to be neglected when Asian learners are being considered.

Our argument in this chapter is, therefore, that we need to recognize the sense in which the development of autonomy forms part of the sociocultural process of second language learning for many Asian learners. As Smith (2001: 73) has argued, "what may be most called for at this point in the 'autonomy in Asia' debate are reports of practice which offer new insights not tied to *a priori* generalizations". In particular, we believe that it is important to examine in more detail the sense in which Asian cultural backgrounds influence individual learners and how this influence may be modified by their ongoing engagement with target language cultures. We also believe that it is important to examine how notions of *individual* autonomy may become relevant to Asian learners as their learning progresses over time.

Our approach to these issues is based on recent research into adult second language users' stories of their language learning. As Pavlenko and Lantolf (2000: 174) have argued, such stories can offer particular insights into the "experiences of people who have both physically and symbolically crossed the border [...] between one way of being and another and perceive themselves as becoming someone other than who they were before". The stories that we will discuss in this chapter belong to two of its authors (Alice Chik and Hye-Yeon Lim) – both adult Asian users of English as a second language who have crossed the kinds of borders that Pavlenko and Lantolf refer to. These stories will first be re-told by the third author (Phil Benson), using extracts from the original written versions. This will be followed by Hye-Yeon's and Alice's reflections on these re-tellings of their stories and a conclusion in which their implications for the debate on autonomy in Asia will be discussed by Phil.

Hye-Yeon's story

I believed that I could only overcome the limits of my Korean educational experience by learning in the target culture.

Hye-Yeon was born in Korea, where she studied English at secondary school and university and worked as an English teacher. After obtaining a Master's degree in Linguistics in Korea she moved to the United States, where she is now a doctoral student in foreign language education at the University of Texas at Austin. Hye-Yeon's story is told in more detail in Lim (2002), where it forms the basis of a discussion of motivational theory.

Hye-Yeon divides her story into three phases, each characterized by a particular environment and mode of learning:

Overall, my English learning environments can be separated into three major phases: formal/school, informal/self-instructional and natural learning environments. The formal learning environment corresponds to the six-year education period in secondary school. The informal/self-instructional learning environment includes the times that I attended a language institute and taught myself English through self-study. It also includes the time that I spent teaching English. The institute learning experience is included in the self-instructional environment because I was the one who chose the institute and could stop at any time I desired to do so. Finally, the natural learning environment is the time that I have been immersed in the target language country. These learning environments have gradually moved from a relatively structured to a more naturalistic environment in which I have more control.

The summary of her story below is divided into the same three phases.

The formal learning environment

Hye-Yeon begins her story by observing that she was motivated to learn English before she began studying it at school. At the age of ten or eleven, she writes,

> I saw an English language show on the television. I was captured by those strange and alien sounds. I wanted to know what those people were talking about. I confess I thought it would be very special to be able to use those words in my own life. So the spark of curiosity was lit.

When she began studying English at middle school a couple of years later, then, she already had "a great curiosity, fondness, and positive orientation to the people who spoke the language". A "belief that English speakers came from an advanced country and that learning English would help me to be like them motivated me to study hard". Hye-Yeon's early experiences of learning English in secondary school did little, however, to support this motivation and in her account of these years she refers to two aspects of her experience that were particular to the Korean educational system.

Hye-Yeon first describes how English classes involved memorizing passages of English and reciting them in front of the class. Initially this was tolerable, but, as time went by, the passages became longer and longer and memorization became a source of frustration:

> I remember one day that I had to memorize a three-page section about the four seasons in Korea. I spent at least six hours memorizing paragraphs about spring, summer, and fall. I was too exhausted to continue to memorize the last paragraph about winter.

She also felt that her experiences of memorization influenced her enthusiasm for learning English at that time:

> I thought that the only way to learn this new language was to memorize every single sentence in the universe. Koreans value memorizing and this is a common feature of our educational process. So, it was normal to think that this strategy was applicable to English as well. However, I am not good at memorizing and so my enthusiasm for learning diminished somewhat at this time. I became ever more frustrated.

In other words, the emphasis on memorization influenced her approach to learning, but not in the sense that it became her preferred learning style. In interaction with her existing motivation, it simply reduced her enthusiasm for learning English. Hye-Yeon describes, however, how she overcame this by 'partitioning' her goals:

> I was not good at memorizing but believed that memorizing was necessary to learn English to obtain good grades. However, since grades were not my focus, memorization may have had less of a negative effect on me. Although I may not have been able to articulate it at the time, or even recognize it, memorizing was not central to meeting my main goal – talking with and understanding people. It seems likely that I partitioned language learning goals at this point – one for me and what started my interest and the other for the formal demands of the school.

"I wonder if I would have been as persistent", she says, "had I not been able to separate good grades from learning English."

Hye-Yeon also discusses the emphasis on effort in the achievement of good grades as a feature of the Korean school system:

> The goal of learning English was submerged for a while as I attempted to be a successful student. English became no different for me than math or social studies. It simply became a grade. As Koreans, we believe that effort determines grades so there was no conflict for me here. I believed that good grades were within my control so I continued to persist in my efforts despite the fact that I knew getting good grades was not really related to achieving my ultimate goal.

By the later stages of her secondary school career, therefore, Hye-Yeon appears on the surface to be a typical 'product' of her cultural background: a learner who applied effort to the task of memorization in pursuit of good grades. Underlying this appearance, however, we can also see a developing sense of autonomy – specifically, a sense that she had her own individual goals in learning English.

Summing up her experience of secondary school learning, Hye-Yeon writes:

> It is difficult to say for sure, but my experience suggests that it is central that a learner discover his own goals and that they not be given to him by someone or something else. It was my belief that I wanted to do something for myself that allowed me to persist. Both success at school and learning English were important for me. Yet I was able to separate these goals and this separation allowed me to persist and become more successful at both tasks.

At this stage in her learning, therefore, Hye-Yeon had already developed both a certain psychological distance from her cultural background, and an awareness of her individuality. Indeed, it was perhaps her feeling that she "wanted to do something for [her]self" that allowed her to make sense of her cultural background and to maintain her personal goal of learning English in order to communicate in the face of educational experiences that did not value this goal as highly as she did.

The informal/self-instructional environment

Hye-Yeon went on to university, where she chose to study English and where, she writes, she was "happy to regain control" of her learning:

> I started trying new things that I thought I would enjoy more for improving my English. I wrote articles in English as a campus reporter, read books and magazines, listened to English pop music, and watched Hollywood and educational programs on TV. I enjoyed what I was doing. I did not know the best way to improve listening and speaking but I liked trying different things and exploring how they worked for me.

The university environment gave her both the opportunity and time to create and explore new contexts for learning that had been unavailable at school. It was also at this time that Hye-Yeon first came into contact with native speakers of English as a result of a decision to attend classes at a private language institute. "Because I had never had a chance to speak with native speakers of English", she explains, "I decided to attend an institute with English classes taught by English speakers." Hye-Yeon describes this as an experience of self-instruction, "because I was the one who chose the institute and could stop at any time had I desired to do so".

The experience proved frustrating, however, because of the teachers' focus on correct pronunciation and error correction:

> I spent about two years in the one-year program because I had to repeat levels several times. I experienced a great deal of frustration while going through that system. I experienced constant failure at communication tasks.

The problem was perhaps that, although the teachers were native speakers, they were not trained teachers and the methods they used were strongly influenced by the Korean school system:

> I was told that perfect pronunciation and sentence structure were essential to being fluent. The same message that I had learned in school was being repeated – perfection.

Hye-Yeon also responded to her frustration by relying on the qualities that had got her through the experience of school:

> Again, I believe that I became instrumentally motivated. I simply wanted to graduate from this institute. This goal became proximal. Additionally, I believed what the instructors were telling me (i.e., that perfect pronunciation was central). [...] So, I persisted in my efforts at this institute to meet my more proximal goal.

One of the consequences of this experience, however, was a temporary sense that she was losing the control over her learning that she had so recently gained:

> While many people acknowledged my high level of proficiency, I was secretly thinking that I was far from my goal and experienced the fear that I might not be able to reach my life's goal because I had not learned the target language in the target culture.

It is significant, then, that this is the first time Hye-Yeon mentions the possibility of learning English overseas. Her frustrations at the language institute, it seems, were related to a dissonance, in the context of her goal, between the opportunity to meet native speakers of English and their teaching methods. This dissonance could only be resolved through the construction of new contexts for her learning, in which she would be able to interact with native speakers beyond the constraints of her background culture.

Hye-Yeon's sense of control was restored first by her experience of working alongside native speakers of English in a Korean school and later by a trip to Australia. In both of these contexts she found that she could communicate with few problems and that she was able to make friends easily with English speakers.

> I started to believe that my English must not be so bad and I didn't have to produce perfect pronunciation and sentences to be understood. Because I no longer believed that perfection was necessary to

communicate, and because I had shown that I could communicate, I now regained control over my own learning.

It is at this point in her story that Hye-Yeon writes: "I believed that I could only overcome the limits of my Korean educational experience by learning in the target culture." Her fear that she would be unable to reach her goal because she had not learned English in the target culture was now replaced by a belief that she would be able to reach this goal by making learning in the target culture the next phase in her learning.

The natural learning environment

Hye-Yeon does not discuss her experiences in the United States in detail. It seems, however, that she was quickly able to deal with the problems that Asian students typically experience when they travel overseas after many years of learning English at home. She writes, for example, of the difficulties encountered in understanding colloquial idioms, cultural references and different varieties of English. In dealing with these difficulties Hye-Yeon was clearly helped by the sense of control that she had developed over her many years of learning English in Korean contexts:

> I discovered that I needed to understand culture and context in a more extensive way. I knew that this was a matter of exposure and time. Both were controllable so I believed that, over time, I would acquire greater language skills.

It is also clear, however, that she was helped by the fact that she was now very close to realizing a goal that had been with her from the outset of her learning:

> I was where I thought a foreign language should be learned: the target culture. Everything that I encountered had to be done in English. I had to use English in daily life: going shopping, paying bills, seeing doctors, calling insurance companies, and so on.

Here, it is important to bear in mind that, for many Asian students, the experience of studying overseas can be traumatic rather than pleasurable. It can also be an experience of significantly failing to communicate with native speakers in everyday contexts. How important was it then, in Hye-Yeon's case, that her being in the overseas context was under her own control?

Alice's story

On a personal level, as a language learner, learning English was more than merely learning a language. It was my own journey to construct individuality.

Alice was born in Hong Kong and began learning English at home as an infant under the guidance of her parents (who were born in Shanghai). Like most Hong Kong students, she had English classes at kindergarten, primary school and secondary school, but unlike most, she also took English literature courses at secondary level. Alice then went to the United States to study Business Administration at the University of Texas at Austin, and after graduation she worked in an investment bank in Austin for eight months. She then returned to Hong Kong, where she has worked as a secondary school English teacher for eight years. For much of this time she has also been studying part-time at the University of Hong Kong, where she has obtained a postgraduate teaching qualification in English and an MA in Applied Linguistics and is now a doctoral student. Alice's story was written for this chapter and is previously unpublished.

Early learning

Alice's early learning of English was influenced by her cultural background in two ways. First, like many Hong Kong students, she was encouraged to learn English by her parents before and during her schooling and, second, the Hong Kong school system had its own part to play. In the first respect, she explains:

> In Hong Kong, it is still commonly believed that people fluent in English will have better career prospects and eventually a better life. Perhaps my parents also thought like that. They took pains to create a favourable language learning environment for me.

Before she began school, therefore, she was already watching Sesame Street on TV, reading books by Dr Seuss and meeting a native-speaker business associate of her father (an Indian man who grew up in England). "The issue of how to learn", she writes, "was very much controlled by my parents."

> They wanted me to understand that English is more than a language used in textbooks, it is used for daily communication. This language rich environment allowed a favourable impression that English is

a communicative tool to express oneself. This also built the foundation for growth later on.

Her experiences of English in kindergarten and primary school, however, were quite different. Like every other learner, she says, she was "forced to copy the alphabet, learn simple vocabulary, learn simple grammatical rules, read EFL/ESL readers and memorize phrases and paragraphs from them".

> The English teachers did not use English to talk to us in the classroom, and teaching was done in Cantonese. The formal schooling explicitly told me that English was a language to be learned only in the classroom from books and tailored materials. I thought that the English teachers I had were so different from the Indian man, the only native speaker I really knew. I began to wonder who was more right when it came to English as a communicative language, my English teachers or the Indian man.

Like Hye-Yeon, then, Alice began learning English with a conflict between her own understanding of what learning was and the methods of learning encouraged in school. In Alice's case, however, it may be that her greater exposure to English outside the classroom gave her a firmer foundation of autonomy in her later schooling.

Because Alice attended an English-medium missionary secondary school, all her English teachers were either native or fluent speakers of English. In junior secondary school, she writes, "I did not attempt to gain any control over my language learning, because I did not see the need." She also writes that, although her academic grades did not reflect her ability to communicate with native speakers, "it didn't worry me at the time, because I was not under any pressure to study very hard". The impetus for the development of her autonomy came from a different source:

> The need for more control came when I began writing my diary in English at 14 or 15. It was a language my mother had not mastered and so I believed I could escape parental surveillance. I found it liberating to write in English as it allowed me to create a private space. This new found private mental space was a big contrast to the small shared space I had in reality.

As a result of her diary writing, Alice says, she gained confidence as a writer and as a user of English outside the classroom: "I was proud of my ability to write down my thoughts in English, and even prouder that

I could escape my mother's surveillance." Privacy was also important because she was sharing a room with her younger sisters.

At around the same time, Alice began reading novels in English, beginning with *Gone with the Wind* ("as I loved the movie"), which she read over a summer holiday.

> The sudden gain of control over my intellectual development was soon out of check, and I stopped reading in Chinese. The reading into different subjects allowed access into a world totally different from my own culture. The idea of language being a communicative tool became a more complex idea of creating a whole new intellectual world.

Privacy was again at issue in her reading of, for example, the 'gay' novels of Edmund White – novels that her mother would have forbidden had she known what they were about! Alice also read for English Literature classes at O-level and A-level, where she enjoyed not only the reading but also the class discussions. The topic of her A-level literature studies was femininity:

> The topic opened up a whole new world and perspective to life and what it meant to be a woman. Every piece of reading was challenging and exciting. Learning how to use English to express complex and political ideas was beyond what other ESL learners were doing in their language classrooms.

The literature class, she says, was "a group of proud language learners and users in an exclusive circle" and "being a literature student was an important label in encouraging me to take control of my own learning". She also came to believe that "no language learner can master a language without being extensively exposed to the literature and culture of that language".

Texas

Like many Hong Kong students, Alice went overseas for her undergraduate studies, where she chose to study Business Administration rather than English. In order to prepare herself for this experience, she took a job in a souvenir shop in a tourist district of Hong Kong. This was, she writes, "the first time that I proved to myself that I could communicate with other native speakers" outside the school and family circle.

Once she arrived in the United States, she experienced similar diffi-culties to Hye-Yeon. However, she too managed to overcome them with relative ease, in part because she took them as an opportunity to learn, rather than as an obstacle:

> As a large state university, UT Austin attracted people from different places and it was forever interesting to listen to people with different accents talk. The three years of undergraduate study were more like learning about people than learning business studies.

She did not, she writes, "have difficulties in understanding the lec-tures or participating in tutorials", but she "had to watch hours and hours of TV programmes to fill my cultural vacuum". For daily survival, she realized, "I did not need to understand Shakespeare, I only needed to understand the jokes made by David Letterman or what was on the Oprah show."

Return to Hong Kong

The first version of Alice's story did not say a great deal about her experiences with English following her return to Hong Kong. After read-ing the summary of her story above, however, she added the following comments:

> In Hong Kong, being a fluent English speaker has given me a new sociocultural label: 'a returnee from overseas'. Returning to Hong Kong after four years, I needed to readapt to the local culture of using primarily Chinese, pushing English back into my private space, in order to survive and bond with my family and colleagues at school.

> When I started my work as an English teacher, students quickly labeled me as 'someone from the West', though I have spent most of my life in Hong Kong. Simply by having been overseas and by speak-ing fluent English, they assumed that I was different from them. This label of being 'Westernized' (or simply, 'non-Chinese') was not a pleasant one that I would like to wear. The students gave me respect as an advanced language learner and user. However, they also believed (or misbelieved) that I was only capable of being so by renouncing my Chinese heritage.

> For these students, it was unimaginable to be both Chinese and English-speaking at the same time. Their belief also made me reflect

on my own growth in and pathways to language learning experiences and proficiency. Contrary to the common belief that fluency in English brings opportunities, it also brings less-welcome consequences. What are the sociocultural consequences I need to bear for being a fluent English speaker in a predominantly Chinese and monolingual society?

As a child, it was understandable that I would not be able to make decisions for myself, practically or intellectually. As a teenager, I chose to read and write in English because it allowed an access to privacy, which in turn motivated and facilitated me to become a more proficient user of the language, hence an even greater degree of freedom. At that time, it was not possible for me to foresee that this choice would create a culturally different identity, as against my parents or peers. It was only as an adult that I came to understand and appreciate that I am different from people around me, and that this individuality was constructed in English, not in Chinese. But this is also a sociocultural identity which needs constant maintenance, reassurance and public reconciliation.

Commentary (Hye-Yeon Lim)

Reflecting on my learning experience as reported above, it is clear that autonomy played a crucial role in my English language learning. I was able to create new views of learning and new situations so that I was better able to deal with frustrations and continue on to my ultimate goal. I had no control over the Korean educational system with its emphasis on accuracy, grammar and memorization. Only as I rejected these emphases and constructed my own rules was I able to learn and enjoy the experience of learning English. Alice, on the other hand, took a different kind of control – finding personal space and developing her own sense of individuality. Nevertheless, only when we both became autonomous learners does it seem that we were able to be in a position to accomplish our respective goals.

For me, the most important part of effective language learning is the creation of a new identity which bridges both the native language and target language cultures. However, this new identity can be a double-edged sword. Being fluent in a language means one has to demonstrate not only linguistic but also sociolinguistic competence. In so doing, it is possible that the sociolinguistic demands of the target and background cultures may clash and learners may be confronted with chaos.

As learners adopt new beliefs, cognitions and practices, old identities will change. Since the new identities will be somewhat alienated from the old ones, learners may have to become more autonomous as they seek ways to reconcile dissonances. As Alice so aptly notes, there are unwanted sociocultural consequences of being a fluent English speaker in a predominately monolingual society.

I suspect that neither of us really knew how much becoming fluent in English would affect us. Yet, it clearly has. Alice notes that her individuality has been constructed in English and this has led to a situation in which her new sociocultural identity needs careful and constant attention. As for myself, I find the situation is much the same. I find myself somewhat alienated from both cultures, not fitting nicely into either but being able to navigate both. Clearly, I must continue to construct my own identity and it will be constructed in two languages.

While autonomy can be conceived of as being completely self-directed in one's own learning, that is an incomplete understanding. As much as one tries to create and retain individuality, humans are ultimately social and cultural products of their societies. Identities and personalities can be constructed through language and interaction. As new language and new cultural understandings are built into old cognitive structures, individuals will also change or will be perceived to have changed by others. Therefore, those who are more constrained by their background cultures may be either less willing or less able to become fluent in a foreign language. This may be particularly true if the foreign language is very different (both linguistically and culturally) from the native language.

I now realize that being a successful and confident language user means more than being in the right environment. It means being willing and able to try to construct a new identity and to be able to look at target and native cultures with different eyes. Being autonomous in language learning involves creating a new identity that is, at the same time, part of and apart from the original. Both Alice's story and mine suggest that we came to this realization late in the process. Nevertheless, the process was perhaps acting on us both before we were cognizant of that fact. Some of the anxiety that other learners may face in learning English could relate to this problem, although it is likely to be misidentified (as it was for me). Therefore, one of the most effective things we can do to help learners acquire a second language is to understand that they may be setting out on a road to greater autonomy and change and to help them navigate the unfamiliar and often uncomfortable terrain. In so doing, we will help them learn how to cope with the challenges they are bound to confront and help them to understand that many of the resources they need are rooted in the language and the culture they are acquiring.

Commentary (Alice Chik)

Reading our two stories, it is indeed amazing to see how Asian learners can mobilize and utilize cultural resources to facilitate their language learning. These stories are personal accounts of how individuals have achieved personal goals. For Hye-Yeon, it was the goal of communication. For me, it was the goal of intellectual privacy. Both of these goals were responses to the constraints of our own cultural backgrounds. We may say these stories are parallel in the sense that the actualization of these goals was achieved by utilizing language as a tool. The linguistic end result of language learning was not as important as the fulfillment of personal goals.

Our cultural backgrounds provided us with a resource pool to draw upon as the starting point in our language learning. Hye-Yeon describes how the Korean school system values memorization, perfection and perseverance. These are not only qualities of a particular school system, they are also cultural norms and values cherished by Koreans. Even the language institute she chose to go to after secondary education reflected these norms and values. Though she may consider her schooling as highly controlled and restrictive in retrospect, it also provided her with a way to start and, later on, with a reason to deviate from the system. In my own experience, the English language curriculum in Hong Kong is distanced from the target culture for historical and political reasons. Language teaching takes place in a 'cultural vacuum'. But in this system, I was also allowed to take the literature class, which was much closer to the target language culture than the contents of the regular curriculum.

Outside the school system, my cultural background also involved strong parental intervention and guidance from a very young age, and my parents created a very positive learning environment for me. From this perspective, we may say that we have both inherited certain cultural norms and values from our early learning. These became the cultural resources we could mobilize when we started to have stronger and more distinctive personal and non-linguistic goals. We may also say that these cultural resources enabled us to move on to the next stage of our learning journey. It is impossible to examine our language learning experience separately from the larger education environment. Hye-Yeon gained good results to enter university, and I did the same. But to have a proficient language level alone would not have enabled us to move on. If this was all we had had, the stories told would have been different.

To be intensively involved with the target language culture (or any foreign culture) means opening up more avenues for learners. In other words, it means more cultural resources to be drawn on. Hye-Yeon's interaction with native-speakers in her teaching and on her trip to Australia enabled her to understand that perfect pronunciation is not an absolute necessity in effective communication. This contradicted the Korean stress on perfection, but Hye-Yeon adjusted to the 'new rule', and became more confident in using English. This also helped her to move towards the fulfillment of her personal goal, or, essentially, to steer herself into a different direction from the prescribed Korean way. My own involvement with the target language culture has allowed me to move beyond the formal language classroom into using English in more authentic communication. Reading on different topics has given me a new understanding of what it really means to use a language to express oneself. It can be said that a closer involvement with the target language culture opens up more cultural resources for learners to formulate their own expression. It also requires a certain degree of individual flexibility, reflectivity and openness to cultural differences and new ideas. Both Hye-Yeon and I fashioned a more individualistic style and approach to language learning because we saw how we could use different resources to fulfill our own goals.

Individual autonomy, then, involves a capacity to mobilize and merge different cultural resources to create a learner's individual identity. It is also connected to the relationship between language learning and culture. In a modern e-communication society like Hong Kong or South Korea, it is impossible to single out formal schooling as the single most important factor in second language acquisition. To focus narrowly on what happens inside the school system would be to limit our academic research to a small aspect of what is going on in individuals' sociocultural and personal worlds. The wide availability of information from different media means the interaction between language learners and target cultures is more intense than ever before. Learners have more choices, and inevitably freedom, to construct their own learning pathways outside school. Perhaps a new emphasis should be placed on how language works as a tool to help learners actualize their personal growth, rather than on the narrower cultural impact of language learning within the classroom.

Conclusion (Phil Benson)

Hye-Yeon and Alice could be described as "expatriate cosmopolitans" (Block, 2002), or individuals who choose to immerse themselves in target language cultures for an extended period of time while retaining the option of returning home at some point in the future (as Alice already has and Hye-Yeon may in the future). As such, they are perhaps not 'typical' Asian learners, the vast majority of whom do not, and perhaps do not want to, cross the borders of their background cultures as Hye-Yeon and Alice have done. They are also untypical of the majority, however, in the extent to which they have succeeded in achieving what is often regarded as the major goal of foreign language learning – a high level of communicative proficiency. The experiences of such learners are, therefore, clearly worth considering in the context of the autonomy in Asia debate discussed earlier in this chapter.

Hye-Yeon's and Alice's learning of English was clearly influenced by their cultural backgrounds, but at the same time their stories show how complex this influence can be. For Hye-Yeon and Alice, the influence of the background culture appears to have weakened as their proficiency developed. But their stories also suggest that the development of this proficiency was a consequence of their own efforts to negotiate the influence of their background cultures to create new contexts for learning as their proficiency increased. It also appears to be particularly significant that both Hye-Yeon and Alice saw the opportunity to learn English as an opportunity to move beyond the constraints of their cultural backgrounds from a relatively early stage. Their desire and ability to take advantage of this opportunity, moreover, appear to have been inextricably intertwined with a desire and ability to develop their individual autonomy.

It also seems likely that Hye-Yeon's and Alice's willingness to engage with English language culture helped, rather than hindered, the development of their individual autonomy. Alice, for example, refers to her reading of a literature, which was – and this is my observation based on my knowledge of the books she read, rather than hers – permeated with models of individual autonomy. Although we can do no more than conjecture upon the influence of this literature, the point is perhaps worth making that Asian learners of Western languages can hardly avoid such ideas and models if they choose to engage with the cultural norms and values embedded within these languages.

Hye-Yeon's and Alice's stories, therefore, suggest that, for Asian learners who succeed in developing a high degree of communicative proficiency in a Western language, the language learning process is one in which questions of cultural identity are inevitably raised. They also suggest that the development of a strong sense of individual autonomy is essential to this process, because it helps such learners establish the critical distance from both the background and target language cultures that a bilingual identity implies. This may be true, moreover, of any learner who takes language learning as an opportunity to expand his/her cultural horizons. And in the light of this observation we may well ask whether the goal of expanding one's cultural horizons is any less legitimate for Asian learners of Western languages for the fact that individual autonomy is more highly valued in Western cultural contexts than in their own.

Reflection/discussion questions

1. As a teacher, how do you think your attitudes to the implementation of autonomy are influenced by the cultural contexts of your own learning history?
2. How do you think knowing more about your own students' learning histories could help your efforts to develop autonomy?
3. How do you think learners' stories could be used as a tool in the classroom for developing autonomy?

2
Changes in Chinese Students' Learner Strategy Use after Arrival in the UK: a Qualitative Inquiry

Xuesong Gao

Introduction

Due to socioeconomic developments in China, there has recently been a dramatic increase in the number of Chinese students studying overseas. In the past, Chinese students tended to enjoy a good reputation for their diligence and academic achievement (Cortazzi and Jin, 1996; Watkins and Biggs, 1996). But with the increase in numbers of Chinese studying abroad, the difficulties they face in their adaptation to a new academic environment appear to be attracting more attention (Barnard, 2002). English language proficiency, being essential to their academic survival and success, continues to be a major problem for many such learners. Thus, there is a clear need for research into how members of the global diaspora of Chinese students cope independently with language learning and use in an English-speaking environment. In this chapter I report on an interview-based study of Chinese students in the UK, investigating changes in their learner strategy use as they cross over from an EFL (English as a foreign language) learning situation to an ESL (English as a second language) context where English is much more widely used in the surrounding environment than in China.

Learner strategies are 'steps' or 'actions' selected by learners either to improve the *learning* of a second language, or their *use* of it, or both (Cohen, 1998: 2). Many researchers assign strategies a crucial role in language learning (e.g. Bialystok, 1981; Rubin, 1981; O'Malley et al., 1985) and strategy research has flourished over the last two decades. For example, using the Strategy Inventory for Language Learning (SILL) survey instrument (Oxford, 1990), Oxford and other researchers have studied learners' strategy use and identified factors that might influence learners' selection of strategies. These studies (e.g. Ehrman and Oxford, 1989; Oxford and Nyikos, 1989; Nyikos, 1990; Nyikos and Oxford, 1993; Green and Oxford, 1995; Yang, 1999) confirm that many learner factors, including learning style, motivation, beliefs, gender, career orientation, personality, and so on, affect strategy use. There are also some studies which suggest that learners in different types of context develop different language learning approaches: thus, Green and Oxford (1995) suggest that EFL and ESL students might employ different patterns of strategies, while Kojic-Sabo and Lightbown (1999) found that the EFL and ESL learners in their study developed different approaches to learning vocabulary. Hsiao and Oxford (2002) consider the influence of learning context on strategy selection to be an important topic for future research using the SILL. Overall, then, there are some suggestions in the literature that different repertoires of strategy use may occur in different environments, but as yet relatively little empirical research has focused on the possible influence of learning environment on learner strategy use.

There also seems to have been insufficient longitudinal research into the development of learners' strategy use over time (Green and Oxford, 1995; Ellis, 1996; Chamot, 2001). There are some studies (e.g. Wenden, 1986; Carson and Longhini, 2002) which use learners' retrospective accounts to offer insights into strategy use, and changes in strategy use over time have been broached in some reports (Wenden, 1986; Oxford and Crookall, 1989; O'Malley and Chamot, 1990; Schmitt, 1997; Chamot and El-Dinary, 1999); however, these studies have not tended to focus on identifying reasons for change.

A study of changes in strategy use when Chinese students come to study in an English-speaking country is therefore justified for two main reasons: (1) as a basis for practical interventions designed to smooth the transition into overseas study for this sizeable group of international students; and (2) as a means of developing insights in two largely neglected areas of strategy research: the influence of learning environment on strategy use, and processes of learner strategy development over time.

The study

When Chinese students come to study overseas in an English-speaking country, they change their learning context, becoming 'ESL' as opposed to 'EFL' learners. It is likely that these students experience many changes in their English learning, which might involve their learning strategy use. In an effort to investigate such changes I undertook an interview-based study of Chinese students who had recently arrived in the UK. The study was originally divided into two phases (cf. Gao, 2002) but I will focus on the Phase Two study in this chapter.

This chapter does not commit itself to studying learner strategies as a whole but aims to answer the following two questions:

1. What happens to Chinese students' vocabulary learning strategy use after their arrival in an ESL context (in this case, a British university)?
2. If there are changes in their strategy use, what factors can be identi-fied as causing these changes?

An initial enquiry prior to the part of the study reported here indi-cated that there were overall changes in Chinese students' learning strat-egy use following arrival in the UK (Gao, 2002). Vocabulary learning emerged as an important topic for deeper investigation, being fre-quently mentioned as an important area by participants in the prelimi-nary study. Clearly, vocabulary learning is related to other aspects of language learning and use (Chin, 1999; McDonough, 1999) and is cru-cial to learners' overall language acquisition (Lawson and Hogben, 1996; Laufer and Hulstijn, 2001). An in-depth focus on one area of learning was also considered likely to be most productive given inconsistencies among existing overall taxonomies of learner strategies (Hsiao and Oxford, 2002).

For this part of the study I interviewed 13 Chinese students about changes in their vocabulary learning strategy use. The interview data were then coded in an attempt to identify factors that might have influ-enced these changes.

All 13 of the interviewed learners had finished their undergraduate education in China and were attending preparatory language or post-graduate academic courses at the University of Warwick, UK. Details of interviewees are presented in Table 2.1.

Table 2.1 Details of participants

Interviewee no.	15	16	17	18	19	20	21	22	23	24	25	26	27
Gender	M	F	F	M	M	M	F	M	F	M	F	F	M
Age	23	26	23	23	27	26	24	23	22	31	23	23	24
Course	MSc	MA	LLM	MSc	MA	LLM	MSc	MSc	IEL	LLM	MA	MSc	MSc

Key: IEL = Intensive English Language Course; LLM = Master degree course in legal studies; MSc = Master of Science; MA = Master of Arts.

I intended this enquiry to provide insights into learners' strategy use from their own perspectives, reducing the problem articulated by Wenden (1986: 186) that data collection and analysis in many learner strategy studies are focused too much on strategies themselves and too little on learners' insights into other dimensions of their language learning experience. Since I wanted not only to identify changes in strategy use but also to discover possible explanations for any changes, retrospective interview indicated itself as a logical choice of research method for this study. Many researchers have been supportive of using interviews for data collection in learner strategy studies, believing that they can produce data of relative depth (Naiman et al., 1978: 221; O'Malley and Chamot, 1990: 118) and enable researchers to obtain information that might not be available through other means (Oxford and Burry-Stock, 1995: 2). Wenden (1986: 189) emphasizes that interviews reveal not only learners' strategy use but also their efforts to "designate, diagnose, evaluate, self-analyze and theorize" their learning behaviours. In this connection, I also felt that using interviews as a research method would best enable me to investigate the developmental process of strategy use over time, via participants' own retrospective accounts.

The retrospective interviews were carried out in a semi-structured way according to an interview guide (see Appendix to this chapter) prepared beforehand. The interview guide was based on the known stages of the cognitive process of obtaining, storing, retrieving and using information (in this case, vocabulary) (Rubin, 1987: 19; O'Malley and Chamot, 1990: 17–18). With questions relating to each stage of the vocabulary acquisition process, each interview lasted around half an hour. Considering the fact that all the interviewees were Chinese, I decided that Chinese was the best language in which to conduct my interviews. Using this shared language helped the interviewed learners to express themselves freely and also enabled me to interpret their messages accurately.

The interviews were recorded, and later transcribed. Then, following the interview analysis procedures recommended by Ryan and Bernard (2000), I carefully read the transcribed data repeatedly and found that ten factors influencing changes in learners' strategy use emerged as salient in their accounts. Then I used a coding process to count the number of interviewees who mentioned these factors in their interviews in order to assess the apparent impact of these factors on the interviewed learners overall. The factors which emerged in this manner are discussed below.

Findings and discussion

Overall changes and factors responsible

Overall, it became clear that the interviewed learners had developed new strategies to deal with vocabulary learning after arrival in the UK. Firstly, it seems that they became less active and more selective in seeking meanings of unfamiliar words. Unless these were key words for their academic study or for social functions valued by them, the interviewed learners were more likely to ignore them than in the past. Secondly, while they had depended heavily on dictionaries before their arrival in the UK, they now used a greater variety of strategies to determine meanings of new words, at the same time appearing to be less attentive than before to aspects of the words other than their contextual meanings. They now tended to use context to guess new words' meanings, or (occasionally) would ask a conversational partner to clarify meaning, while consulting a dictionary tended to become a strategy only of last resort. Thirdly, most learners came to rely on consolidating their vocabulary learning through use, by reading, writing and, relatively rarely, speaking. After arrival in the UK they seldom employed the reviewing or rote learning strategies many of them had utilized for consolidation of vocabulary learning in China.

These were general trends among the 13 interviewed learners, although two were found to have experienced little change in their strategy use, and this was apparently due to the uniqueness of their previous learning experiences (discussed further below). In addition, two of the 13 learners reported that they had developed new methods of organizing their learning in order to cope with new learning needs for their academic studies and social interaction in the UK – this counteracts the general trend towards *less* active deliberate learning noted above.

Through analysis of the transcripts, I identified ten factors that learners reported as influencing their strategy use (Table 2.2).

Together the first four factors above might be termed 'learner factors' since they relate primarily to learners themselves and the other six 'contextual factors' since they form part of the students' learning context. I shall discuss these factors separately below although, as will become clear, there was frequent interaction among them.

Learner factors

Many previous studies have been devoted to discussing the relationship between individual learner factors and strategy use (e.g. Ehrman and

Table 2.2   Factors influencing change, and their impact

Factor	Impact mentioned by
Motivation	All 13 interviewees
Learning beliefs	8 interviewees
Proficiency	8 interviewees
Prior learning experience	2 interviewees stood out in comparison with the others because of their unique learning experiences
Language input	All 13 interviewees
Language production opportunities	12 interviewees
Learning needs	All 13 interviewees
Academic priorities	10 interviewees
Academic culture	Although mentioned by 4 interviewees, it had a perceptible impact on all
Application of technology	10 interviewees

Oxford, 1989; Oxford and Nyikos, 1989; Nyikos, 1990; Nyikos and Oxford, 1993; Green and Oxford, 1995; Yang, 1995). While supporting previous findings on relevant learner factors, this study also sheds light on the relationship between these factors and changes in learners' strategy use, with rich insights having been provided from the interviewed learners' perspectives.

Motivation

Motivation has previously been reported to have a pervasive influence on learners' strategy use (Oxford and Nyikos, 1989: 295). A review of recent motivational research by Dörnyei (2001) shows that motivation has a dynamic character and varies over time. This indicates the need to adopt a process approach in studying motivation and – I would add – the relationship between motivation and strategy use. From a process perspective it is to be expected that changes in learners' strategy use correspond to changes in their motivational level. Indeed, the interview data provide some evidence supporting such a hypothesis: the learners in the study did report adjustments in their strategy use in response to motivational changes.

Interviewee 16 represents a good case in point. Before she came to the UK, she used to spend considerable time on her English learning, reviewing vocabulary lists, reading short articles to consolidate her vocabulary learning and practising test questions. She regularly arrived at her office earlier than other staff in order to study, even after working overtime till late the night before. After her arrival in the UK, she found that she was not motivated to learn new vocabulary because it was simply "too much" for her. She explained the change in her learning behaviour as follows:

> At that time, I was thinking about studying abroad [...] I just wanted to change my life. [...] [But now] I feel that I am not energetic enough to cope with these [i.e. learning English and academic work]. I am probably too old for it. Anyway, I am too lazy for it. Maybe humans are lazy in the first place. I just got to realize it [i.e. that I am also lazy] now.

Not all the students were like interviewee 16. Being in an English-speaking country was, by contrast, a learning incentive for students such as interviewees 15, 22 and 23 because of increased possibilities of interacting with people in English.

Learning beliefs

My findings seem to indicate that there were two layers in the students' belief system: their fundamental learning beliefs and their beliefs in best practice. I found that the students in my study did not change their fundamental belief in the essential importance of repeated exposure to a new word in order to remember it, but they developed different beliefs regarding the best way to put this fundamental belief into practice. In the past many learners accepted that the best way to memorize words was to use rote learning strategies, particularly via visual repetition (in other words, repeatedly seeing a word, usually in a word-list). Quite a few learners (for example, interviewees 18, 24, 26) referred to a widely-circulated 'myth' in China: a person can memorize a word if s/he repeats exposure to it (particularly visually) seven times. After they arrived in the UK, they realized that the best practice in learning new words was to "use them" (interviewee 19) through reading (e.g. interviewees 25 and 27), writing (e.g. interviewees 17 and 18) and/or "interacting with people" (e.g. interviewees 21 and 26). However, this does not mean that they have changed their fundamental belief in repeated exposure. The following interview extract provides a good illustration of this change in beliefs in best practice, and at the same time the underlying constancy of a belief in repeated exposure:

> [There are] two kinds of repetition [...] the first is conscious repetition, which is to memorize a word without context [...] we write it down again and again [...] the second is unconscious repetition.

When we are reading something, that word appears. When we read on, that word appears again. Then again and again. I believe that the second kind of repetition is much better. (interviewee 24)

For these learners, the two sets of strategies seemed to be context-specific. In China, especially to prepare for exams, they felt they had to use rote learning strategies and tended to equate 'learning' with 'memorizing'. Even interviewee 24 (quoted above), as well as many others (interviewees 23, 26, 27 etc.), considered that "conventional strategies", by which she meant rote learning strategies, were more reassuring and worked better for exams. Although in the UK interviewees came to realize that they could improve their learning most effectively by *using* newly learnt words, they did not have the illusion that being in a language-rich environment automatically leads to increased proficiency in English. The key revelation for them was that frequently encountering a new vocabulary item is essential for learning the item. This revelation justified – retrospectively – how they had learnt and memorized new words in China at the same time as indicating the new direction of learning via "unconscious repetition".

Proficiency

Learners' proficiency is normally considered to have a positive causal relationship with strategy use (Wenden, 1986; Green and Oxford, 1995). The present study confirmed that the interviewed learners tended to use strategies more often because of their improved English proficiency but also revealed a more complex picture. Interviewees 15, 26 and 27 found themselves using more inferencing strategies since they found that their "guessing results were much improved" (interviewee 15). However, as learners' language proficiency increased, reaching a point at which they thought that they had sufficient language knowledge, this awareness of proficiency caused some to decrease their strategy use since they felt less motivated to learn new vocabulary. Before interviewee 26 took an important English test in China, she spent a lot of time on intensive reviewing and memorization of new words. In this manner she had learnt a large amount of academic vocabulary and she subsequently found that her vocabulary knowledge was sufficient for coping with academic study in the UK. She then became less motivated to learn more words, even though she admitted that she found it difficult to use academic words and was ignorant of words for use in daily life. Other interviewed learners reported similar problems (interviewees 19, 21, etc.). I conclude from this phenomenon that learners' relative proficiency, or perceived proficiency in relation to their learning needs, rather than learners' language proficiency per se, seems to affect learners' strategy use after arrival in the UK.

Prior learning experience

Two learners in the present study (interviewees 24 and 27) emerged as different from the others in terms of stability of strategy use pre- and post-arrival in the UK. There may be various possible explanations, but their prior learning experience seemed to be the most likely cause. Both of them had experiences of using their English to solve practical problems in their work or academic studies before coming to the UK, while the other interviewees only started having such experiences after their arrival. Interviewee 24, who used to be a construction project negotiator, told me that he had to learn English because:

> [...] my job forced me to do so. We had to compile English documents, which were always very thick. They had a lot of new words inside [...]. When we designed projects for new customers, we then had to deal with new words related to the new project.

As a committed professional, he tried to use every possible strategy to improve his language proficiency. His strategy repertoire contained strategies that had been well tested and which he continued to regard as useful.

Interviewee 27 engaged in baccalaureate studies at an International College in Hong Kong. He described his experiences in Hong Kong in the following manner:

> This was my biggest challenge in language learning. [...] The language of instruction in Hong Kong is English, which literally means that I had to do all my academic work as well as live my daily life in English. [...] It was very painful at the beginning.

Interviewee 27 had developed a sophisticated metacognitive understanding of language learning. Based on his experiences in Hong Kong, he saw that there were two important prerequisites for successful language learning: a good language environment and learning awareness. He believed that "if a learner has such an awareness, he or she can learn by guessing in the language". This global statement describes how he acted in Hong Kong and continued to act in the UK.

Contextual factors

Oxford and Nyikos (1989) note the existence of interaction between learners' internal factors (particularly motivation) and external variables, while Kojic-Sabo and Lightbown (1999) propose that contextual differences might be the reason for the differences in strategy use between the ESL and EFL learners in their study. Indeed, the interviewees in the present study appeared to be particularly conscious of the contextual impact upon their learning. Below I discuss the contextual factors that emerged in their retrospective accounts.

Language input

Bacon and Finnemann (1990) suggest that authentic language input indirectly improves learners' strategy use. I found that the learners in my study generally claimed to have benefited from a dramatic increase in authentic language input in the UK. It seems that they considered this a major incentive for studying in the UK and were more motivated to learn English, at least at the beginning of their stay. However, rich language input alone might be insufficient to maintain an active approach to language learning among some of the interviewed learners.

After arrival in the UK, interviewees learned that "everywhere there are new words" (interviewee 25) and thus many opportunities to learn new vocabulary. Therefore, some learners employed new strategies, such as learning new words from native speakers.

> I always said "throw away" something in the kitchen. Then one day my [native speaker] flatmate asked me whether I meant *"chuck"* [something] away. I asked her what it meant. Then I came to know that I should use the word 'chuck' instead of 'throw'. (Interviewee 19)

But how much these learners can benefit from being in such an input-rich context seems to depend on their desire to utilize the new learning opportunities, which depends on other variables. For example, some learners (interviewees 17 and 18) used to shop with an electronic dictionary to learn the names of relevant goods in their first month in the UK. Soon they gave up this new strategy, as it was not necessary for them to know these new words in the supermarket ("we all know what meat looks like": interviewee 18). Interviewee 16 tried to memorize names of vegetables by having a list in the kitchen but failed to do so because she was insufficiently motivated ("I always take vegetables off the counter without a thought"). In general, indeed, the richness of language input in the new learning context seemed to break down the continuity of these learners' vocabulary learning processes. After encountering a new word, most learners were no longer interested in memorizing or consolidating its acquisition but chose to wait for it to appear again in the environment so that they might decide on its importance before finally learning it.

Language production opportunities

The study suggests that learners who are involved in active language production activities may be relatively likely to develop new strategies and increase frequency of strategy use: it appeared overall that those who were actively involved in social exchanges with non-Chinese were relatively more motivated and well-organized in their vocabulary learning. However, many reported interacting in Chinese much more than in English overall.

Thus, although it might be assumed that learners would experience many more language production opportunities as a result of coming to the UK, apart from academic writing activities I found that the interviewed learners' utilization of language production opportunities seemed to be rather limited. Indeed, a lack of language production activities reduced the interviewees' learning needs and had a negative effect on their motivation, inhibiting their strategy development as a result.

The type of people they had access to for (typically, brief) social conversations were reportedly confined to their flatmates, coursemates and cleaning staff. Most learners referred to some occasions when they sought meanings of new words from their coursemates or flatmates. Other language production events referred to in their interviews were largely confined to academic presentations and discussions.

Interviewee 19 believed that individual learners themselves were responsible for such a paradoxical phenomenon ("if you are willing to speak, you might have more opportunities"). I suspect that some learners suffered from initial setbacks in interacting with people in English because of their vocabulary problems. Interviewee 26 found that the cleaner of her room "never uses the words that are basic words in our understanding". This is probably one of the reasons why most learners sounded most comfortable interacting with their coursemates on academic matters. It is also possible that they were more concerned with their academic studies than seeking interaction opportunities to practice English. Although none of the 13 learners specifically mentioned this, it is also likely that they had cross-cultural communication problems as revealed in other interviews (Gao, 2002). As a group of learners dislocated from their homes, I was not surprised that they preferred interacting with other Chinese for emotional and social support. Hence, I reasoned that it was inevitable for them to create their own Chinese communities and spend most of their free time in these communities in the UK, which further reduced opportunities for them to interact with people in English.

Learning needs

New learning needs, generated in the new environment, might drive learners to adopt new strategies, while disappearing needs might make learners less motivated to use old strategies.

For most interviewed learners (all except interviewee 24), the value of English was as an important academic subject, "essential to our success in universities" (interviewee 26), aside from being important for finding jobs. Most learners had developed strategies to increase their vocabulary in order to pass exams, especially gatekeeper exams such as TOEFL or GRE. Their vocabulary learning had been guided by the numerous published study materials for these exams.

Although these exam-oriented learning activities prepared these students with quite a large vocabulary, their vocabulary was still not problem-free after their arrival in the UK. In the case of interviewee 20, "loads of new words were upon me all of sudden. [...] I could not even understand my lecture handouts." Responding to this urgent problem, he engaged in systematic use of vocabulary learning strategies including note-taking, periodical reviewing and consolidating newly learnt words by using them.

On the other hand, disappearing needs contributed to a reduction in some learners' use of strategies that they had used in the past. The disappearance of language tests might partially explain why learners were found, overall, to use much fewer deliberate vocabulary learning strategies such as note-keeping and visual repetition (interviewees 15, 16, 17, 18 etc.). In the case of interviewee 25, as an English major student in China she used to look up words in a monolingual dictionary to understand English definitions because she would be asked by her teachers to "explain words in English in her class". Since there was no longer such a need in the UK for her, she looked for Chinese definitions of new words more often than English ones when using a dictionary.

Furthermore, learners became more selective in their vocabulary learning because they evaluated the relevance of encountered new words to their future needs. They believed that it was not necessary for them to learn some words because they were "not going to become an

expert on words" (interviewee 21) and would not be involved in professions "that purely rely upon the use of English language" (interviewee 19).
As a result, these learners were inclined to use fewer vocabulary learning
strategies than before, and, rather, put their vocabulary problems aside.

Academic priorities

Learning priorities are decisive in learners' selection of strategies, with
learners being inclined to use strategies to solve the language learning
problems that they regard as priorities (Wenden, 1986: 194). This study
confirms Wenden's observation: the interviewed learners' vocabulary
learning clearly became subject to necessities in their academic learning,
since English changed from being the core content of learning (in
China) to being an *instrument* for core content learning (in the UK).

This change in the status of learning English was recognized as important by the interviewed learners themselves. Interviewee 26 said that
"academic learning in the university in China was virtually English-
learning", and some interviewees (for example, 21 and 27) mentioned
the pride that they used to have in their English when they were in
China. The learners understood clearly that their English learning no
longer had such prestige in itself and should serve their academic studies in the UK. Therefore, most interviewees' vocabulary learning seemed
to focus on the academic words relevant to their own fields, and most
developed new strategies in response to their academic needs. In terms
of dictionary-using strategies, interviewee 19 mentioned his increased
consultation of a Chinese–English dictionary to aid in assignment-
writing. Others (for example, interviewees 16, 22 and 26) found
themselves using dictionaries more often but spending less time on each
consultation since they needed to get themselves through the reading as
quickly as possible. They had little intention to learn the new words that
they came across in their reading. After all, academic study had always
been the top priority in these interviewees' learning culture (see below),
and its focus had now shifted away from English.

Academic culture

The concept of 'cultures of learning', as introduced by Cortazzi and Jin
(1996), is particularly important for understanding the learning behaviours of Chinese students. Changes in academic culture, especially in
assessment methods, may tend to have a very significant impact upon
Chinese students' strategy use.

For most learners in China, what is to be learnt is largely defined by what is to be examined. Consequently, the interviewed students' strategy use had been related in the past to the exams that they had to take. Exams had dominated their past learning experiences, as interviewee 26 commented: "Our English-learning is exam-oriented. We took one exam after another. And also we took important exams such as TOEFL and GRE." English exams did not have entirely negative effects on the learners. In fact, good grades in language tests had always been inspiring targets, as exhibited in some learners' accounts (e.g. interviewees 16, 18, 22, 26). These students had not only tended to choose strategies appropriate to the way that they were examined in English tests but also in other academic examinations. For instance, the general prevalence of closed book exams had required them to engage in memorization, while multiple-choice testing formats encouraged them to use guessing strategies. In the UK, these students – familiar as they were with an exam-oriented academic culture – found it harder to learn English independently without the specific goals which exams had used to define clearly for them. Some started wondering why they had to learn more English at all (interviewees 19 and 21). Furthermore, changes in academic assessment methods also affected their perceptions of learning needs. For example, open-book exams or assignments allowed them to use dictionaries. This reduced their desire to memorize words: "We do not have to memorize [words], for we do not have to spell them" (interviewee 26).

Application of technology

An additional feature of learning context deserves mentioning here: that is, the dominant presence of computers in these students' lives in the UK. Interviewees did most of their academic work on or near a computer. I also discovered that most of them had language learning software, particularly dictionaries, installed on their computers. Five learners mentioned using dictionary software to learn new words (interviewees 15, 16, 19, 23 and 26). Others mentioned using vocabulary learning software with self-testing functions (interviewees 23 and 24). It seems likely to have been a universal phenomenon, also, that these learners used the Microsoft Word spell-checking facility when writing assignments. They also tried to increase language production opportunities by using English as a communication medium in online chat rooms, message boards and e-mails. Indeed, most of my own e-mail communications with the interviewed learners were carried out in English.

However, some learners did not seem to be aware that using these technologies could represent an important part of their learning. Thus, I was asked by one doubtful learner whether he could regard himself as using a dictionary 'if I just used dictionary software' (interviewee 15). Interviewee 23 found it 'interesting' to use vocabulary learning software at the beginning but soon found it 'boring' and gave it up after a short while. It is likely that such technologies open up new possibilities in language learning. However, there seems to be some distance to travel before learners such as those interviewed integrate technology into their conceptualization of language learning and develop their ability to utilize these technologies effectively for independent learning purposes.

Implications and conclusion

The study reported here examined changes in Chinese students' vocabulary learning strategy use after arrival for further study in the UK. The findings require further corroboration through other research methods (for example, a questionnaire survey with wider distribution), but it has shown that the study of changes in learners' strategy use is a worthwhile field for further investigation. Based on an analysis of interview transcripts, it was possible to identify four learner factors and six contextual factors that might have caused the overall changes that were noted. The study not only confirms previous findings on the importance of learners' motivation, proficiency and beliefs in influencing strategy use, it also shows how changes in learning context can influence changes in strategy use. A list of contextual factors which have not received much attention in previous studies was presented, involving consideration of the impact of language input, language production opportunities, learning needs, academic priorities, academic culture and technology upon learners' choice of strategies.

This study has both theoretical and practical implications. In the theoretical dimension, it seems important to continue research to confirm and develop the list of factors that might cause changes in learners' strategy use, map out a more comprehensive picture of their interaction, and eventually develop a theoretical framework for learners' selection of strategies and development of their strategy use as called for by McDonough (1999: 14). More importantly, perhaps, such research might help us to understand better how learners manage the developmental process of change in strategy use and establish a clearer picture of how they negotiate interactively with their learning context in such a process. As has emerged from this study, then, future learner strategy research needs to consider possibilities of taking a process approach and paying greater attention to the contextual factors that might influence changes in strategy use. It is also indispensable to consider the sociocultural background of learners to understand better the reasons for their strategy selection. Hence, a holistic, qualitative research approach which focuses on the dynamic and evolutionary nature of learners' strategy use can be adopted with profit in future studies.

In practical terms, the findings of this study imply that educators need to be more aware of the difficulties learners face in bridging differences between academic culture in China and Western academic settings. Chinese educators might need to work differently to keep learners oriented on the right track towards learning English, attempting to change the predominantly exam-oriented academic culture by introducing authentic language input and learning tasks, new assessment methods, and so on. On the other hand, educators in the UK need to provide appropriate support to Chinese students on how to learn English in a new context, for example, via appropriate language learning strategy training, social and cultural support packages, and so on. These can be incorporated into intensive language learning courses prior to or in parallel with their academic studies. Chinese students need further support in overcoming initial difficulties in communication, in balancing English learning and academic needs, and in developing independent language learning strategies appropriate to the new learning context. As the academic culture of Chinese students has always been dominated by examinations, educators in both countries could, on the basis of research data such as that presented here, set up realistic and practical language learning targets as well as strategy training approaches that might help to bridge their respective contexts.

Acknowledgement

I wish to express my heartfelt gratitude to the editors and to Rebecca Oxford for their helpful comments on an earlier draft. However, I assume full responsibility for any remaining inadequacies.

Reflection/discussion questions

1. Which of the factors identified in this chapter are likely to influence the learning strategy use of learners in a context you are familiar with?
2. How well-prepared are the same learners for managing necessary changes in strategy use when changes happen in their learning context?

3. How can we help students better to negotiate changes in their learning roles (and in their learning strategy use) across different contexts?

Appendix: interview questions

1. Where did you normally encounter or learn new words in China?
2. Where do you normally encounter or learn new words now?
3. What did you do with new words in China?
4. What do you do with new words here?

If learners mention dictionary use in their answers, follow up with questions 5–8:

5. How often? In what contexts?
6. What did you look at in the dictionary at that time?
7. After you looked up a new word in the dictionary, what did you do with your findings?
8. What about now? Why is it different (if different)?.

If learners mention guessing the meanings of the new words, follow up with questions 9–10:

9. How did you guess the meaning of a word?
10. What about now? Why is it different (if different)?

If learners mention taking notes, follow up with questions 11–13:

11. Did you keep a list of new vocabulary? Did you use the vocabulary lists published in textbooks or other books?
12. In what form did you write down these words? What about now?
13. What did you do with these written-down words? What about now?

If the learners answer that they memorize(d) these words, follow up with questions 14–16:

14. How did you memorize words? (Prompts: By sound, form or meaning. Using oral repetition, visual repetition, association, imagery, visual encoding, word structure, semantic encoding, auditory encoding, contextual encoding.) What about now?
15. What did you do in order to consolidate your memory of new words? What about now?
16. If different, why is that so?

3
Learner Autonomy as Agency in Sociocultural Settings

Kelleen Toohey and Bonny Norton

Introduction

Second language learning literature (and discourse in other fields) often constructs learners as individuals who act, think, and learn in accordance with innate, specifiable characteristics, independently of the social, historical, cultural and political-economic situations in which they live. From this perspective, these 'autonomous' learners have variable motivations, learning styles, cognitive traits, strategies and personality orientations that are seen as causal of their success or failure in language learning. We have seen particular interest in specifying the characteristics of successful language learners (e.g. Naiman et al., 1978). More recently, however, as Canagarajah (2003) points out, there has been a 'social turn' in our literature that places emphasis on the ways in which sociocultural factors and larger societal processes are involved in the construction of individuals and their learning (Hall, 1993, 1995; Rampton, 1995; Auerbach, 1997; Pavlenko and Lantolf, 2000; Pennycook, 2001). Another thread in this discussion has related to learners' agency, their embodied experiences, and their individual histories situated in sociocultural contexts (e.g. Benson, Chik and Lim, this volume).

Here, we wish to present our research on two language learners – one adult (Eva) and one child (Julie) – and to consider what factors in the learners' environments enabled or disabled their access to learning. We also wish to examine how Eva and Julie exercised agency in resisting and shaping the access to learning provided by their environments. By focusing on learners' situated experiences, we seek new insights into the dialectic between the individual and the social – between the human agency of these learners and the social practices of their communities.

In keeping with the theme of this collection, we wish to invite readers to consider language learning as increasing participation in communities of practice (Lave and Wenger, 1991), to understand 'autonomy' not so much as individualized performance but as socially oriented agency, and to conceptualize 'cultures' as specific settings with particular practices that afford and constrain possibilities for individual and social action in them.

Two successful language learners

We wish here to examine two cases of successful language learning within our own independently conducted studies of language learners in Canada in the 1990s (Norton Peirce, 1995; Norton, 2000; Toohey, 1996, 1998, 2000). Norton's work was with adults; Toohey's with children. Both studies were qualitative and used a variety of data-gathering techniques: journals and interviews (in the adult study) and participant observation, interviews and videotaping (in the child study). In both cases, we were less interested in individual characteristics of the learners than in their social interactions, as well as the ways in which opportunities to engage in interaction in their specific situations were structured. Drawing on our data, there are two central questions we wish to explore: (1) What kinds of access to participation in the social networks of these settings were provided for learners?; and (2) How did these two particular learners manage their own access to the social networks of their anglophone peer groups?

Eva: an adult language learner

In a study conducted with five immigrant women (Norton Peirce, 1995; Norton, 2000), there was one language learner, Eva, a young Polish woman, who could be considered more successful than the others. During the course of the study, the five learners were assessed with the use of a cloze, dictation, dialogue, crossword, short essay and oral interview. Although each of the learners had arrived in Canada with little experience of speaking English, Eva's performance on these measures was outstanding relative to that of the other learners. Previous research approaches might explain Eva's learning as being a result of her particular cognitive traits, affective orientations, motivations, past experiences and individual learning strategies. However, we would prefer to theorize her learning trajectory as being due to the particular circumstances of her language learning situation, her situated position in her social networks, her personal embodied history in other social networks, and her agency in negotiating entry into the anglophone social networks in her workplace, despite initial difficulties.

Eva worked at Munchies, an upmarket fast food restaurant, where she was the only non-English speaker and the only recent immigrant to Canada. As she said, "[Munchies] was the first place that I had to be able to communicate in English. I was having a hard time with understanding, speaking and making conversation with somebody." Activities in the restaurant for workers included: taking orders from customers, passing orders on to other workers, taking cash from customers, preparing food, cleaning the restaurant, keeping supplies current, and communicating with management. The only activities that were not dependent on spoken interaction were cleaning the floors and tables, clearing out the garbage, and preparing drinks. Significantly, it was precisely these latter activities, "the hard job[s]", that were Eva's assigned responsibilities when she first started working at Munchies. This was solitary work, in which she had little interaction with anglophones. "I'm just alone and everybody doing something else – who can I talk to?", she asked.

Eva understood that in order to practice speaking English, she had to become part of the social network within the workplace; she had to form social relationships with her co-workers. However, the work she was assigned limited her access to that network. Eva had a job that often isolated her spatially from the other workers, and it carried little status in her community. As a result, she felt her co-workers had little respect for her and did not interact with her: "I think because when I didn't talk to them, and they didn't ask me, maybe they think I'm just, like [not worth talking to] – because I had to do the worst type of work there. It's normal." The relevance of such relationships for language learning was clearly articulated by Eva: "When I see that I have to do everything and nobody cares about me, because – then how can I talk to them? I hear they doesn't care about me and I don't feel to go and smile and talk to them."

After a period of months, however, Eva managed to develop relationships with her co-workers and to enter their social network. These relationships developed because of certain affordances in the social hierarchies of her workplace, as well as Eva's agentic action in (and outside) her workplace. The fast-food company sponsored monthly outings for employees outside the restaurant, and on those outings, Eva was able to challenge her workplace position as a 'stupid' person, only worthy of the "worst kind of job". Outside the restaurant, Eva's attractiveness, youth and charm were valued symbolic resources. Also on these occasions Eva's partner would help provide transportation for her fellow employees. Outside the institutional constraints of the workplace, Eva's identity in the eyes of her co-workers became more complex and their relationship to her began to change. Had these outings not been a part of company policy, it is doubtful that Eva would have developed social outside-work relationships with her co-workers.

With reference to activities that took place in the restaurant, Eva was gradually given greater responsibility. As she was given more status and respect in the workplace, she felt more comfortable speaking: "When I feel well, then I can talk to the others," she said. Eva explained that it was not that she wanted a job that was "better" than those of her co-workers, but one in which she would have an equal status. This in turn would open up possibilities for shared conversation.

Eva described in interviews that she listened to the way her co-workers spoke to the customers and participated in social conversation. Having access to the expert performances of her native English-speaking co-workers, and the kind of job that required continual practice, Eva quickly developed fluency in work-related English. She also came to participate more actively in coffee-break conversations with her co-workers. On one occasion, for example, she took the opportunity to teach a co-worker some Italian so that the co-worker could surprise her husband. Eva also described how she would claim spaces in conversations, with the intention of introducing her own European history and experiences into the workplace.

Conversations in Eva's workplace were initially not easily accessible to her, but the company practice of worker outings allowed Eva access to social conversations with her co-workers. Her workplace was one in which it was possible to move from "hard jobs" where there was little opportunity for social interaction, to jobs in which speaking English was required. With a shift in her job responsibilities, Eva, although not initially an active participant, could hear conversations between experienced English speakers, both co-workers and customers. After some time, then, Eva was able to claim both space and time in conversations with her peers. She ingeniously brought her own resources to the attention of her co-workers and she invited them to invest in a relationship with her. She was able to do this despite her immigrant status, the nature of the work she was initially assigned, and her imperfect English. Eva's success in her endeavours is poignantly captured in a conversation she overheard a few months after starting work at Munchies. One worker, turning to another, said in passing: "I don't like working with people who aren't Canadian." When his companion replied "Except Eva," he repeated: "Except Eva."

Julie: a child language learner

The second learner to be considered is Julie, who was, at the time reported on here, a five-year-old child of Polish-speaking immigrant parents. Julie had not attended an English pre-school program, but she and her younger sister had attended a Polish-medium Sunday school from an early age. Julie (as well as five other children of minority language backgrounds) was observed in a public school over the course of three years for a study aimed at discovering how these children came to be participants in school activities (Toohey, 2000). Julie was initially identified as an English as a second language (ESL) learner and she subsequently attended, in addition to her regular kindergarten, a supplementary afternoon ESL kindergarten. By the end of kindergarten, her teacher assessed her as being enough like a (in the teacher's words) "normal" (i.e. English-speaking) child linguistically and academically, that she would have a good year in Grade 1, an assessment that in effect 'graduated' her from ESL. In view of her mother's opinion that Julie started school speaking Polish appropriately for her age, but that she knew only "a few words [of English]...not much", her progress seemed extraordinary. No formal English proficiency tests were administered to the children, but Julie's teacher's assessment of her as linguistically and academically able, and the evidence that she participated in a wide variety of classroom interactions, are the basis for the selection made here of her experience as a relevant case of successful language learning.

Like workplaces, classrooms might be seen as having desirable and not-so-desirable activities and resources. While workplaces often differentially assign workers to particular resources and activities, classrooms are at least putatively organized so as to provide equitable access for children to all resources and activities. While Julie initially was quite quiet in her classroom, and spent a good deal of time watching and listening to other children, she appeared nevertheless to have relatively easy access to many classroom interactions and materials quite early in her kindergarten year. Before discussing Julie's particular negotiation of access, it will be useful to discuss some characteristics of activities in Julie's kindergarten.

Activities in Julie's kindergarten might be seen as of two broad types: activities in which the teacher was a participant (and often, leader) and "play", in which the teacher was not involved. Teacher-led activities in this classroom were primarily in the form of "Circle Time", when children sat on the floor in a circle around the teacher and she led them in chanting, singing, talking and literacy activities. Many of these Circle activities were choral, and each child could participate in them to varying extents, depending on expertise and/or inclination. In solo activities (e.g. when children were asked if they had anything to "share", or when they were asked to give individual answers to teacher questions), participation was also voluntary and the teacher 'protected' each child's turn with prompts and scaffolds, and reminders to other children to listen.

While these circumstances were the case for all the English language learners in the classroom, not all of them showed increasing ease in participation. Julie was early on a rather inactive participant in choral activities (like the other English language learners in her classroom), but with access to hearing the expert performances of her anglophone classmates over time, she (as well as most of the other English language learners) began to participate in the chorus. While initially also a reluctant performer in solo speech activities, later in the kindergarten year, Julie participated more actively in "sharing" and reporting on home events, with the support of her teacher, and after having heard models of expert performance from other children. Not all her English language learner classmates displayed such participation in solo performance.

Kindergarten play, unlike Circle, rarely involved the teacher. In play, children were together, speaking or not to one another, manipulating the materials of the room (puzzles, cars, blocks, dressing-up materials, materials in playsites like the housekeeping centre, computers, and so on) and taking more or less full roles in that play. Although talk usually accompanied play, talk was seldom or never the only mediator. Instead, play materials often seemed more crucially important than talk. Children needed to secure access to materials and also to playmates, and their access to either was by no means universally secure. But in kindergarten play, unlike in coffee-breaks in Eva's case, access did not appear dependent primarily on experience in English; children who were inexperienced speakers of English sometimes appeared desirable, or at least tolerated playmates, and they also sometimes had access to desirable play materials. This is not to say that all children were always welcome in interactions with all other children, nor that they always got access to materials they liked; this was definitely not the case – some children (including experienced English speakers) were forcefully rejected by others as playmates and some children rarely got access to desirable materials. This was, then, a community in which it was possible to be successful or unsuccessful in gaining access to some social networks and to some desired resources.

Julie socialized actively with other children in her classroom. While she rarely appeared to seek to play with those anglophone girls in her classroom who appeared very powerful there (the girls who dominated the 'housekeeping' playsite), Julie did seem able to play with or beside the children whom she sought as playmates. She was particularly friendly with another second language learner, a boy, as well as an anglophone girl classmate. Was Julie's active interaction due to her inherent sociability (as concluded in some other child second language acquisition (SLA) studies, viz. Wong Fillmore, 1979), or were there characteristics of Julie's community that enabled her success there?

This question stimulated examination of moments of conflict in the classroom: moments when children's access to materials, to desirable identities or to playmates was in question (Toohey, 2001). While children's play in this kindergarten was often 'harmonious', it was also characterized by conflict (like the play analysed in detail by Goodwin, 1990) over materials or activities or access to play. Sometimes, children engaged in what appeared to be 'subordination' moves, in which they attempted to denigrate or subordinate other children, so as to command ownership of classroom materials or to exclude others from play. It was interesting to note that some children were unsuccessful in countering attempts by others to appropriate classroom materials or to exclude them from play. Julie, however, often ignored exclusionary/subordination attempts, or countered them with exclusionary or subordination moves of her own. She was able to do this with the aid of allies, other children who sometimes 'spoke for' her or who intervened on her behalf in disputes. While she was usually successful in her counter-moves, other children who used, in many cases, exactly the same language that Julie used, were not so successful. Exclusion from play meant removal from opportunities to hear other children speaking, or to practice themselves. Julie, however, often with the aid of her particular friends (mentioned above), was usually able to stay in play. So, this was a community in which it was possible to be excluded from play, one of the community's primary activities; and a community in which it was possible to be successful or unsuccessful in countering attempts by others to exclude one from those activities.

As well as making allies of children, Julie was successful in creating alliances with adults in her classroom. As an experienced Sunday-school attendee, Julie was familiar with school conventions of, for example, silence upon adult command, expeditious movement through transitions, 'appropriate' body demeanour and adept use of the tools of schools (scissors, paste, and so on). She appeared quiet on demand and her speech volume was low when required. She often greeted adults in her classrooms with excited smiles and hugs. These behaviours seemed to contribute to the adults who worked with her deeming her a "pleasant and easy-going" child, a "nice little girl", whose behaviour was 'mature' enough for Grade 1. Again, not all the English language learners in her class were so designated.

Eva, the adult language learner discussed above, was able to negotiate for herself an identity at the parties held outside the workplace, an identity which was in some ways at odds with her workplace identity. Aspects of Julie's outside-school identity might also have influenced her classroom access to peers. The afternoon ESL kindergarten which Julie attended also included her cousin Agatha and several other Polish-speaking youngsters. Agatha was a proficient speaker of Polish, but she was also an experienced English speaker because of her pre-school attendance at an English-speaking daycare centre, and she was, thus, another powerful ally for Julie. In the afternoons and on the playground, and in their homes, Julie and Agatha played together often.

By the end of the kindergarten year, Julie's teacher saw her as a student who was ready for Grade 1, at least as adequately prepared as other "normal" students. Not all of her English language learner classmates were so evaluated: some of these children, children who had had a much more problematic time in kindergarten, were deemed by the teacher to have further need of ESL instruction in Grade 1, and they would be removed from their classrooms for specified amounts of time for such instruction.

Workplaces and school classrooms: different 'cultures' for language learning

We referred earlier to sociocultural perspectives on L2 learning that focus not so much on individuals as on how practices in specific social, historical, and cultural contexts afford or constrain the access of learners to community activities and thus to learning. This approach, based on what is variously termed sociocultural, sociohistorical or cultural-historical theory, aims to "reflect the fundamentally social nature of learning and cognition" (Kirshner and Whitson, 1997: 1). Inspired by the early twentieth-century work of Vygotsky (1978) and that of more contemporary cultural psychologists, anthropologists and educators, second language researchers with interests in sociocultural theory have urged that our traditional focus on individuals and their functioning needs to shift to a focus on activities and settings and the learning that inevitably accompanies social practice (e.g. Gutierrez, 1993; Donato and McCormick, 1994; Lantolf and Appel, 1994; Willett, 1995; McGroarty, 1998; Toohey, 2000). These researchers conceptualize language learning as increasing participation in the activities (including linguistic activities) of particular communities, rather than in terms of control of wider varieties of linguistic forms or meanings.

Fundamental to a sociocultural approach is the assumption that "learning and development occur as people participate in the sociocultural activities of their community" (Rogoff, 1994: 209). From this perspective, learners of English participate in particular, local contexts in which specific practices create possibilities for them to participate in community activities, and in so doing, use one of the community's tools, language. Lave and Wenger (1991) propose the notion of a "community of practice" ("a set of relations among persons, activity and world", p. 98) as a way to theorize and investigate social contexts. Social contexts in their view can be viewed as complex and overlapping communities in which variously positioned participants learn specific, local, historically constructed and changing practices involving the use of particular tools. This view shifts attention away from questions about, for example, the personality traits or learning styles of participants, to questions about community organization, with respect to how participants' engagement in community practices, and use of the community's tools, is enabled or constrained.

The work of Mikhail Bakhtin also has been taken up in studies of L2 learning from a sociocultural perspective. Bakhtin (1981: 294) spoke to the need for speakers to wrest language away from "other people's mouths" and "other people's intentions". For him, speakers try on other people's utterances; they take words from other people's mouths; they appropriate those utterances and gradually those utterances come to serve their needs and relay their meanings. Bakhtin speaks about this process of appropriation as a struggle involving "the meeting and clash of divergent interests and the points of view to which these interests give rise" (Packer, 1993: 259).

From this perspective, second language learning is seen not simply as a gradual and neutral process of internalizing the rules, structures, and vocabulary of a standard language. Rather, differentially positioned learners are seen to appropriate the utterances of others in particular historical and cultural practices, situated in particular communities. Thus, researchers need to pay close attention to how communities and their practices are structured in order to examine how learners' access to the linguistic tools of their communities is facilitated or constrained. Attention thus shifts from the cognitive and emotional resources and strategies individual learners bring to second language learning situations, to a consideration of the learning situation and its everyday practices, and how these enable and constrain learning. It is with this in mind that we will examine the practices of Eva's workplace and Julie's classroom.

Munchies was a workplace with differentiated practices for workers, and Eva – positioned as newcomer, immigrant and English language learner – was seen by her boss and co-workers as an appropriate performer, at least initially, of hard, solitary work tasks. Doing these tasks blocked her access to conversations with her co-workers and customers, and thus limited her opportunities to engage in community practices like talking while working. Eva did have access to coffee-break conversations, but they were not very lengthy and they required expertise in English usage that Eva, as a relatively inexperienced speaker of English, did not have. If Eva's English proficiency had been tested at this point, when her workplace community had blocked her access to practice with more experienced participants, she might not have appeared to be a successful language learner. However, the workplace community of practice overlapped with another community of practice, the outside work social contacts in which workers participated. In this context the division of labour, spatial relationships, role possibilities and so on were different; Eva was able to bring valued resources to bear, and she could participate in a fuller way than she was able to in her workplace.

Julie's community was also structured hierarchically, in that the teacher was clearly the director of activities there. As director, however, the teacher invited and scaffolded children's access to classroom activities and conversations, at least in those interactions in which she was involved, and she explicitly desired and encouraged talk (within specified limits). When the teacher was involved, all community activities and resources were potentially, at least, accessible to all the children, and there were few solitary tasks required of children. When children played with one another, however, their interactions were often mediated by material resources that were not accessible to all. Julie was able to secure access to classroom resources and to talk with peers relatively easily, and her path to this access seemed less fraught with difficulty than Eva's and, indeed, less fraught than the paths of other English language learners in her classroom. As a participant with adult and child allies, previous experience with classroom materials and behavioural conventions, and as a person whose resistance to domination was (allowed by others to be) successful, Julie was able to participate in most interactions to which she sought access. Her kindergarten experience was thus relatively comfortable, not only because of what she brought with her, but also because of the way in which community practices in her classroom were structured. Had the expertise of her community, her cousin and her allies been less available to her, or had the resources she brought to the community or her allies been less symbolically valued, it is possible that her language and academic learning would have been evaluated differently.

Although both Eva and Julie were successful in gaining access to the conversations of their milieux, they had to struggle for this access. As we shall now discuss, we have found current post-structural and critical theory about identity and agency helpful in understanding how these language learners differentially engaged with the struggles they encountered in their respective communities.

Autonomy, identity and human agency

Previous researchers might have seen Eva and Julie as gradually developing appropriate strategies for interaction in their respective linguistic communities by, for example, monitoring their linguistic performances more diligently and exploiting the target language more systematically. Our research paints a more complex picture, however. Rather than focusing on language acquisition per se, both learners sought to set up counter-discourses in which their identities could be respected and their resources valued, thereby enhancing the possibilities for shared conversation. Thus Eva, initially constructed as an 'ESL immigrant', sought to reposition herself as a 'multilingual resource' with a desirable partner; Julie, initially constructed as an 'ESL learner', became seen as a "nice little girl" with allies. It was their success in claiming more powerful identities (either consciously, as in Eva's case, or perhaps unconsciously, as in Julie's case) that seems central to their success as good language learners. This is not to say that proficiency in English was irrelevant in the process of accessing peer networks, particularly in Eva's case, but rather that struggles over identity were central. Such an analysis is informed by recent work on identity and language learning in the field of SLA (see Norton and Toohey (2002) for an overview).

During the past few years, scholars such as Goldstein (1996), McKay and Wong (1996), Norton (1997), Angelil-Carter (1997), Stein (1998) and Harklau (2000) have demonstrated in their research that the conditions under which language learners speak are often highly challenging, engaging the learners' identities in complex and often contradictory ways. They have focused, in particular, on the unequal relations of power between language learners and target language speakers, arguing that SLA theory has not given sufficient attention to the effects of power on social interaction. The notion of 'investment' (Norton Peirce, 1995; McKay and Wong, 1996; Angelil-Carter, 1997) has been helpful in signaling the socially and historically constructed relationship of learners to the target language, and their sometimes ambivalent desire to learn and practice it. Re-conceptualizing the established SLA notion of 'motivation', some researchers argue that when learners 'invest' in a second language, they do so anticipating that they will acquire a wider range of symbolic and material resources, which will in turn enhance their conception of themselves and further their desires for the future.

Pierre Bourdieu (1977, 1984), a French sociologist, focused on the importance of power in structuring speech. He argued that "speech always owes a major part of its value to the value of the person who utters it" (1977: 652). For him, because of unequal power relations between speakers, the ability of speakers to "command a listener" (p. 648) is concomitantly unequal. Both Eva and Julia had shifting degrees of ability to command listeners in their respective communities. Eva initially had difficulty in commanding the attention of her listeners: a person who carried out the garbage was a person of limited value; a person who was not Canadian had very little power to impose reception in her community. Nevertheless, Eva was highly invested in learning English because she wanted better relationships with her co-workers (symbolic resources) as well as improved job prospects (material resources) which would in turn give her a greater sense of self-worth. Julie was similarly invested in mastering the shifting set of practices that would position her as a successful student and a desirable and powerful playmate. She may have been initially silent in her classroom, but silence or 'ESL-ness' was not a stigmatized category there; her silence, simply, was not particularly noticeable. Her community granted her (but not everyone) the right to participate in community activities, and this access helped her to claim the right to speak fairly soon after entry into kindergarten. Eva struggled for months for equivalent success.

Theories of identity as multiple, changing, and a site of struggle are comprehensively developed by Christine Weedon (1996), working within a tradition of feminist poststructuralism. Weedon (1996: 32) notes that the terms 'subject' and 'subjectivity' signify a different conception of the individual than essentialist views associated with humanist conceptions of the individual dominant in Western philosophy. Poststructuralism depicts the individual – the subject – as diverse, contradictory, dynamic and changing over historical time and social space. Our data demonstrate convincingly that the subjectivity of the language learner is crucial to an understanding of the conditions under which a language learner speaks. Eva could not speak from the position of the person who carried out the garbage: she had to reposition herself in the eyes of her co-workers before she could claim the right to speak and, more crucially, impose reception on her interlocutors. Likewise, Julie needed to position herself as someone with allies, and as someone resistant to subordination, so as to continue to claim space in the play of her classmates.

Discussion

Let us return, then, to our two central questions: (1) What kinds of access to participation in the social networks of these settings were provided for learners? And (2) How did these two particular learners manage their own access to the social networks of their anglophone peer groups? We believe the answers to these questions lie in the dialectic between agency/autonomy and community/culture and we summarize our thinking on these matters below.

Eva and Julie were able to gain access to the social networks of their particular communities because of practices in the communities in which they were located and through their own agency/efforts to position themselves as persons worth talking/listening to. Eva was able to counter her positioning as an undesirable immigrant with an undesirable job, because her community was one in which mobility in work assignments was possible. Her community also supported different constellations of value in outside-work outings. Julie participated in a community in which participation in choral performance was always accessible, but not compulsory for her. Her community was also structured so that solo performances for the teacher were protected and scaffolded. In interactions with other children, when community practices might have sequestered Julie from peer interaction, her community accepted her efforts to counter subordination. In both cases, we wonder what data we would have collected had Eva and Julie not been blonde and white-skinned, slim, able-bodied, well-dressed and attractive to Western eyes. In this regard, while her co-workers were ultimately happy to work with Eva, they remained reluctant to work with other immigrants. And in the classroom, other English language learners (notably a South Asian female student in the study) were not as successful as Julie in resisting subordination, even though they used in many cases exactly the same language to attempt this resistance.

The other question raised by our studies is the relationship between access to second language networks and second language learning.

We think both studies demonstrate that access to second language networks, and increasing participation in them, is coincident with second language learning. In the adult study, Eva had more access to an English-speaking Canadian network than the other women reported in Norton (2000); she also showed the best progress and proficiency in English language assessments. In the child study, Julie moved from very little preschool experience in English to 'graduation' from ESL in one year, unlike the other children in Toohey (2000), whose access to a peer network was less secure. Like Lave and Wenger (1991) and Wenger (1998), we believe that learning to use the tool of language, like learning to use the tools of other activities, is primarily a matter of access to skilled performance, practice and access to identities of competence. Our data, from learners of different ages and in different environments, support this claim.

Concluding comments

In this chapter we have argued that our studies of two successful language learners demonstrate that there was nothing inherently good about them as language learners. In another work place, Eva might have remained a 'non-Canadian'; in another classroom, Julie may have joined other English language learners on the margins of social life. Our research and recent theoretical discussions have convinced us that understanding language learning requires attention to social practices in the contexts in which learners learn second languages. Further, we have argued for the importance of examining the ways in which learners exercise agency in forming and reforming their identities in those contexts. We see this dual focus as necessary to understand good language learning. Further, learners' investments in learning a second language, as well as the ways in which their identities affect their participation in second language activities, must also be matters of consideration in future research.

Drawing on our data, we conclude this chapter with a comment on the way conceptions of SLA theory may evolve in the future. We believe it is significant that both Eva and Julie were able to access the social networks in their respective learning communities, albeit at different rates. We would like to underline here that the reception both learners received in their different learning sites was more favourable than that given to other English language learners with different physical and cultural characteristics. Accordingly, we hope that future research, drawing on diverse methodologies, will develop insights into issues of race, the body, and language learning.

Reflection/discussion questions

1. Describe a particular language learning setting with which you are familiar. What practices in this setting enable or disable learners' participation in community activities?
2. Consider your own second/foreign language learning trajectory. Did you struggle to re-position yourself within your learning setting? How did you do this?
3. From your own experience, what generalizations can you make about differences between child and adult second language learning settings?
4. Think about a second language teaching situation with which you are familiar. What do you think are the implications for learning and for autonomy of *compulsory* participation in second language activities?

Note

This is a substantially revised version of B. Norton and K. Toohey (2001). Changing perspectives on good language learning. *TESOL Quarterly* 35/2: 307–22.

Part II
Theoretical Perspectives

4
Toward a More Systematic Model of L2 Learner Autonomy

Rebecca L. Oxford

> *Oh! Blessed rage for order, pale Ramon,*
> *[...] rage to order the words of the sea [...]*
> *and of ourselves and of our origins.*

(Wallace Stevens)

Introduction

The theoretical framework of learner autonomy in our field, and probably in others, is far from coherent. Although L2 learner autonomy has benefited from many expert contributions (e.g. Holec, 1980, 1981, 1988; Dickinson, 1987, 1988, 1992; Little, 1991, 1995; Wenden, 1991; Dam, 1995; Benson and Voller, 1997a; Karlsson et al., 2001), it is still beset by conflicting ideologies, roiling inconsistencies, and fragmentary theories. Even the most basic terminology is full of semantic conflicts. For instance, Dickinson and Holec used different (and reversed) meanings for autonomy and self-direction. For Dickinson (1987), 'autonomy' referred to the learning situation in which the individual manifests an attitude of responsibility, and 'self-direction' was the attitude of responsibility. In contrast, Holec (1979) defined 'autonomy' as the learner's ability to be responsible for his/her learning and later (1980) referred to autonomy in regard to the learner's attitude of responsibility, while he used 'self-direction' to refer to the learning situation or mode in which the attitude of autonomy is displayed.

Conflicts in terminology were still unresolved by 2001, when yet another distinction emerged between autonomy and self-directed language learning. Rivers (2001: 287) used 'autonomy' to refer to L2 learners' "requesting and demanding substantive changes to every aspect of the course, and especially to the course content and structure" and employed 'self-directed language learning' as the label for "behaviors directed at the amelioration of the learner–teacher and learner–learner style conflicts, and at the individual's need for learner autonomy". For Rivers, "autonomy is a prerequisite for self-directed language learning" (p. 286).

Other clashes have been more ideological than semantic. For instance, Allwright (1990) took a psychological stance, asserting that autonomy involves an attitude of willingness to take responsibility, the necessary ability, and concrete action; but Pennycook (1997) resoundingly decried the psychological approach to autonomy. Benson's (1997) attempt at a systematic model of L2 learner autonomy proved helpful in some ways but remained at best quite fragmentary. That model, in line with Pennycook (1997), contains three "versions": (a) technical, encompassing situational conditions for autonomy; (b) psychological, involving the individual's characteristics, such as attitudes and behaviors; and (c) political, dealing with competing ideologies. However, the model clearly privileges the political version; a necessary piece, the sociocultural perspective, is missing; learning strategies are located only in the technical version, although logically they should be part of each version; and finally, the model does not systematically show how the important constructs of context, agency, and motivation relate to different versions of autonomy.

A "blessed rage for order" at last convinced me to try to sort out the currently ambiguous and conflicting frameworks of L2 learner autonomy. The "rage to order the words" – the theories and terminology of learner autonomy – became a quest to develop a more systematic and comprehensive theoretical model than has previously existed. I offer this model, summarized in Table 4.1 below, to stimulate discussion and further refinement of concepts of L2 learner autonomy. This chapter is organized as follows: (1) overview of the model; (2) conceptual definitions of key terms; (3) explanation of each of the four perspectives in the model; and (4) implications of the model for further research.

Overview of the model

The model (Table 4.1) contains four perspectives on autonomy, each with a different focus:

- *Technical perspective*: focus on the physical situation.
- *Psychological perspective*: focus on characteristics of learners.

Table 4.1 A model of learner autonomy

Perspectives on autonomy	Themes			
	Context	Agency	Motivation	Learning strategies
Technical Autonomy is seen as skills for 'independent' learning' situations, such as in a self-access center.	Context is viewed as literal surroundings, typically in a self-access center.	Agency is viewed as *total* by some advocates of self-access. However, agency is viewed as *limited* by critics of self-access.	Motivation is variable, depending on the situational conditions and the response of the individual to those conditions.	Learning strategies are considered as tools that are 'given' by the teacher to the student through learner training (strategy instruction).
Psychological Autonomy is seen as a combination of characteristics of the individual. Contributions include attitudes, ability, learning strategies, and styles.	Context refers to the generalized environment (foreign vs second language environment), than referring to the specific details of the immediate setting.	Agency is a psychological characteristic of the individual.	Motivational intensity (for L2 learning) is often seen as a relatively static characteristic of the person, although self-efficacy (an aspect of motivation) changes through strategy instruction. Recent, complex L2 models reveal multiple aspects of motivation.	Learning strategies seen as psychological features of the individual that can change through practice and strategy instruction. Optimal strategy use relates to task, learning style, goals, etc.

(Contd.)

Table 4.1 (Contd.)

Perspectives on autonomy	Themes				
	Context	Agency	Motivation	Learning strategies
Sociocultural I Autonomy is self-regulation, gained through social interaction with a more capable, mediating person in a particular setting. Mediation can also occur through books, technology, and other means.	Context is seen as the relationship between the learner and more capable others, as well as specific social and cultural settings.	Agency is viewed as the power to control one's learning through self-regulation.	Motivation is linked to becoming a self-regulated individual.	The term 'learning strategies' is not typically used, although metacognitive, cognitive and social learning strategies are clearly implicit in Vygotsky's work.
Sociocultural II (often overlaps with political-critical): Autonomy is not the primary goal. The primary goal is participation (at first peripheral and then more complete) in the community of practice. Mediated	Context is viewed as communities of practice, as cognitive apprenticeship, and as larger social and cultural environment.	Agency is reflected in a cognitive apprenticeship and in participating actively with expert practitioners.	Motivation is linked to becoming part of a community of practice. Motivation is investment in an 'imagined' (desired) community.	Learning strategies grow out of the practices of communities. In cognitive apprenticeships, learners gain strategies from expert practitioners. Also, learners already have

learning occurs through cognitive apprenticeships. *Political-critical* Autonomy involves gaining access to cultural alternatives and power structures; developing an articulate voice amid competing ideologies.	Context is an arrangement of ideological positions, instantiated in a specific interaction, relationship, or setting.	Agency is power to control one's situation, be fully heard, be free from oppression, and have choices.	Motivation is associated with becoming free to have one's own voice, ideological position, choice of cultural alternatives. The individual is also motivated to seek redress from social inequalities of race, gender, class, etc.	many strategies from their initial communities. Learning strategies are hardly discussed in the political-critical perspective, except to say that they do not belong there (see Pennycook, 1997). However, learning strategies can help open up access within power structures and cultural alternatives for learners.

- *Sociocultural perspective*: focus on mediated learning. (Note: Two forms of the sociocultural perspective are included, labeled here as Sociocultural I and II.)
- *Political-critical perspective*: focus on ideologies, access, and power structures.

Consideration of all relevant perspectives is likely to provide a stronger, richer understanding of learner autonomy. Four important themes – context, agency, motivation, and learning strategies – run through each of the perspectives.

Conceptual definitions of key terms

'*Context*' comes from the Latin 'contexere' (to weave together, join, or connect). In this chapter, it refers to the whole situation, background, setting, or environment relevant to L2 learning. Some perspectives view context as more general, while others see it as more specific and local. In the political-critical perspective, context also refers to ideological positions manifested in specific settings, relationships, or interactions. The context provides "opportunities for learning to the active, participating learner" (van Lier, 2000: 253). These context-based opportunities can be called 'affordances' because each opportunity "affords further action (but does not cause or trigger it)" (ibid.: 252).

'*Autonomy*' is derived from the Greek 'autónomos' (living under one's own laws, self-governing). The original political meaning was applied to city-states, but the meaning has expanded into other realms. Autonomy and self-regulation (a Latin-based equivalent) refer to the same condition of being self-ruled or capable of regulating one's own thoughts, learning, and actions.

'*Agency*' comes from the Latin 'agēre' (to do, act, lead, or drive). 'Agency' means the quality of being an active force in producing an effect, and an agent is one who has this quality. Psychologically speaking, a learner is an agent if s/he acts intentionally (Bandura, 1997: 3), which implies an intention or goal. However, in a broader context, a person's sense of agency can be blocked or encouraged by social and cultural conditions.

The root of '*motive*', '*motivate*', and '*motivation*' is the Latin 'movēre' (to move). 'Motivate' means to provide with a 'motive', that is, an inner drive, impulse, intention, or goal that causes a person to do something or act in a certain way. 'Motivation' is the condition of being moved to action or the internal desire to take action. 'L2 learning motivation', or 'L2 motivation', means the desire to learn another language.

'*Strategy*' is from the Greek 'stratēgía' (command of a general). In ancient Greece, strategy involved a general's plan to win a war. 'Strategy' now means a plan oriented to meeting a goal. 'L2 learning strategies' are specific plans or steps – either observable, such as taking notes or seeking out a conversation partner, or unobservable, such as mentally analysing a word – that L2 learners intentionally employ to improve reception, storage, retention, and retrieval of information. Learning strategies should not be confused with learning styles, which are broad approaches to learning, such as intuitive-random versus concrete-sequential, or visual versus auditory.

I now turn to the first perspective on learner autonomy, the technical. This perspective reminds us of the need to consider external surroundings.

Technical perspective on learner autonomy: focus on situational conditions

The technical perspective emphasizes the situational conditions under which learner autonomy may develop. Most often the literature treats these as 'other-created' conditions, not conditions initially generated by the learner. Context in this perspective consists of literal surroundings, such as a self-access center, a classroom, a home setting, or a travel environment. The self-access center is the most frequently mentioned context in the technical perspective and will be the focus of the discussion here. Dickinson's (1987: 11) definition of autonomy illustrates the technical perspective: "the situation in which the learner is totally responsible for the decisions concerned with his/her learning and the implementation of these decisions. In full autonomy there is no involvement of a teacher or an institution [...] [nor] specially prepared materials." However, this view, if carried to its logical extreme, would preclude even the possibility of using an institutionalized self-access resource center. Later Dickinson (1992) showed how teachers in formalized classrooms can promote some degree of learner autonomy.

Within the limits of context (literal, physical conditions) as defined in this perspective, the development of agency is "merely a matter of handing over the reins, of giving students greater control over the curriculum, of giving them greater control over or access to resources, of letting them negotiate what, when, and how they want to learn" (Pennycook, 1997: 46). However, agency is not a gift that can be delivered to the learner (Freire, 1972). Merely changing situational conditions – especially 'giving' students full responsibility for their learning – cannot by itself create agency. Many self-access centers offer only low-level, scripted, non-communicative, uncreative L2 tasks (Littlejohn, 1997), which are not autonomy-fostering or agency-inspiring. However, as described by Karlsson et al. (1997), the University of Helsinki self-access center has successfully developed agency in L2 learners through 'user support groups' working on meaningful L2 projects with help from committed advisors. Moving far beyond physical conditions and dealing directly with psychological, social, and cultural issues, this appears to be a truly redefined, agentic self-access center.

Learner autonomy's technical mode, if viewed as the extreme situation in which the person learns alone and makes all instructional decisions without support from a teacher, advisor, or institution, can be either motivating or demotivating, depending on the learner's goals (see Dörnyei, 2001) and learning style (see Ehrman, 1996; Reid, 1998). If the learner wishes to read more effectively, solo learning might be satisfactorily motivating, especially if the person has an introverted style and therefore often enjoys working alone. However, if the learner – especially an extroverted learner (who needs interaction) or a concrete-sequential learner (who craves guidance) – desires to develop speaking competence, then solo learning can be demotivating. For many learners, motivation emerges via having at least some interaction with peers or with a language counsellor or teacher (Riley, 1997).

The technical perspective on autonomy treats learning strategies merely as tools that the teacher can 'give' to the student via learner training or strategy instruction (Benson, 1997). However, learning strategies are not mere tools that can be handed over, just as agency or empowerment cannot be simply granted. Effective strategy instruction requires the teacher's knowledge of learners' current strategy use, needs, and cultural beliefs; it also demands learners' full participation in the process of strategy development (Oxford, 1990, 1996a). This process goes well past the external, physical conditions highlighted by the technical perspective.

The technical perspective, with its emphasis on external conditions, has value. After all, a rich description of literal, physical circumstances is often very important for understanding psychological, social, and political factors in a learning situation. We must not, however, be romanced into thinking that external conditions alone can develop learner autonomy. Without psychology, the next perspective to be discussed, the technical perspective would be inert.

Psychological perspective on learner autonomy: focus on characteristics of learners

The psychological perspective examines mental and emotional characteristics of learners, who are viewed either as individuals (individual psychology) or as members of a rather generalized social or cultural group (social psychology). The psychological perspective uses neither the sociocultural – meaning 'interactionist' – nor the political-critical lens.

Psychological research indicates that autonomous learners have characteristics such as these: high motivation; self-efficacy, that is, "beliefs in one's capabilities to organize and execute the courses of action required to produce given attainments" (Bandura, 1997: 3) – and thus a sense of agency; a desire to seek meaning (Frankl, 1997); positive attitudes; need for achievement; and a combination of extrinsic and intrinsic motivation (Deci and Ryan, 1985; Wigfield et al., 1998). Students are 'extrinsically' motivated when learning is done for the sake of rewards (such as grades or praise) that are not inherently associated with the learning itself. In contrast, students are 'intrinsically' motivated when the reward for learning is enjoyment of the activity itself or a feeling of competence in doing the task. In intrinsically motivating tasks, students may experience 'flow', an in-the-moment, optimal sensation of enjoyment and competence (Csikszentmihalyi, 1991). Motivation depends greatly on the context, people involved, and specific circumstances (Pintrich and Schunk, 1996). Severe performance anxiety mitigates against autonomy and motivation, though mild anxiety may sometimes enhance them (Young, 1998).

In the psychological view, context often refers to the generalized second versus foreign language environment, rather than the details of the immediate setting. A 'second' language is learned in a setting where it is the main means of daily communication by most people, while a 'foreign' language is learned in an environment where it is not the everyday vehicle of the majority's communication (Green and Oxford, 1995). Compared with a foreign language environment, a second language environment 'affords' many opportunities to encounter and use the target language. Early studies (Gardner and Lambert, 1972; Gardner, 1985) showed that second language learners who wanted to integrate into the target culture (having 'integrative orientation') were more motivated and more proficient than those who were 'instrumentally oriented' for reasons of academic or job advancement. However, integrative orientation proved far less important in foreign language settings, where instrumental motivation held greater sway (Au, 1988; Crookes and Schmidt, 1991; Oxford and Shearin, 1994).

In the 1990s, researchers studied a greater range of reasons for L2 learning: friendship, travel, cultural and media interest, concern for world affairs or peace, career improvement, intrinsic interest, and others (Clément et al., 1994; Oxford, 1995). In a Canadian study, adult learners considered 'autonomous' were intrinsically motivated to learn L2 as though it were a puzzle or game but did not show much social desire to use the language (Noels et al., 2000).

A number of recent models of L2 motivation have a bearing on learner autonomy, although autonomy is not their focal point. For instance, Dörnyei's (1994) model of L2 motivation includes three levels: (a) the *language level*, reflecting social and cultural attitudes toward the language and involving integrative and instrumental reasons for language learning; (b) the *learner level*, concerning the individual's characteristics, such as achievement needs and linguistic self-confidence (this is where autonomy resides); and (c) the *learning situation level*, containing course factors, teacher factors, and group factors. Tremblay and Gardner (1995) presented an empirically based, expanded model of L2 motivation. See Dörnyei (2001) for a summary of recent models.

Motivation to direct one's own learning may be related to learning style (Ehrman, 1996; Reid, 1998), defined earlier as a broad approach to learning. For instance, compared with concrete-sequential learners, who prefer to have an authority figure to guide their learning in a step-by-step way, intuitive-random learners want to be free to play by their own rules while learning. Therefore, intuitive-random learners may be more motivated to become autonomous and may also find it easier to do so. Certain learning styles appear to predominate in particular cultures, and these styles depend on typically unquestioned and sometimes unconsciously held beliefs (Yang, 1992). Differences across cultures' belief systems may help explain why learner autonomy can differ in value from one culture to another. As Pennycook (1997) noted, learner autonomy may not be a universal good.

Learning strategies, specific steps or plans people use to enhance their learning, are often viewed as a psychological gateway to L2 learner autonomy (Oxford, 1990; Wenden, 1991; Dickinson, 1992; Littlewood, 1996b). Outside the L2 field, Zimmerman and Martinez-Pons (1988, 1990) identified and categorized the learning strategies of autonomous learners as follows: self-evaluation, organization, goal-setting, planning, information-seeking, record-keeping, self-monitoring, environmental structuring, giving oneself consequences for performance, rehearsing, memorizing, seeking social assistance, and reviewing. Use of learning strategies relates to language performance, achievement, proficiency, and autonomy beliefs (see, for example, O'Malley and Chamot, 1990; Oxford and Ehrman, 1995; Pressley and Woloshyn, 1995). Learning strategies are successfully teachable through strategy instruction or learner training, which can improve learners' sense of agency, self-efficacy judgments, motivation, confidence, and L2 performance (Chamot and O'Malley, 1996; Chamot et al., 1996; Dadour and Robbins, 1996; Oxford and Leaver, 1996; Nunan, 1997a).

Motivation was the key factor in learning strategy use in very large-scale investigations of foreign language learning in Egypt, Singapore, Taiwan and the USA (Oxford and Nyikos, 1989; Ku, 1995; Schmidt et al., 1996; Wharton, 2000). Students motivated to use the new language outside of class as well as in class, as compared to just in class, employed more creative and effective learning strategies (Hsiao, 1995; Oxford and Ehrman, 1995; Oxford et al., 1993). We might assume that students who were more motivated to use the language outside of class were more autonomous learners.

The psychological perspective on learner autonomy offers many riches, such as an understanding of various forms of agency, models of motivation, and autonomy-encouraging styles and strategies. However, the psychological viewpoint does not look in depth at the details of any given sociocultural context, nor does it consider the crucial role of mediated learning. That is why the sociocultural perspective that follows is so important.

Sociocultural perspectives on learner autonomy: focus on mediated learning

This perspective on learner autonomy consists of two related aspects, Sociocultural I and II, both of which involve socially mediated learning. The perspective has been called by various names: sociocultural, sociocognitive, and social-interactionist. Unlike the psychological perspective, the sociocultural perspective emphasizes social interaction as a major part of cognitive and language development. Unlike the political-critical perspective, the sociocultural view does not focus primarily on issues of power, access, and ideology; it centers instead on the development of human capacity via interaction. Both aspects, but especially Sociocultural II, can be linked with the political-critical perspective, involving ideologies and access to power, although they can also be understood in a less political light, as shown here.

Sociocultural I

Sociocultural I centers mostly on the work of Vygotsky (1978; for applications of Vygotsky's work in L2 learning, see especially Lantolf (2000) and Lantolf and Pavlenko (2001)). In the Sociocultural I perspective, context is important in two ways. First, learning is situated in a particular context – that is, a social and cultural setting populated by specific individuals at a given historical time. Second, context also consists of a particular kind of relationship, that of mediated learning. Mediation involves dynamic interaction between the learner and a 'more capable other' (although mediation can also occur with a book, cultural artifact, or physical model). For Vygotsky, cognitive development consisted of the conversion of social relations into mental functions through mediated learning. Mediation helps the learner move through the zone of proximal development (ZPD). The ZPD represents the difference between (a) the learner's performance without assistance and (b) the learner's performance with assistance.

In the Sociocultural I view, agency is tantamount to self-regulation (Vygotsky, 1978). In Vygotsky's theory, the 'more capable other', often a teacher or parent, wants the learner to develop self-regulatory abilities that allow him/her to act intentionally and independently. The more capable other provides the learner with scaffolding consisting of various types of assistance, which can be removed as the learner becomes more self-regulated. Through the use of appropriate scaffolding at just the right times, the more capable other helps the learner move through the ZPD. Scaffolding is not a one-time thing, and neither is its removal. It is a spiraling, cyclical movement that involves both social engagement and separation.

Motivation is not highlighted as a key feature in the Sociocultural I perspective, but it is quite important. The Sociocultural I view implies that the learner is motivated to become a self-regulated learner. The more capable other must start by accepting learners where they are but must also motivate and guide them to greater competence. The learner's motivation is intensified because of the meaningfulness of the learning and the nature of the mediated-learning relationship.

In Vygotsky's theory, self-regulation is "the process of planning, guiding, and monitoring one's own attention and behavior" (Berk and Winsler, 1995: 171). Planning, guiding, and monitoring oneself, along with organizing and evaluating one's own learning, are collectively known as 'metacognitive learning strategies', though Vygotsky did not use the term 'strategies'. Vygotsky mentioned a variety of higher-order cognitive functions, such as analysing and synthesizing, which other researchers often call 'cognitive learning strategies'. Such strategies are internalized via social interactions with more competent others, thus requiring the use of 'social learning strategies', such as asking questions for clarification and learning with others. For more information on these different kinds of strategies, see Oxford (1990, 1996a), Chamot and O'Malley (1996), and Cohen (1998).

Sociocultural II

Sociocultural II stems from the work of Rogoff and Lave (1984), Lave and Wenger (1991), Rogoff (1996), Wenger (1998), and Wenger et al. (2002). Norton (2000, 2001) has revealed its importance in the L2 arena. Like Sociocultural I, Sociocultural II relies on mediated learning, which is meaningful and situated in a particular place and time. However, in Sociocultural II, the individual is not as central as community participation; and this perspective emphasizes the context of autonomy rather than the individual exercising it. In Sociocultural II, context is the *community of practice* (Lave and Wenger, 1991; Wenger, 1998; Wenger et al., 2002), the relationships that occur in that community, and the larger social and cultural environment. Learners (newcomers) *participate peripherally* in communities of practice through *cognitive apprenticeships* (Rogoff and Lave, 1984; Rogoff, 1996) with practitioners (old-timers). This interaction can only occur if old-timers are willing to provide insider knowledge, cultural understandings, practice, and strategies to newcomers.

Norton (2000, 2001) discussed L2 immigrant learners' symbolic and emotional investment, that is, their motivation to enter particular 'imagined (desired) communities'. Sometimes the emotional investment was so strong that learners were afraid of using the L2 in the presence of gatekeepers to the imagined communities and therefore lapsed into non-participation. Yet, with proper support, some learners were able to move from non-participation to peripheral participation and gradually to more complete participation in the communities to which they wished to belong. Learners felt increasingly agentic, able to have an effect, as they moved toward more complete participation in the community.

Lantolf and Pavlenko (2001: 146) expressed the necessity of meaning in the Sociocultural II perspective on learner agency:

[H]uman agency is about more than performance, or doing; it is intimately linked to significance. That is, things and events matter to people – their actions have meanings and interpretations. It is agency that links motivation, more recently conceptualized as investment by Norton Pierce (1995), to action and defines a myriad of paths taken by learners. Self-reflection enables us to change our dispositions toward action and involvement.

In the Sociocultural II sense, the practitioners or old-timers can help the learners or newcomers to gain the strategies, meanings, and artifacts needed to enter the community of practice. In a sociocultural study of L2 learning strategies, Levine et al. (1996) described immigrants to Israel from the former Soviet Union. Old-timers were immigrants who had left their homeland earlier, were by then full participants in the Israeli culture, and were less tied to Soviet-style rote-memorization strategies. Self-observed strategies of the new immigrants, as compared with those of the old-timers, tended to be more rigid and less creative. Newcomers gradually relaxed their strategy use as they became acclimatized to their new cultural community in Israel.

In L2 learning histories (Oxford, 1996b), learners discussed using learning strategies as a key means of gaining access to their imagined communities, which were as seemingly mundane but as personally significant as the local restaurant-bar in a Spanish city, a particular group of more proficient peers learning Spanish for the Peace Corps in Guatemala, and a two-person (tourist and native farmer) interaction in France. Learning strategies, which created greater proficiency and self-efficacy, thus enabled the learners to access their imagined communities.

In sum, both the Sociocultural I and the Sociocultural II categories contribute ideas concerning mediated, meaningful, situated learning that involves a sense of agency. Motivation is important in both Sociocultural I and II, but in Sociocultural II its characterization is particularly insightful: investment in the imagined community. Learning strategies play somewhat different, but still significant roles in the two aspects of the sociocultural perspective. The Sociocultural II category often overlaps with the political-critical perspective, which is discussed next.

Political-critical perspective on learner autonomy: focus on power, access, and ideology

The political-critical perspective centrally involves issues of power, access, and ideology. Pennycook's (1997, 2001) work illustrates this perspective (or rather set of perspectives). Pennycook (1997) skewered 'mainstream autonomy' for its false assumption that student-centered, individualistic, and autonomous learning is universally appropriate. He also argued that it was wrong for liberal-humanists to de-radicalize Freire's (1972) and Illich's (1979) "marginal and politically engaged concept" of learner autonomy (p. 41). "[T]he wider social, cultural and political concerns of language education" have been largely forgotten in the "reductionist" shift toward a student-centered focus "on the psychology of the language learner in cognitive isolation" (ibid.). In the political-critical perspective, context refers to ideologies and attitudes found in specific locations, situations, groups (related to age, gender, religion, culture), institutions, and socioeconomic levels. Context is viewed in a highly political way, reflecting issues of oppression, power, control, and access. Power operates not only "at the macro level of powerful institutions" but also at the micro level of "everyday social encounters" and ordinary discourse (Norton, 2000: 7).

Yet contextual adversities such as ethnic oppression are not necessarily insuperable barriers to claiming personal power and mental autonomy. According to Andrew Cohen (personal communication, November 2002), the refusniks in the former Soviet Union learned Hebrew, including the spoken language, using dictionaries and textbooks, often without live models for pronunciation. In other examples provided by Cohen, his father-in-law, imprisoned in Auschwitz, learned German by listening to the guards; and Albert Valdman, seeking refuge from the Nazis in France in a barn owned by a Resistance family, learned English from a Sears and Roebuck catalog. Frankl (1997) kept himself alive in the Nazi concentration camp by searching for personal meaning. As Lantolf and Pavlenko (2001: 145–6) state (emphasis added):

> As agents, learners actively engage in constructing the terms and conditions of their own learning. [...] Change in one's habitus [disposition] is possible because human agents are capable (given the right circumstances) of *critically analyzing the discourses which frame their lives, and of claiming or resisting them according to the effects they wish to bring about.*

In Pennycook's (1997) political-critical viewpoint, development of autonomy and agency must involve becoming "an author of one's own world" (p. 45). To do this, learners must "struggle for cultural alternatives" (ibid.), that is, "meanings in [the L2] that run against the class, gender, race and cultural assumptions linked to different contexts of language use" (p. 53) and must develop "*insurgent* voices [...] amid the cultures, discourses, and ideologies within which we live our lives" (p. 49). This seems to be exactly the route taken by the refusniks, Cohen's father-in-law, Valdman, and Frankl, all of whom were insurgents in their idiosyncratic ways.

However, not all groups or individuals believe that power or autonomy is within their grasp. For instance, Ogbu's (1991) research showed that in countries around the world, *voluntary* (immigrant) minority groups and *involuntary* (non-immigrant) minority groups differed in their cultural models about power. Voluntary minority groups believed they could advance in their new societies and often showed high motivation that led to school success and power. In contrast, involuntary minority groups believed that the society's rules for self-advancement would exclude them unless they were willing to give up their own cultural identities. Thus, voluntary and involuntary minority groups differed greatly in motivation for schooling and in beliefs about the possibility of success, given their different social worlds.

The political-critical perspective shakes us by the shoulders, forcing us to question assumptions and to critique existing power structures. It causes us to think hard about accepting the status quo. It creates an internal (and sometimes an external) struggle. It reminds us that we can critically analyse the discourses that frame our lives, we can create new alternatives for ourselves, and we can challenge our students to do the same.

Discussion and implications for future research

The model of L2 learner autonomy above contains four perspectives: technical, psychological, sociocultural, and political-critical. Each of these perspectives has four strands or themes: context, agency, motivation, and learning strategies. Without one or another of these themes and perspectives, the model would have been incomplete. Even the technical perspective, with its emphasis on immediate, physical conditions, has value, although such external conditions do not automatically lead to learner autonomy.

Future research should combine as many perspectives as possible in any given study. No single perspective should be considered antithetical to any other perspective, although some theorists would have us believe that antagonism is inevitable. For instance, a tendency to privilege the political-critical viewpoint at the expense of other relevant viewpoints would be a sad waste, although it is important to recognize that the political-critical perspective is very important and was ignored for too long within applied linguistics.

To shed light on L2 learner autonomy, quantitative and qualitative research should work together to produce a larger, clearer picture of what occurs – and what should optimally occur – in various contexts, with different people, and under contrasting belief systems. We must not be satisfied only with quantitative research tools that distance the investigator from the context and hide cultural assumptions within webs of abstraction and generalization. On the other hand, we must not accept the idea that the only way to do research is through qualitative methodologies, whose results cannot easily be generalized. Investigations can combine both qualitative and quantitative techniques to present a clearer view of learner autonomy.

Truly rich research can emerge when we use multiple methodologies to uncover deeper meanings for context, agency, motivation and learning strategies, all of which should be part of the tapestry of learner autonomy. Let us explore the model in this chapter as a means of talking about learner autonomy in fresher, more expansive, and more systematic ways. I hope others share with me a "rage for order" that can spur our field to greater discussion of autonomy's breadth and depth.

Acknowledgements

I am grateful for the helpful suggestions made by Andrew Cohen and David Palfreyman concerning this chapter.

Reflection/discussion questions

1. Has the model of autonomy presented in this chapter clarified any uncertainties you had about the meaning of autonomy? What uncertainties still remain?
2. In what ways is the concept of 'agency' important to the idea of learner autonomy? Can learner autonomy exist without a sense of agency?
3. Think about a learning situation with which you are familiar. Which themes – context, agency, motivation, and strategies – are most strongly emphasized in this situation? Try to think of examples.
4. Is Pennycook (1997) right in suggesting that learner autonomy may not be universally good for all cultures? Why/why not?

5
Self-Access as Access to 'Self': Cultural Variation in the Notions of Self and Personhood

Philip Riley

> *I often think it's comical*
> *How Nature always does contrive*
> *That every boy and every gal,*
> *That's born into the world alive,*
> *Is either a little Liberal,*
> *Or a little Conservative!*

(W.S. Gilbert, Iolanthe)

Introduction

The processes through which personal identities are constructed are so hidden, out-of-consciousness, that the results, as W.S. Gilbert points out, often seem simply natural. But, of course, far from being innate, or just a matter of wondrous coincidence, individuals are socialized into categories like 'Liberal' and 'Conservative', 'Man' and 'Woman', 'electrician' and 'shopkeeper', 'Geordie' and 'Cockney', and a myriad more. The processes of socialization – the 'ways we bring up children' in the widest possible sense – vary from one period, one society and one group to another, as do the social categories available (for example, 'Liberal' and 'Conservative' were available, but, say, 'ecologist' or 'Member of Gay Pride' were not to Gilbert's boys and 'gals'). The components and architecture of identity, and thus identity itself, are cultural variables.

In this chapter, I propose to look at certain aspects of the socialization process and the construction of identity, and to suggest how they might relate to the main topic of this book: autonomy across cultures.

First, though, we will clearly need to look at the meaning of the term 'identity' itself, and so I will briefly outline an approach which has been developed over recent years with colleagues at the CRAPEL (Centre de Recherches et d'Applications Pédagogiques en Langues), University of Nancy.[1] This approach is an eclectic one, but has its main roots in anthropological linguistics, philosophy and social psychology: more detailed references will be found in the discussion which follows.

An approach to the notion of identity

The expression 'personal identity' can be seen as a superordinate term for an entity including two primary constituents: *person* and *self* (see Figure 5.1). In very general terms, 'person' refers to public, social aspects of the individual, addressed by others as "*you*", and it will be treated here as synonymous with social identity. 'Self', on the other hand, refers to private, subjective aspects of the individual. This fundamental difference, though widely acknowledged, has always been a major source of problems, since it seems to confer on 'identity' two mutually exclusive meanings, social identity being based on characteristics which are shared with others (Liberal, Conservative, etc.), whilst self is the essence of the individual, reporting as "I" – what makes me *me*, different from everybody else. The individual as person (participant in social interactions) goes through successive synchronic states, playing different roles such as teacher, customer or son according to the situation; but the individual as self is the continuing, diachronic subject of these varied experiences.

Person: Social identity (*What sort of* individual?)	Self: Numerical identity (*Which* individual?)
Public, social	Private, subjective
Addressed as "you"	Reports as "I"/"me"
A set of roles	The agent of my actions
Member of groups	Essential individual
Participant in interactions (synchronic focus)	Continuity of memory (diachronic focus)

Figure 5.1   Identity, person and self

At the risk of trivializing an immensely subtle problem, consider the example of what we might say when we introduce one person to another:

This is Sally Cattermole. She's a teacher.

Here, the proper name is used to pick out or specify the numerical identity, the individual self, whilst the category 'teacher' is selected as a situationally relevant or salient aspect of social identity. (The fact that this linguistic distinction is culture-specific, that there are societies which adopt very different systems of nomenclature and address, only serves to underline the closeness of fit between language and the structuration of identity.)

Philosophers are interested in 'conditions of sameness': criteria for saying that an entity (a human being, say, or a stone) continues through time. They can therefore discuss 'identity' as a quality which entities 'have' without reference to other entities, since it is intrinsic. To put it simplistically, a stone does not need another stone to tell it what it is.

Socially speaking, though, 'identity' is a quality which is ascribed or attributed to an individual human being by other human beings. We do need other people to tell us who we are, and, as we shall shortly see, they do so all the time: waiters and doctors, siblings and bus conductors, colleagues and friends all constantly bombard us with instructions concerning the positions and roles we occupy, what groups we are and are not members of. And, as we shall also see, we ourselves jockey for position, sending out a stream of identity claims.

Rather than trying to argue that the difference is superficial, or that one or other of self or person is the 'real' locus of identity, the approach adopted here embraces the seeming paradox, accepts it as the consequence of our human nature: we are both separately incorporated individuals and members of society (cf. Figure 5.1). With a few sad exceptions such as wolf children and the autistic, every individual lives as a member of an array of social groups or figurations. These include Liberal and Conservative, boy and girl, but also ecologist, man and woman, electrician and shopkeeper; and the list could be extended to include hundreds, possibly thousands of other terms in an encyclopaedic repertoire of social categories: religious, political and professional groups; socioeconomic figurations; groups based on place of residence, class, level of education and lifestyle; age cohorts; speech communities; ethnic, kinship and family structures; sporting associations and teams; and so on (cf. Figure 5.2).

Obviously, no single individual can ever belong to more than a relatively small selection of such groups. Partly, this is because many of the

Aspect	Figuration
gender	male, female
age	teenager, pensioner, middle-aged, ...
audition	deaf, hearing, ...
residence	Londoner, Liverpudlian, ...
occupation	lawyer, welder, cashier, ...
religion	Plymouth Brethren, Muslim, atheist, Catholic, ...
politics	Green, socialist, conservative, ...
pastime, sport	chess player, swimmer, ...
marital status	married, single, divorced, ...
ethnicity	Jamaican, Irish, Pakistani, ...
language(s)	speaker of Urdu, French, Arabic, English, ...

Figure 5.2 Parameters of social identity

categories are mutually exclusive: man/woman, Catholic/Mormon, hearing/deaf, for example. Partly, too, because the practicalities of life may act as a filter, so that certain combinations of categories become difficult to achieve, membership of one category limiting access to one or more others: a poor, black, female President of the USA? An illiterate member of the Académie Française? Again, some categories are permanent (you can't do much about your parents or place of birth) whilst others can be changed by happenstance or deliberate effort, by chance or nature's changing course untrimmed, as we get married or divorced, celebrate an eighteenth birthday, win the National Lottery or an election, obtain a driving licence or a diploma in brain surgery. (En passant, it is worth noting that society recognizes the relative importance of these shifts, modifications or additions to identity through the kinds of rites of passage which ratify them.)

Let us illustrate this notion, and the way it relates to language, by examining the following utterance:

Mary Smith is a thirty-six-year-old mother of two who works as a cashier for Lloyds, votes Labour and sings in East Chester choir.

In this statement, Mary is categorized in terms of her

- age cohort
- gender and family

- occupation
- political affiliation
- residence
- leisure activity.

All of these categories are related to language in at least two different ways:

(i) They are encoded in language: expressions such as 'occupation', 'cashier', 'mother' and 'Labour' are selected from the repertoire from which identities can be constructed, different languages and societies having in varying degrees different repertoires.
(ii) These different aspects of Mary's identity are likely to influence the ways she talks and the ways people talk to her – as mother, cashier, chorister, and so on.[2]

Any individual, then, accumulates a specific configuration of memberships of social groups, so that his/her social identity can be defined as '*the sum of the social groups of which the individual is a competent and recognized member*'. As we shall see later, since membership of specific groups confers the rights or duties to enact particular roles, our social identity is very closely linked to the nature of our participation in communicative situations. For the moment, though, I will limit myself to three points which indicate the relevance of this discussion of social identity to 'autonomy' and 'self-direction':

Firstly, included in the list of social groups of which any individual is a member we will sometimes find the category '*language learner*'. However, in the approach to personal identity adopted here, although this might be the salient category in a particular communicative situation (such as the classroom, or a counselling session) it can in no way be dissociated from the rest of that individual's identity. To do so would, in fact, be to fall into the trap which has bedevilled so much discussion and research on second language acquisition over the past thirty or more years, where the term 'the learner' has been used as an abstraction, a simplified representation or personification of *the learning process*, devoid of any truly individual and social dimension and, therefore, conceptually unsuitable for analytic reflection on problems of learner autonomy.

Secondly, we need to keep reminding ourselves that the 'auto' in autonomy means 'self', and that 'autonomy' is just one of a raft of related terms mapping out the field: self-instruction, self-evaluation, self-direction, self-access, self-image, etc. This is clearly not just a freak of etymology, as many of the other terms employed – not just in the field of autonomy, but in language learning in general – 'memory', 'needs', 'motivation', say – clearly entail the existence of an individual person, an identity, someone real who has those memories, needs and motivations.

Thirdly, the various constitutive aspects of identity need to be learnt or acquired as part of the process of socialization, providing an overarching framework for personal development and education, so that any attempt to understand particular learning paradigms, such as autonomous or self-directed learning, must be situated within that wider context.

However, if the suggestion made earlier that the two meanings of 'identity' refer to complementary aspects of human nature is to be anything more than simply playing with words and diagrams, we have to be able to say something about the relationship between 'self' and 'person' which is more than a simple affirmation that they exist, and that this distinction reflects our nature, that each of us has a kind of dual nationality, that as sociopolitical animals we are both members of society, and embodied individuals. If, that is, our theory of 'identity' is to have any kind of explanatory or even descriptive power, we have to be able to say something about the sources of selfhood and personhood and the relationship between them.

I would like to suggest that as the result of work, much of it empirical, carried out in a wide range of the social sciences, we are now in a position to do just that: to make principled and cogent claims about the sources of identity, its architecture and the processes through which it is constructed. This is an immensely complex field, so much so that there is probably no single person fully competent to deal with all the approaches and issues involved. As it would be quite impossible to give any kind of overview or summary of all this work in the space available, I will just give a very limited sample from three of the major disciplines concerned: anthropology, social psychology and linguistics.

Anthropology: concepts of personhood

In a sense, the whole aim of anthropology is to ask "What does it mean to be a human being?" What, that is, are the parameters and limits, the degrees of variability, of human nature? So it is not surprising to find the self, personhood and identity at the very centre of anthropological inquiry, with its sister discipline ethnography adding the question "– and what does it mean to be French, English or Cantonese?" (Sperber,

1982). Together, then, these disciplines examine the essential and local forms and processes shaping 'identity' (Duranti, 1997; Foley, 1997). Precisely because these issues are so central to anthropology, the relevant literature is vast, and concepts, terminology and theories proliferate confusingly, making generalizations of any kind perilous. Moreover, the account sketched here is highly selective, as it is only one strand in a discussion of autonomous second language learning, a topic to which anthropologists do not normally attend. *Caveat lector.*

Most people working in this area would agree that the agenda for modern anthropological discussion of selfhood and personal identity was set by Mauss (1938). Mauss puts forward a theory according to which there existed in the past bounded societies consisting of totemic clans, each clan having a fixed stock of names ('personnages') transmitted by recognized procedures, the bearer(s) of a name being reincarnations of their predecessors back to mythical times, and dancing out the fact at rituals. Children are recognized as reincarnations of particular ancestors:

> The individual is born with his name and his social functions [...] The number of individuals, names, souls and roles is limited in the clan and the line of the clan is merely a collection of rebirths and deaths of individuals who are always the same. (cited by Allen, 1985: 33)

One way of understanding this idea is to look at aristocratic societies, where one is born into a title and its properties and functions: The Ninth Lord Shawfield of Effingham inherits the name, rights and duties and property of numbers one to eight by right of birth. His title and the kind of identity it indexes precede and survive the individuals who bear them, and are unrelated to individual abilities, temperaments, qualifications, and so on. Mauss cites examples of such societies in Africa, Polynesia, Malaysia, North America and Australia, but pays closest attention to the Romans, who gave the 'persona' a legal and moral status: slaves could not be personae, as they had no legal existence and in some societies the old, the infirm, the young, and unmarried (or childless) women might be excluded. The age and conditions whereby the individual attains personhood also vary from one society to another. For example, there are societies where the individual only becomes a full person at death.

Mauss argues that the concept of a form of identity which survives the individual after death was picked up by the Church (via Aristotle) as the idea of an immortal soul. However, the Christian apologists added the notion that all individuals, not just those recognised by society as personae, but children, women and slaves, possessed metaphysical and moral value, that persons were sacred. In the seventeenth and eighteenth centuries, sectarian movements developed a philosophy of this person, the self, positing and examining ideas of individual freedom, conscience, and agency – ideas that influenced the big gun philosophers like Leibniz, Descartes, Spinoza, Hume, Berkeley, Fichte, Kant and led to the Declaration of the Rights of Man and the French Revolution. Anticipating in detail, and with far more evidence, certain ideas of Michel Foucault and the postmodernists, Mauss insists that this interest in the notion of an autonomous self is a characteristic of modernism and unique to Western thought.

In the seventy years since it was published, Mauss's theory has been extremely influential and there have been many anthropological studies of the concepts of person and self and of the construction of identity in specific societies (useful general discussions will be found in Lévi-Strauss, 1977; Shweder and Levine, 1984; Carrithers et al., 1985; Giddens, 1991; Levine, 1992). La Fontaine (1985) provides an extremely useful set of examples and a cogent review of Mauss's ideas, and extends the theory with her own powerful suggestions concerning the main source of variation in the concept of the person. She discusses published ethnographies of four traditional societies, all agricultural peoples without centralized political institutions. There are many differences between them, but

> overall they resemble one another in their concepts more than they resemble the individualist West. [...] In these four societies, human beings are seen as composite creatures; in all four, the individual human being is composed of material and immaterial components [...] concepts of the person serve to identify and explain a wide range of behaviour, emotions and events. None of the concepts are strictly comparable with the concept of person which characterises individualism, for the elements are not unified into a whole which of itself has significance. (p. 126)

All four concepts are based on different ways in which the individual participates in tradition. Let us look at one of her examples, the Tallensi of Ghana, in slightly more detail. For members of this society, a human being has 'sii', which is not life itself, but which constitutes the living body as a unique identity, an individual in our terms. An individual's possessions are imbued with their sii, and taboos prevent conflict between sii of eldest son and father. Siis attract and repulse one another, giving rise to likes and dislikes. Sii vanishes at death. The living body distinguishes persons ('niriba') from ancestors, ghosts and non-human spirits; the immaterial aspects distinguish men from animals (except for some sacred crocodiles, since they are manifestations of the ancestors and therefore persons).

Individual men are distinguished from one another by their distinct sii, not by names, for names identify an individual with (a) an event in the life history of his family (the public name) and (b) an ancestral guardian (the private name). A 'personal identity shrine' embodies the fate already prepared for its owner and is associated with a set of ancestors; it thus distinguishes him as an individual, but in terms of a place in a system of social relations.

In such societies, the concept of person refers to a 'moral career'. The completed person is the product of a whole life:

> In Western societies, the conferring of a name serves to achieve the same end: personhood and individuality are thus identified from the beginning. But for the Tallensi, personhood is finally validated at death. It is the completion of a proper life which qualifies an individual for full personhood, for marriage and the birth of children are essential prerequisites [...] no individual qualities of behaviour or temperament can disqualify a parent from personhood; conversely, no matter how loved and admired an individual may be, if he or she fails to fulfil the ideal pattern of life and leaves no children, then full personhood has not been attained. (p. 128)

La Fontaine concludes that Mauss's conclusion has been validated by subsequent ethnographic work. The concept of the social personality allows us to see Tallensi ideas as concepts of the person: the sum of statuses.

However, the concept of the person in individualism is different. In individualism, the 'person' implies a general moral status accorded to human beings by virtue of their humanity, which recognises their autonomy and responsibility for their actions. As Mauss said, it is the extension into the moral sphere of the unique nature of the individual. By contrast, the Tallensi, for example, do not generalize but particularise, and personhood varies according to social criteria which contain the capacities of the individual within defined roles and categories.

In the West, for example, society is constituted of autonomous equal units and the institutions which reflect this vision are based on a rule of law (the state) where persons are citizens, all people (ideally even rulers) being subject to law. As Weber (1921/1978) pointed out, this principle is the defining characteristic of bureaucratic organization. The main features of such structures are: a clear distinction between office and officeholder, and hence between individual and social role; and the allocation of authority on the basis of fitness for office, fitness being of course a quality of individuals. The equality of persons and competition for office are thus integral to the structure of Western society. Hierarchy and inequality are conceptualized as attributes of social roles; all individuals are equal as persons. By contrast, the Tallensi, for example, base their concept of society on tradition, established once and for all – society is the projection over time of the original founders, heroes or ancestors; in such a society each new baby has a position defined at birth.

La Fontaine's conclusion is that the Western concept of the individual is unique. However, as this summary of her article shows, so is every other society's. Personal identity and the self are malleable. Any form of social intervention which aims at engaging with the individual (including self-direction, self-access and learner-centred approaches of any kind) must therefore attend to the types of personal identities involved. This is particularly true in situations where the social intervention has an intercultural dimension, as is necessarily the case in second language learning. Although the example of a traditional African society we have been looking at is worth quoting because it is particularly striking, it should not be imagined that there is no variation in the structure of personal identity even within the Western world. This can be recognised in everyday stereotypes (distant Englishmen, stuffy Germans, warm outgoing Italians, etc.) but it is also supported empirically by studies such as Budwig's (n.d.).

The overall thrust of this line of argument is that any discourse-based practice aimed at promoting autonomy (for example, caretaker talk, counselling) will have to be sensitive to local notions of personhood if they are to be successful.

Social psychology: the social origin of selves

A number of social psychologists have arrived at similar conclusions to those of the anthropologists, but by a very different route. They take as their starting point the theory of the sociologist George Herbert Mead on the social origin of selves. Mead (e.g. 1934) argued that minds and selves can only emerge as a result of communicative interaction via language, and that what is called 'the mind' is in fact an internal conversation based entirely on language and social meanings. We can see this in terms of an 'I' and a 'Me', where both are part of the 'self', but where the 'I' is the individual as having consciousness, the 'Me' is the individual as an object of that consciousness, including the internal, subjective representation of the Person. This representation of the person to the self is possible because the child is able to reproduce subjectively in intra-action the discursive processes acquired intersubjectively in interaction.

Over the last decade or so, this theory has been resurrected by social theorists in various forms and combined with ideas borrowed from a very diverse group of thinkers (Vygotsky and Bakhtin; Foucault and Althusser; Elias, Mannheim and Schütz; Lévi-Strauss) who share this vision of discourse as the primary mechanism of socialization and the construction of selves. These theorists include Fairclough (1992) and Billig (1987). A masterly synthesis of this approach is provided by the neo-Marxist Ian Burkitt, who argues that

> The self is social in its entirety. Only if we begin from the study of social relations can we truly understand how individuals are social selves [...] social life is the source of individuality and human beings only develop as truly human within a social context. (1991: 215)

This has important implications for any kind of constructivist theory, where learning is seen as a socially mediated activity, since it provides a clear bridge between interpersonal and intrapersonal, showing that 'social' and 'individual' aspects of the learning process, far from being contradictory, are essentially similar.

Burkitt's formulation may well strike you as overly deterministic, so it is important to remember that certain of the membershipping strategies mentioned below are clear evidence of our individual ability to resist, negotiate and manage our identities. In addition, metalinguistic activity of almost any kind can be seen as strategies for the reconfiguration of identities, for redefining the speaker's ethos or self-image (Goffman, 1969; Amossy, 1999).

There is, then, an increasing weight of evidence drawn from disciplines across the board that identity is socially constructed, that our sense of self can only emerge as the result of communicative interaction with others. Children raised outside society do not acquire language – though they have the capacity to do so – and, for that very reason, they fail to form selves.

Linguistics

Both of the above approaches insist on the importance of language and discourse as the primary mechanism for the construction of identities, so it is not surprising that linguists should have been keen to examine in real detail just how that mechanism functions. At least three major lines of investigation have been opened up. The first concerns the role of language as a component of ethnic identity, and there is already a copious literature on this topic, much of it related to multilingual communities (Fishman, 1977; Haarman, 1986). The second, an offshoot of anthropological studies of rearing practices (Jahoda and Lewis, 1988), deals with the ways adults speak to children in different cultures according to social expectancies of competent adult persons (Ochs and Schieffelin, 1984).

The third, relatively recent and relatively neglected line concentrates on deictics and address systems in general and pronouns in particular. An especially interesting and detailed study is Mühlhäusler and Harré (1990). They examine the pronominal systems of dozens of languages from all round the world and present convincing evidence that they vary in the social space, positions and functions allocated to the 'I' and that these correlate with variations in the ways in which identities are conceived and configured, represented and enacted. 'Identities' are constructed appropriately through the acquisition of certain practices, particularly those involved in taking and assigning responsibility: individuals have to learn a local theory of personhood which is to a large extent both summarized and instantiated in the pronoun system and other communicative practices.

Despite widespread belief to the contrary, not all languages have pronominal systems with three 'persons' (!) and two numbers. There are languages where 'self' may include close members of one's family, and there are languages which have sets of pronouns marked for different tenses, contradicting Western notions of physical continuity. There are also languages such as Inuit and Japanese which are group- rather than speaker-oriented, so that individuals speak first and foremost as representatives of their collectivity. This seems congruent with the Inuits' collective behaviour (documented by Mühlhäusler and Harré, 1990): when one laughs, all laugh, when one cries, all cry.

My own attention was drawn to this issue by a Burmese student of mine as early as 1985. Although he was a specialist in French, he confessed to me that he was having problems because he found French "such an impolite language". Somewhat surprised, I pressed him for examples.

"The word 'je'," he replied. "In my language, I have an 'I' for when I am superior or inferior to you, for when I am pleased with you or angry with you, so that when I speak French, I always feel like a bull in a chinashop, never respectful, never expressing my attitudes appropriately."[3]

At discourse level, there are a number of ways in which language is related to the construction, specification and expression of discourse: membershipping strategies and identity claims, the use of domain-specific discourse, and metaphorical recategorization. Let us look at these points briefly (a more detailed discussion of the first two will be found in Riley (2002), from which some of my examples are taken).

To illustrate the ways in which speakers select situationally salient aspects of their addressee's identity, the philosopher Louis Althusser cites the case of a policeman being called to the scene of a crime. His uniform and his revolver confer on him both symbolic and real power, so that when he shouts at a person running away "Hey, you, stop!" that person becomes a criminal because the policeman says so. The runaway, that is, is both the subject of and subject to the policeman's discourse: "Ideologies interpellate individuals."

If that were all, as some postmodernists claim, it would be a very deterministic, very pessimistic account of personal identity. However, if you look at discourse, at actual examples of situated communicative interaction, what you find is that the individual is consciously and constantly trying to affirm his/her sense of identity. Our attempts are not always successful, of course, and this can give rise to conflict, but the very existence of conflict disproves the thesis of absolute social determinism.

Identity claims are utterances in which individuals affirm their membership of specific social figurations or sub-groups in order to foreground them with reference to the matter in hand and thereby orient their audience's behaviour and expectations. In English, such claims are commonly, but by no means exclusively, made by using the expression "(speaking) as an X, I...":

"Speaking as an economist, I..."
"Speaking as a single mother, I..."

Other expressions include "I am an X"; "You're talking to an X"; "We/Us Xs"; and there are, of course, numerous indirect strategies:

"Those of us who have the privilege to work in higher education..."
"Look, I've spent half my life in the tropics..."

Other strategies include:
"Well, wearing my hat as Treasurer of the Sports Committee..."
"Are you asking me for advice as a lawyer or as your friend?"
"I'll have you know you are talking to someone who spent thirty years in India."

Membershipping strategies are speakers' attempts to identify and/or impose membership of specific social figurations on their interlocutors.

"Are you ready to order, sir?"
"Why do you Northerners (women, Catholics, teachers, etc.) always..."
"Non-EU nationals."
"Pregnant women should consult their doctors before using this medicine."
"Place your hand on the Bible and repeat after me..."

As these examples show, such strategies are very often employed for positioning the addressee in a specific role and thereby eliciting particular types of behaviour which the speaker desires or expects. However, it is important to note that individuals who are the subjects of another's membershipping strategy may refuse to accept the identity or role being attributed to them. One of the commonest ways of this resistance, it seems to me, is to lay a counter-claim to a different identity or role:

"Look, I'm the secretary here, not the tea-lady."

As is to be expected, membershipping strategies frequently occur at the beginning of relationships and interactions and counsellor–learner discourse is no exception. For example, where I work in France at least, counsellors are used to being told:

"I need someone who will really make me work."
"Just tell me what to do and I promise to work hard."

The role-relationship implied in such utterances shows that here they are being membershipped as teachers. Counsellors may have a range of resistance strategies of varying degrees of force and tactfulness, including:

"Why don't you tell me what it is you want to do?"
"I'm afraid I'm not much of a slave-driver."

"Well let's just say I'll try to help you learn."
"You have to remember that I can't learn things for you."

The use of domain-specific discourse, including technical language and slang, is one of the most common and powerful forms of identity claims and membershipping strategies. As I mentioned earlier, any of the categories of identity can correlate with language, though not necessarily in the same ways, of course. We have also seen that many of the categories of identity available in a society are lexicalized in relatively transparent ways ('man', 'old-age pensioner', 'teacher', 'card-carrying member of the Winchester Young Conservatives', 'asylum-seeker', for example). One of the most strikingly familiar examples is the close relationship between 'occupation' and vocabulary. Individuals demonstrate their membership and knowledge of trades, professions, gangs, political movements and the like by their use of technical terms and jargon.

This point is immediately relevant to counsellor–learner discourse, where the participants can often be seen to be accommodating to one another's terminology. Over the course of several counselling sessions, learner A, for example, began using several expressions which had clearly been picked up from his counsellor, such as 'language skill' and 'oral comprehension'. The counsellor took this metalinguistic development as a hopeful sign, as being at least a precursor of metacognitive development. On the other hand, counsellors will sometimes go to great lengths to use the learner's own words, with the aim of making their intervention less intrusive. In either case, these metalinguistic strategies are part of a wider process of role and identity negotiation.

Metaphorical recategorisation: Speakers are always free to recategorise their interlocutors metaphorically:

"Be an angel, ..."
"You are an absolute jellyfish!"

As these examples show, this recategorisation involves the identification of one thing with another. We use language in this way to resituate objects in semantic ('quality') space by providing them with new linguistic coordinates (cf. Fernandez, 1986). The metaphors learners and counsellors use about themselves, their relationship, and about language and language learning, and the ways they develop can be extremely informative. For example, English-speaking language learners often have recourse to a conceptual metaphor LEARNING IS A JOURNEY (Lakoff and Johnson, 1980; Riley, 1994) which generates linguistic metaphors such as

"I'm making good progress."
"I've made great strides."
"I've fallen behind."
"I'm completely lost."

So when learner B says "I'm a plodder" and learner C says "I keep going off in all directions", they are using this metaphor for self-description, providing the counsellor with a valuable glimpse of their self-image.

Conclusion

In this chapter, two basic points have been made. The first is that 'identity' and its primary constituents 'person' (social identity) and 'self' are to some extent at least cultural variables: personhood involves a sense of self and a range of competences which satisfy a society's expectations and requirements of the ideal member. Secondly, it has been argued that the primary mechanism of this process is language, since it encodes those culturally specific concepts, and is the dynamic locus for the inter-individual negotiation and enactment of social identity, and for the intra-individual dialectic from which the self emerges.

The implications of this line of argument for autonomous or self-directed learning schemes and for counselling for language learning are profound, though not, it has to be admitted, always clear. In fact, until considerably more research has been done on the discursive construction of identity in general and on the negotiation of roles in the counsellor–learner dyad in particular (cf. Clemente, this volume), only the most general and tentative conclusions can be formulated.

The first is that there can be no one 'best' form of counselling, or even one that is applicable over a wide range of cultural contexts. In research terms, this means looking at communicative practices in general and the 'language of counselling' in particular in a number of different cultures. Clearly, the model of discourse analysis used will have to be sensitive to intercultural variation, which argues strongly in favour of ethnographic approaches such as those developed by Hymes (1974) for the 'ethnography of communication' and Gumperz (1982) for 'interactional sociolinguistics'. If the argument developed here is followed, priority will be given to strategies used in the negotiation of roles and identities, and to the relationships between discourse and metacognition (with language awareness and self-awareness seen as opposite sides of the same coin).

This certainly does not mean, however, that the nitty-gritty of coun-selling should be neglected, nor its importance underrated: by focusing on the ways in which specific decisions are taken concerning the con-stitutive elements of the learning programme – materials, activities, organization, forms of evaluation, and so on – we will develop both a better understanding of counselling as practice and of the ways in which roles are realised in specific settings.

Secondly, there have to be serious reservations about the wisdom of counselling in a language other than the learner's mother tongue, and where this is inevitable for practical reasons there should be constant monitoring of the counsellor's cultural assumptions concerning his/her own and the learner's respective roles. The principal danger is, of course, that the asymmetric distribution of knowledge is exacerbated by unequal linguistic competence. In these circumstances any attempt to establish free and fair relationships, empowerment and mutual respect is seriously threatened. However, to finish on a more positive note, there are ways of reducing this risk, such as recruiting the help of successful learners as peer tutors, or developing relevant mother tongue materials and instruments for the learners to use themselves. Again, both of these tasks imply further research.

Reflection/discussion questions

1. Draw up a list of the social sub-categories to which you belong, and another list for one of your students (cf. Figure 5.2). What are the main differences between the two lists? How do you think these might relate to different ideas of personhood?
2. What membershipping strategies do you and your learners tend to use with one another? How do they reflect (or not) your ideas concerning your respec-tive roles, and concerning learner autonomy in particular?

Notes

1. More detailed discussions of this approach will be found in Riley (1999, 2002). The colleagues in question are the members of GREFSOC (Groupe de Réflexion Sociolinguistique): Hervé Adami, Virginie André, Sophie Bailly, Désirée Castillo, Francis Carton, Maud Ciekanski, Jeanne-Marie Debaisieux, Marie-José Gremmo, Florence Garcia-Poncet. I am indebted to my discussions with them.
2. In fact, there is an important third possibility: Mary might be a member of more than one speech community. In other words, she might enact different memberships in different languages. For example, let me add the information that Mary Smith is also Mrs Benali. She met Rachid, a Frenchman of Algerian origin whilst on holiday in Paris. They use both French and Arabic at home

and because of her language skills, Mary is regularly called on to help in the Foreign Exchange department. Like all bilinguals, she code-switches between her languages according to the specific roles she is called upon to play, according, that is, to the situationally salient aspect of her identity. However, I shall not be pursuing this point here.

3. I understand that Burmese does not in fact have any pronouns strictly speaking, using conventional nominalized expressions as terms of address, etc.

6
Social Autonomy: Addressing the Dangers of Culturism in TESOL

Adrian Holliday

Introduction

This chapter will explore how we need to rethink current associations between 'autonomy' and language students, in order to address a reductive culturism which I believe pervades TESOL. I shall begin with a critique of two dominant conceptualizations of student autonomy. The first is characterized by a long-standing 'us'–'them' native-speakerism. Although the second is based on a more critical cultural relativism in which native-speakerism is seen as untenable, I see both as being equally culturally reductive. I shall then argue for a third position in which autonomy is defined in the terms brought by students from their own worlds outside the classroom. I suggest that we routinely fail to see this social autonomy because of preoccupations with our own professionalism.

Because my discussion is based within a complex politics of how educators and students with diverse identities see each other, I need to explain how I am using "'us'–'them'", "we" and "our" in the above paragraph. "We" and "our" here, and throughout this chapter when used in unmarked form, refer to the whole *profession* of TESOL. There is no doubt that we (TESOL people throughout the world, e.g. teachers, writers, curriculum developers and publishers) are ourselves divided by the dominant position of the English-speaking West (cf. Phillipson, 1992; Holliday, 1994; Pennycook, 1994, 1998; Canagarajah, 1999; Jenkins, 2000). However, I believe that we do also have a common, though diversified, international, professional-academic identity, which is manifested in the way that, from our different backgrounds, we come together in faculties, projects and conferences across the world and share a specialist discourse. In contrast to this, the 'us'–'them' polarity is an aspect of the particularly divisive *ideology* of native-speakerism which works against our common identity. I define 'native-speakerism' as a set of beliefs supporting the view that 'native-speaker' teachers represent the ideals both of the target language and of language teaching method-ology. Although TESOL native-speakerism originates in a specific set of educational and development cultures in the English-speaking West (Phillipson, 1992), and is an easy position to adopt particularly for those who conceptualize themselves as 'native-speakers', it has had a massive influence and exists to a greater or lesser degree in the thinking of all TESOL people. In this chapter I will therefore argue that the way that we TESOL people commonly think about 'autonomy' both feeds and is derived from this 'us'–'them', native-speakerist ideology, which is cul-turist and which works to divide us; and I shall explore ways of undoing this ideology.

Throughout I shall use inverted commas to mark the way in which 'us' and 'we' (here, meaning native-speakerists, rather than all TESOL people) and 'our' ('native-speaker') culture are conceptualized within the ideology of native-speakerism as distinct from 'them', 'they' and 'their' ('non-native-speaker') culture. Here, 'native-speaker' is an ideo-logical term denoting someone who is awarded (within the ideology) a special status connected with ownership of the language, and a native-speakerist is someone, from the English-speaking West or elsewhere, who promotes this ideology (cf. Holliday, forthcoming).

An 'us'–'them' discourse of participation

The commonly held notion of autonomy in TESOL is, I think, repre-sented in this statement from Harmer's (2001) *The Practice of English Language Teaching*, which might be considered a standard text on TESOL pedagogy:

> However good a teacher may be, students will never learn a language – or anything else – unless they aim to learn outside as well as during class time. [...] To compensate for the limits of classroom time and to counter the passivity that is an enemy of true learning, students need to develop their own learning strategies, so that as far as possible they become autonomous learners. This does not always happen automat-ically. Attitudes to self-directed learning are frequently conditioned by the educational culture in which students have studied or are studying [...]; autonomy of action is not always considered a desir-able characteristic in such contexts. (p. 335)

There are several elements here which are problematic. "Passivity" is placed in unquestionable opposition to "autonomous learners" and "true learning". Then, "educational culture[s]" or "contexts" are cited as conditioning influences *against* "autonomy of action". The implication is thus that 'other' educational cultures or contexts negatively influence students, who are presumed not to have autonomy, whereas "true [language] learning" is located in a place where autonomy can be 'developed' through "learning strategies". It seems, then, that the educational origin of the student is seen as Other to that of TESOL; and there is a strong native-speakerist implication that "corrective training" (Foucault, 1991) will need to be provided for 'foreign', 'non-native' students from Other contexts.

The opposition between passivity and autonomy which is revealed in the above quotation also seems to underlie the following examples of TESOL discourse that I have heard in and around conference events:

(a) "Students from [country X] are passive" (teacher referring to students used to a transmission, lecture mode, who did not say enough in a more 'participatory' classroom);
(b) "She's a problem student because she never says anything" (teacher);
(c) "The class went well. It was very lively" (teacher). (Holliday, 1997b: 409–10)

In these examples, the concept of autonomy is embedded in notions of participation and liveliness. Statements (a) and (b) give an impression that some students have come to the class with the inappropriate behaviour they have brought from Other educational cultures, which statement (a) locates in the specific country X. What the students referred to are accused of lacking is the quality of 'liveliness', which is praised in statement (c).

Despite my criticisms, such views are deeply embedded in my own professional development. When I worked as a curriculum consultant in Egypt and Syria in the 1980s I did not question the British Council agenda that what had to be changed was the 'passivity' of students in 'local' university language classes. There was a very strong feeling at the time that 'passive' students (i.e. not speaking, only listening) lacked the autonomy to learn effectively. I always felt that the best classes were the ones where the students were orally 'active', and that the less successful classes were the ones where the students were quieter and 'less active' (Holliday, 1994: 83). And one may wonder exactly what the issue is here, as the truth of what Harmer and the people at the conference say may seem self-evident, especially to those teachers who have struggled with non-forthcoming language students from different parts of the world. However, there is an increasing body of discussion which suggests that this type of characterization of 'foreign' students is native-speakerist, unfounded and the product of essentialist cultural overgeneralization (e.g. Spack, 1997; Kubota, 1999; Holliday, 1999a).

Racism or culturism?

Kubota (1999, 2001) is one of a growing number of applied linguists who follow the anti-essentialist literature in the social sciences which links the manufacturing of exotic 'cultures' by the West to its colonial narrative of making the foreign Other look primitive and in need of civilizing (for example, Sarangi, 1995; Pennycook, 1998; Holliday, 1999a; Canagarajah, 1999). She critiques the current TESOL narrative, in which Asian students from the Pacific Rim are constructed as lacking in the autonomy and critical thinking which are seen as necessary for effective pedagogy:

> The intellectual qualities posed as ideal for US students are independence, autonomy, and creativity, and students should ideally develop analytical, objective, and critical thinking skills. [...] These qualities are presented as diametrically opposed to the characteristics of Asian students, who are described as being intellectually interdependent, inclined to preserve rather than create knowledge, reluctant to challenge authority, and engaged in memorization rather than analytical thinking. [...] Asian students allegedly plagiarize because they do not share the Western notion of text authorship that stresses originality, creativity and individualism. Asian students are described as reticent, passive, indirect, and not inclined to challenge the teacher's authority. [...] Their written communication style is often characterized as indirect, circular, and inductive. (2001: 14)

Kubota (2001: 17–20) discredits this view by describing how US educators, who report a 'crisis' in some US secondary school and college classrooms, use the same terms to describe US students – terming them "passive, docile, and compliant rather than active, creative and autonomous" (p. 19). Kubota therefore suggests that although the image of passivity may appear to specify a particular non-US cultural group, it is in fact used indiscriminately to describe the unsatisfactory Other of the day, whatever that may be.

Kubota attributes the indiscriminate othering of the foreign to "the persistent racism of contemporary society" (p. 28). While I agree with Kubota's overall argument, I prefer the term *'culturism'* to 'racism' as the root process we need to consider here. By culturism I mean reducing the foreign Other to simplistic, essentialist cultural prescriptions (Holliday, 1999a: 245, 2002a: 186; forthcoming). Culturism is thus very like racism in that both reduce and judge a strange Other according to negative stereotypes, but different in that it applies to the othering of cultural groups which are not necessarily racially distinct. Kubota focuses largely on the way in which a racist dominant discourse of TESOL within the English-speaking West perceives 'non-white' TESOL people and students from the East. I would like to extend and refine this focus to the way in which native-speakerism perceives teachers and students who 'come from other cultures' outside the English-speaking West, even within Europe – especially where these 'other cultures' are perceived as discouraging autonomy.

Whether we are talking about racism or culturism, I find very apposite Kubota's (2001: 28) reference to the way in which prejudices are hidden by the "contemporary discourse of liberal humanism", especially in "a nice field like TESOL" (Kubota, 2002: 84). It can be argued that 'nice' middle-class people from comfortable societies think that by talking about 'cultures', and admiring their 'exotic' qualities, they are 'accepting' and 'being tolerant' and 'understanding' of them – whereas in fact they are simply reducing them to stereotypes. Jordan and Weedon (1995: 149–50) assert that the 'commodification' of racial and cultural difference is "a marked feature of the radical twentieth-century avant-garde". 'Nice' TESOL people can thus enjoy their exotic students who bring them the opportunity of "discovering another culture". 'Other cultures' thus become objects to be 'nice' about instead of groups of real people with whom 'we' can interact and be equally people.

A further point made by Kubota (2001: 10–11) is that "the Othering of ESL/EFL students by essentializing their culture and language presupposes the existence of the unproblematic Self as a monolithic, normative category". Thus, in Harmer's statement (cited above), while the (Other) students, from other educational cultures, are seen as problematic, the Self of the teacher remains unproblematic. This 'unproblematic Self' within TESOL is consonant with its history of being so positivistically self-assured in the efficiency of its teaching technology that it can overlook social and political context (Phillipson, 1992; Holliday, 1994; Coleman, 1996b) – as a technologized discourse which presents itself as "'context free', [and] as usable in any relevant context" (Fairclough, 1995: 104).

Three approaches to autonomy

In Table 6.1, I summarize three approaches to autonomy in TESOL, the first two of which can be linked to the state of affairs which Kubota describes. Approach A is native-speakerist in the way in which native-speakerist 'we' perceive 'them' from 'other cultures'. I think this approach is linked with the two non-political versions defined by Benson (1997). (See also Oxford's discussion of these versions in this volume.) It certainly promotes the Self of the teacher as unproblematic. Students are considered autonomous when they behave in ways which conform to an image of the 'native speaker' and his/her culture. Although the native-speakerist approach is ostensibly 'learner-centred', it falls into the trap of conceptualizing what is good for the 'learner' in the terms of the language learning activities which the *teacher* constructs (Holliday, 1999b). Surely it is not possible for teachers, who are not themselves 'learners', and who do not therefore belong to, and cannot easily understand the world of 'learners', to be 'learner-centred'. The conceptualization of 'learner' is in itself problematic in that, rather than being viewed as a whole person, she is an operative within a teacher-constructed environment, defined by, limited and therefore reduced to measurable skills and needs (Usher and Edwards, 1994; Clark and Ivanič, 1997: 84; Holliday, 2001a). The outcome is a control of 'learning' through planned tasks which serve the technical needs of the discourse rather than the real student. Anderson (in process) demonstrates this in his ethnography of a British university teaching centre which reveals how, despite a discourse of learner-centredness, lessons are highly controlled.

Approach A suits the objectives of professionalism as described in Harmer (2001, as cited above), through which teachers can be trained to deliver 'learner training', and which has given birth to a wide range of 'how-to-do-it' literature for teachers (for example, Nunan, 1997b). This thinking also encourages native-speakerist teachers to be crusaders in their quest to *change* their students into 'better' thinkers and 'learners'. It is deeply culturist in its vision of 'our' superior 'native-speaker' culture; and leads many teachers to despair at the unsolvable problem of not being able to teach in the way they wish because their students 'from other cultures' 'refuse', or are 'unable' to comply.

Approach B is related to critical linguistics in that it recognizes the political side of autonomy (Benson, 1997) and the changing ownership of English which confirms the untenability of native-speakerism. Kubota nevertheless critiques a version of approach B in referring to

Table 6.1 Three approaches to autonomy

Approach	[A] Native-speakerist 'Learner autonomy' 'Learner-centred'	[B] Cultural relativist 'Critical linguistics'	[C] Social autonomy Pre-existing social autonomy People in society
Assumptions	'We' (native-speakerists) must teach 'them' (from 'other cultures') how to be autonomous in 'our' educational settings. Autonomy needs to be induced by means of learner training – in the image of 'the native speaker' and 'his/her culture'. Constructed by teacher-created learning activities.	'We' (from the English-speaking West) cannot expect 'them' (from 'other cultures') to be autonomous like 'us'.	Everyone can be autonomous in their own way. Autonomy resides in the social worlds of the students, which from they bring with them their lives outside the classroom. Often hidden by learning activities.
World view	'Our culture' is superior.	One 'culture' cannot be like another.	Culture is uncountable and negotiable.
Problem (as perceived by owners)	'They' cannot be what 'we' (native-speakerists) want them to be because 'their culture' does not allow them.	It is unrealistic to expect 'them' (from 'other cultures') to be like 'us'.	We (all TESOL people) always tend to be culturist, reducing 'them' to cultural stereotypes. Our professionalism prevents us from seeing people as they really are.
Solution (as perceived by owners)	Learner training or acculturation.	'They' or 'we' must develop special methodologies that suit 'them'.	We must stop being culturist and learn to see through our own professionalism.

Atkinson and Ramanathan (1995) and Atkinson (1997). Atkinson (1997: 72) claims there is an opposition between critical thinking and "many cultures [which] endorse modes of thought and education that almost diametrically oppose it", an opposition which resonates with that drawn between autonomy and other cultures in my initial quotation from Harmer (2001), above. There is also a hint of native-speakerism in Atkinson's (1997: 79) labelling of the people who come from these "non-Western cultural groups" as "nonnative thinkers". This is, however, different to approach A in that language educators need to be wary of imposing the "individualism, self expression and using language as a tool for learning" which are "deeply implicated in critical thought", and which may "marginalize" rather than improve the learning of language students (Atkinson, 1997: 89). Approach B is culturist in that autonomy is seen as a Western phenomenon which 'we' (from the English-speaking West) should therefore not expect 'non-native' students to adopt because of 'their' cultural origin. Although native-speakerist corrective training is felt, in approach B, to be unjust on the grounds that all 'cultures' are equal, students from some 'cultures' are excluded from the educational treatment given to students from others, and therefore treated divisively. There is a complex dilemma here which is expressed by Pennycook (1997). He rightly advocates that students from other places should find "cultural alternatives" to Western constructions of autonomy, perhaps with non-native-speakerist forms which allow for the "silent, unobserved resistance" that I describe in the second part of this chapter, and/or which allow for *choosing* to be taught in a "teacherly way" (p. 43); but at the same time he seems to fall into a cultural relativist trap of expecting, on the basis of essentialist descriptions of cultural difference, that students who do not come from the West cannot participate in a "concept of individual autonomy" (p. 36), and that, somehow, silent resistance is not individual. There is still a sense in approach B of 'us' 'native-speakers' denying 'them' (from Other cultures) 'our' imagination of autonomy, according to 'our' imagination of 'them'.

Jones' (1995) account of setting up a university self-access centre in Cambodia seems to be a good example of approach B.[1] He is culturally relativist in his statement that "the concept of autonomy is laden with cultural values, particularly those of the West" (p. 228). He then makes a massively over-generalized culturist presumption that it is therefore not appropriate to expect "full autonomy", not only of Cambodians, who he says are "dependent and authority-oriented", but of people from "many countries between Morocco and Japan" who find it difficult to accept "the individual responsibility and freedom" derived from "Western values" (p. 229). He therefore sets up the self-access centre to allow group as well as individual work; and, although he observes that the students manage this very well, with "as often as not eight students at a time gather[ing] around a listening post in order to do an exercise together" or consulting newspapers in the reading corner (p. 231), his overall conclusion is that their preference to work collaboratively erodes the ideal of "individual autonomy".

In my view there is every evidence that the students in Jones' study are being autonomous, but in a way of their own which they have brought with them, with which they inhabit the space provided by the self-access centre. That Jones does not see this as 'full' or 'real' autonomy may relate to his preoccupation with the existing professional discourse (cited by him in some detail), which prescribes for him what autonomy is and which people from which 'cultures' can fulfil its requirements.

Approach C in Table 6.1 can, I believe, escape this trap of culturism by introducing three disciplines:

1. not *beginning with* an essentialist cultural description of students from a certain part of the world, and not *presuming* that autonomy is the domain of a Western (or any other) culture;
2. trying to see through and beyond a TESOL professionalism which is influenced by native-speakerism, to search for the worlds which the students bring with them.

If there *is* any presumption in approach C, it is:

3. presuming that autonomy is a *universal* until there is evidence otherwise – and that if it is not immediately evident in student behaviour, this may be because there is something preventing us from seeing it – thus treating people equally as people.

I shall now try and demonstrate how approach C leads to an appreciation of autonomy as a pre-existing social phenomenon.

The regime of the native-speakerist classroom

A further point made by Kubota (2001), which resonates with my own experience, is that there is a tendency in the othering of foreign students (in approach A) to blame the student, or the student's culture, for behaviour which might instead be attributed to other factors external to the student such as "an unwelcoming atmosphere" (p. 31). In a qualitative study of a small fragment of video sequences of Japanese high school classrooms (Holliday, 2002b), I observed students engaging in a considerable amount of personal talk, which was not part of the formal part of the lesson but used by students as an autonomous means for dealing with the pressures of the classroom and sometimes to support colleagues who were nominated to speak by the teacher. Personal talk occurred, then, within the social interaction domain of the classroom. At the same time, students said very little within the transaction domain of the lesson (I am using Widdowson's (1987) terms here, where 'transaction' is what passes between the teacher and students as part of the pedagogic plan of the lesson, and 'interaction' is the social, non-pedagogic aspect of what happens in the classroom). In contrast, in British classes students are expected only to talk in the transaction part of the lesson, and only when the teacher is not talking to the whole class – when the teacher specifies, in other words, either in individual responses or in organized group activities. The proper place for talk in the British class is thus controlled by the teacher, and personal talk which is not authorized by the teacher is prohibited. I therefore hypothesized that the often observed quietness of Japanese language students in Britain is brought on by the strangeness (to them) of the way in which talk is expected in the unfamiliar classroom regime. Unable to indulge in personal talk in the social interaction part of the British lesson, tension rises amongst Japanese students, and they subsequently become more silent and less able to engage in the talk which is required in the transaction part of the lesson. They may thus appear 'passive' and lacking in autonomy, but it is more the impact of the strangeness for them of British lessons that brings about reticent behaviour than the 'culture' which the students bring with them.

The regime of the TESOL classroom can therefore be a major factor in inhibiting student behaviour and hiding their autonomy. I refer to this regime elsewhere as the native-speakerist "learning group ideal" (Holliday, 1994: 53) which gives primacy to teacher-controlled oral interaction in the classroom and measures both the ability and the self-esteem (see below) of the student in terms of oral expression. (Cf. Pennycook's (1994: 122) discussion of phonocentrism.) This kind of classroom is at the heart of the native-speakerist approach A to autonomy. The connection between autonomy and oral activity can also be traced to the way in which learner-centredness in TESOL has been equated with share of classroom talk, and to the oral-dominated lockstep of audiolingualism (Holliday, forthcoming).

The impact of the regime of the classroom on student behaviour is also addressed in Hayagoshi's (1996) qualitative study of why Japanese students are so 'silent', and by implication lacking in autonomy, in British university language classrooms, when she would normally expect them to be noisy from her experience as a teacher in Japan. She observes a marked change in the students' behaviour as soon as the British teacher leaves the classroom:

> The quietness of these seven Japanese definitely dominated the atmosphere of the classroom. There was nobody to throw a stone into this quietness.
>
> They were very slow to react and rarely express their opinions. [...] The teacher went out for a while [...] I felt that the tense (hard) atmosphere [...] suddenly changed dramatically to a mild gentle one. Actually, I heard one Japanese student sigh with relief. However, this mood vanished when the teacher returned. They were quiet, tense and stressed, again. (Lesson observation 1.)
>
> After the class, these quiet Japanese became *normal* students [...] friendly and, of course, quite talkative!

Later, she

> asked some Japanese students why they were quiet in the classroom. One student answered that "there are some invisible walls around me which prevent me from speaking in the class". (Hayagoshi, 1996, her italics)

It is clear to me that the dramatic change of atmosphere and the self-perceived "invisible walls" are more *imposed* on the students by a régime external to them than by aspects of their cultural personality which they bring with them. Hayagoshi places the responsibility for this phenomenon on the British teachers. It is *their* perceptions which she finds problematic rather than the attitudes of the students.

This difference between what teachers imagine about 'culture' and what students bring from and feel about their own social world is demonstrated in Chang's (2000) interview study of five British applied linguists and four Taiwanese students connected with a study skills course at a British university. The study took place a year after the end of the study skills course when the students were about to finish the MA TESOL programme for which it had prepared them. Two of the applied linguists had taught them on the study skills course and three had taught them on the MA TESOL. As with Kubota and Hayagoshi (cited above), Chang was driven to carry out this study by the way that 'Asian students' are misinterpreted by applied linguists from the English-speaking West to the extent that the absence of autonomy is perceived as a 'cultural shortage' (p. 42).

Table 6.2 shows how different the perceptions were. While both the study skills teachers and the MA TESOL lecturers seemed fairly unanimous in thinking that the students needed to be more 'autonomous' and generally to improve their learning skills, the students seemed equally unanimous that what *they* wanted was more information about what they were supposed to do, in a situation where they did not really have the English to understand their tutors' instructions. Chang reports that the students were already autonomous in their learning in the sense that they were very happy to work independently out of class, as they had been used to doing in Taiwan, and that they lacked confidence only because of lack of information (p. 42).

Chang's findings resonate for me with the experience I had with Iranian trainee ship engineers at Lancaster University in 1980 (Holliday, 1994: 144). After several months of despairing at how incapable the students were at doing technical drawing, it became clear that all they really lacked was information about exactly what they were supposed to do. As soon as they received the simple phrase in Farsi which made this clear, they were able to produce excellent drawings, like the ones they were used to at high school in Iran. It was our own teaching which had confused them! One of the problems with the activity-discovery approach – "look at the … and find out how to … " – inherent in much native-speakerist TESOL is that exactly what participants are supposed to do is not always transparent to people not brought up in this particular professional discourse.

Table 6.2 Differences in perception (adapted from Chang, 2000: 45)

British applied linguists	Taiwanese students
think that the students:	think that they:
need more 'self-access' time to become 'autonomous' learners;	need confidence from appropriate instructions, and then they can study 'autonomously' as teachers wish;
need to learn how to consult teachers;	need to consult teachers more often;
need to develop study skills.	need to develop language skills.

Autonomous coping

These studies by Hayagoshi, Chang and myself draw attention to a social autonomy which students already possess (as perceived in approach C in Table 6.1), which is inhibited by the native-speakerist regime. The sources of this social autonomy can be observed in a wide range of classroom settings outside native-speakerist TESOL. Significantly, as I observed in my Japanese fragments (Holliday, 2002b, cited above), these sources may be clear in the non-formal interactional parts of lessons and therefore not recognized by the native-speakerist regime of approach A. My first experience of students' social autonomy was in the very Egyptian university classrooms (referred to above) in which I was employed to get rid of passivity. Whereas students appeared only to be sitting and listening, 'spoon-fed' by 'dominating' lecturers, they were in fact far from passive. Like the high school students in my Japanese fragments, they were doing a great deal in what I termed the 'informal order' of education: organizing seating, distributing lecture notes, forming informal learning groups, negotiating with lecturers, and generally coping with a considerable scarcity of resources, as well as assenting to and appreciating the nature of power bestowed upon the lecturer. Hany Azer harnesses these capabilities in his methodology for independent communicative study in very large classes (cited in Holliday, 1994: 184–91). Shamim (1996) illustrates something similar in a secondary school in Pakistan, where students show considerable autonomy in the way they organize their seating in different parts of classroom, as does Mebo (1995) in her description of students' attitudes towards colleague competition in finding seats in large classes in a Kenyan university. Tong (2002) also describes in detail how students in secondary school classes in Hong Kong are not the 'passive' people they seem to be at first sight, but in fact demonstrate considerable autonomy:

> It is important to note that students in this study have also been found to engage in different kinds of private work, e.g. student reading, working and looking up words in the dictionary, which needed little or no oral interactions, in which students seemed to communicate with the materials and the illustrations. Students looking up words in the dictionary might indicate their initiative and their willingness to be independent life-long learners. [...] Students participated, answered or asked questions. Students expressed their opinions or clarified confusions with teachers. Students took opportunities to interact with the researcher. All this shows the students'

motivation, confidence, creativity and feeling. Students were not all the time conforming to the will of their seniors. Students reacted to teaching with some disruptive behaviour when they lost interest. Students collaborated with their fellow students when they were asked to speak out in English. (Tong, 2002: 254)

These examples of autonomous student action take place in "hidden sites of critical learning" which are similar to those observed by Canagarajah (2002b). He demonstrates this in his observation of Sri Lankan university students writing stories from their own society into the margins and illustrations of a foreign Western textbook. They authenticate the textbook in their own way, but in the interactional 'underlife' of the classroom, out of the transactional sight of the teacher (Canagarajah, 1999: 89–90).[2]

Lacking in self-esteem?

A basic tenet of the native-speakerist approach A to autonomy is that 'passive', non-autonomous students lack self-esteem (for example, Harmer, 2001: 335). Although it may be presumed by the native-speakerist observer that the Japanese students in Hayagoshi's study (cited above) lack self-esteem, or the autonomous initiative to "throw a stone" into the silence of the classroom and do something about it, there is no evidence in the study that there could be anything but a temporary loss of self-esteem specific to the confines of the particular classroom regime. In the same way, Tong (2002) finds that the Hong Kong secondary school students in his study *appeared* passive when they were dealing with specific aspects of classroom life, for example "when they lost interest in teaching content and withdrew from classroom activities", and when they "were conscious about making errors and possibly being shamed by the teacher or their classmates, losing face, and being disgraced" (p. 254).

These observations raise the question – why should any student who has not been involved in setting up the system and has no ownership in the design of the regime be expected to participate in its perpetuation? I began to understand this in relation to a group of undergraduate Hong Kong students who came to Britain for an English immersion programme. It took me a while to encourage any of them to be open with me about why they were so reticent in my classes, while at the same time I found them remarkably forthcoming in non-class settings, when encountered on the campus, in the town or on school attachments, and also, to a lesser extent, in meetings and tutorials (Holliday, 2001b). Then, eventually, one of the students announced that he was not prepared to expose his English ability for scrutiny in a formal classroom setting, as though this was a very unsound survival proposition. This may be contrary to native-speakerist pedagogical principles – that you cannot learn unless you take part orally. On the other hand, students who make this choice are practising a large degree of social autonomy which is independent of the vision of the teacher and his/her pedagogy. Autonomy cannot therefore be *created* in the educational setting. It can only be encouraged, perhaps nurtured, or perhaps capitalized upon, because its origin is elsewhere, within the world which the student brings with him/her. I think this is what Breen and Mann mean when they say:

> Autonomy is seen as a way of being in the world: a position from which to engage with the world. [...] We are proposing that autonomy is not an ability that has to be learnt [...] but a way of being that has to *be discovered*. (1997: 134, my emphasis)

I emphasize "be discovered" here because in my view this type of autonomy is not something that is easy to see in any TESOL context where there is a very powerful professional discourse standing between the teacher and the students. The regime, not only of the native-speakerist classroom, but of any classroom which is organized along teacherly lines, thus becomes a barrier to seeing the world of the student (Holliday, 2001a: 171). Hence, social autonomy may be actually *hidden* by classroom activities – or by what teachers believe these activities ought to be.[3]

Finding social autonomy

Although I believe there is clear evidence of a social autonomy which students of all types and from all sorts of places utilize both in their daily lives and in dealing with the exigencies of education, it can be invisible to teachers who are preoccupied with their own professional agendas. The studies cited in the second half of this chapter show that the autonomous qualities of students are not always appreciated by their teachers. This is not only the case with 'native-speaker' teachers. In Tong's study (cited above), it is the discourse of Confucianism among Hong Kong teachers which presents the culturist notion that Hong Kong students cannot behave in certain ways. On the other hand, these studies go some way to fulfilling the disciplines listed within approach C by employing a qualitative methodology which helps the researcher look directly at student behaviour and attitudes. Hayagoshi's and Chang's studies, and my own of Japanese classroom fragments (all cited above), are very small; but the value of such qualitative studies of individual instances of social action is very gradually to build a picture sufficient to throw doubt on existing discourses. The interpretive paradigm insists that one allows meaning to emerge from direct observation while putting aside, or bracketing, taken-for-granted and essentialist notions of the foreign Other (Baumann, 1996: 2; Gubrium and Holstein, 1997: 40; Holliday, 2002a: 185), and that the researcher must state his/her ideology (Janesick, 1994: 212; Holliday, 2002a: 53). I try to do this explicitly in my study of Hong Kong students (cited above), where I state that, as someone brought up in native-speakerism, "I bring with me a discoursal baggage" which "is pre-occupied with a 'learner autonomy' that resides in a certain type of oral participation in the classroom" and "tends to explain the behaviour" of the students "by reducing them to prescribed, 'culturist' national or regional cultural stereotypes" (Holliday, 2001b: 124). Also, that:

> This involves trying to see the Hong Kong students first and foremost as university students rather than 'Chinese' [...]. Whether or not 'Chinese culture' has anything to do with what I observe is thus something to be discovered last rather than considered first. (ibid.)

Thus, the research has a major moral objective of recognizing and dealing with my own prejudices and representing the students from Hong Kong as rounded, fully and naturally autonomous human beings.

Changing ideologies

The native-speakerist discourse of TESOL is complex and deep, and is within all of us – from the English-speaking West or elsewhere – who have been brought up in its tradition, whether we are critical of it or not. I feel that the straight 'us'–'them' view of native-speakerism is slowly becoming a thing of the past as the ownership of English changes and we begin to appreciate more the worlds of others. When reading recent papers on the issue of autonomy, I see that there is indeed a clear movement towards writers taking care not to 'otherize' their students. Many use sensitive phrases which acknowledge what students from different backgrounds bring with them, such as "to support autonomy" (Pemberton et al.,

2001: 23), "promoting autonomy" (Carter, 2001: 26), "capacity for autonomy" (Lai, 2001: 35), and "engagement of their autonomy" (Champagne et al., 2001: 45), much of which is within a "discourse of advising" (Pemberton et al., 2001: 24). Nevertheless, I feel that the struggle must go on – to see our students more generously as people and not as confined either to culturist stereotypes or to teacherly constructs of the 'learner' located within 'our' teacher-created activities. Because racism and culturism pervade all aspects of all our societies, we must look more deeply into the values of our ordinary professionalism, and struggle not so much to build systems for ourselves, but to understand others.

Reflection/discussion questions

1. Try and establish in your mind that all descriptions you have heard about national cultures are nothing but groundless rumours. Try not to think of your students as Chinese, Japanese, Iranian, etc. How does this change your vision of your students' behaviour?
2. Think of examples of sexism, racism and culturism. How are these concepts similar? Why might a woman teacher prefer you not to explain her shortcomings in the classroom in terms of her gender? What does this have to do with culturism?
3. If you are from the English-speaking West, how would you feel if you heard a Japanese person saying this to his/her colleague about you?: "We can't expect him/her to collaborate with the other students because s/he comes from an individualist culture. We will have to let him/her work on his/her own rather than asking him/her to do pair work." If you are not from the English-speaking West, try to imagine a corresponding situation involving yourself.

Notes

1. Jones (1995) is an old paper; and I apologize to the author, who may well have moved on from the position he expresses there. I am using it because it is a good example of a trend which I feel is still prevalent.
2. The relationship between autonomy and authenticity is important here, but beyond the scope of this chapter. I discuss this in detail elsewhere (Holliday, 1999b, forthcoming).
3. There is, of course, the element of students discovering aspects of their own autonomy, which could be new to them in the unfamiliar business of language learning; but I am more concerned here with how teachers discover it.

Part III
Practical Interventions

7
Pedagogy for Autonomy as (Becoming-)Appropriate Methodology

Richard C. Smith

Appropriate methodology and autonomy

Concerns regarding the inappropriate transfer of teaching methods and materials from Western to non-Western contexts have been frequently expressed in ELT circles in recent years (cf. Phillipson, 1992; Holliday, 1994; Pennycook, 1994; Canagarajah, 1999). In this climate of opinion, as the concept of learner autonomy has risen to prominence in mainstream ELT discourse some writers have been quick to draw attention to the dangers of its possible imposition on non-Western, particularly Asian contexts (for example, Ho and Crookall, 1995; Jones, 1995).

Mostly reports relating to the notion of 'appropriate methodology' have focused on critiquing the *inappropriate* transfer of particular methods or materials. However, some writers have presented alternative solutions for particular contexts, with adaptations of Western approaches or materials tending to be justified according to generalizations about national cultural characteristics (for example, Flowerdew, 1998). In relation to learner autonomy, also, some suggestions have been made for appropriate methodology on the basis of national stereotypes, with a particular focus on the supposed group-oriented tendencies of students in different Asian countries (for example, Farmer, 1994; Ho and Crookall, 1995; Jones, 1995). Others have seen research into national or regional learning styles as a key to the potential development of appropriate methodology (Oxford and Anderson, 1995; Littlewood, 1999). However, given the variety of types of social or cultural factor which impact on particular classrooms (cf. Holliday, 1994: 28–31), and possible dangers in this area of 'orientalism' (Said, 1978; Pennycook, 1998), such

129

generalizations or even 'hypotheses' derived from them (Littlewood, 1999) appear to represent an insufficient basis on which to develop appropriate local practices (cf. Smith, 1997, 2001). It is regrettable in this connection that, with only a few exceptions (notably, Holliday, 1994, 1997a; and Canagarajah, 1999, 2002a), there has been so little discussion of general principles which might inform the development of appropriate methodology by teachers, for their own contexts, without reference to a priori generalizations.

Criticisms relating specifically to the 'transfer' of the concept of autonomy to Asian contexts may tend additionally to reflect the misleading view that autonomy itself is a new method or that its promotion entails particular procedures. Rather, as stated in Little (1991) and as argued further in Aoki and Smith (1999), autonomy should more properly be seen as a possible educational goal, being a willingness and/or ability to take charge of one's own learning which learners may already possess or not possess in varying degrees. Thus, the promotion of autonomy does not entail the use of a particular method or technology. Instead, as Benson (2001: 107–78) illustrates, a wide variety of possible approaches can be envisaged. Following on from this, if learners in a particular context do not appear to respond well to a particular approach to developing autonomy, this – in itself – is no reason to assert that they lack autonomy or that the goal of autonomy is inappropriate: it might be the approach which needs to be criticized, not the students or the validity of autonomy itself.

In this chapter I wish to argue that one kind of approach to the classroom development of learner autonomy might – potentially – be more appropriate in non-Western contexts than others. I base this argument on my own experience with students in a Japanese university (reported on below) and on a distinction (see Figure 7.1) between two methodological tendencies, which I shall characterize here as 'weak' and 'strong' versions of pedagogy for learner autonomy.

'Weak' versions of pedagogy for autonomy, in this characterization, tend to view autonomy as a capacity which students currently lack (and so need 'training' towards), and/or identify it with a mode of learning (for example, self-access) which students need to be prepared for. The underlying assumptions tend to be that students are deficient in autonomy (and/or currently unable to make effective use of self-access resources), but that autonomy – as conceived in the mind of the teacher, syllabus designer and/or institution – is nevertheless a goal worth pursuing with them. The rationale for these assumptions, as well as guidance regarding the contents of instruction (the 'learning strategy

Approach	Goal
'Weak version':	
Awareness-raising ('training'/ 'preparation' for self-directed learning/learner autonomy)	→ Self-directed learning/learner autonomy (as envisaged by the teacher/syllabus/institution)
Learning strategy syllabus	
Presentation and practice of discrete 'good learning' strategies	
'Strong version':	
Exercise of students' own (partial) autonomy (via (partially) student-directed learning + reflection)	→ Awareness-raising (enhancement of student-directed learning/ ← development of students' own autonomy)
Negotiated syllabus	
Experience of and reflection on student-directed learning	

Figure 7.1 'Weak' and 'strong' versions of pedagogy for learner autonomy

syllabus'), may tend to come from research into and/or beliefs regarding 'good language learners', or from a belief in the potential efficacy but current under-use or misuse of self-access facilities. Thus, instruction may tend to consist in presentation and practice of strategies which are considered, according to background research or other conceptualizations of 'good learners', preferable to students' current learning behaviours (cf. Holliday's 'approach A', in this volume). In sum, instruction tends to be based on a deficit model of students' present capacities, while autonomy is seen as a deferred goal and as a product of instruction rather than as something which students are currently ready to exercise directly.

A 'strong version' of pedagogy for learner autonomy, on the other hand, is based on the assumption that students are, to greater or lesser degrees, already autonomous, and already capable of exercising this capacity (cf. Holliday's 'approach C'). The methodological focus here is on co-creating with students optimal conditions for the exercise of their own autonomy, engaging them in reflection on the experience, and in this manner (rather than via transmission of a 'good learning' strategy syllabus), developing their capacities, which are then brought to bear in further exercise of learner autonomy. This could be described as an experiential approach (cf. Kenny, 1993) in the sense that awareness-raising is based firmly on students' own experiences and insights. It is also developmental and 'process-oriented' (cf. Breen, 1984, 1987; Legutke and Thomas, 1991: 202–4) in that the goal is ongoing improvement of existing learning capacities, rather than delayed attainment of autonomy as a 'product' of instruction.

From the point of view of appropriate methodology, a weak version of pedagogy for autonomy, in which learning arrangements tend to be determined by the teacher, syllabus and/or institution rather than being negotiated with learners, can certainly be criticized. This version tends to be based on conceptualizations of 'good language learning' which are, ideally, relevant to students' own needs and priorities; however, the more distant the context(s) in which these conceptualizations were originally formed, the less appropriate they are likely to be. Thus, criticisms might justly be levelled against the export (if this is what is happening) of pre-packaged approaches, materials or technologies for developing learner autonomy from 'centre' to 'periphery' contexts. Strategy training approaches, learner training materials or self-access models which have been developed in Western countries might need to be particularly critiqued in this manner. As others have indicated (for example, Jones (1995) for self-access and Benson (1995) for learner training), these may run a grave risk of being ethnocentric and inappropriately imposed outside the contexts for which they were originally developed.

Rather than developing this kind of critique in new ways here, however, I wish to focus on a positive methodological alternative (the 'strong version' of pedagogy for autonomy identified above) and analyse what appears to have made it appropriate in one particular non-Western context. Below, then, I devote some space to describing in a concrete way how classroom-based negotiation of student-directed learning has shown itself to be feasible and apparently appropriate in my own practice in a Japanese university. I then derive some implications from this account of practice for the development of appropriate methodology by teachers more generally, and I conclude by considering the feasibility of this kind of approach in other contexts.

A 'strong version' of pedagogy for autonomy in practice

Background

The approach I shall describe was developed over a period of five years' teaching in a Japanese university, with seven separate classes of – on average – 35 to 40 undergraduate students each. These classes were all timetabled to meet for one and a half hours each week, for one academic year (two semesters) in total. I took the first steps with classes of first year students majoring in a variety of languages other than English (see Smith (2001) for an account of my first year of experimentation). Subsequently I extended the approach to classes for English majors in their third and fourth years at the university.

Prior to this five-year period I had already taught for eight years in Japan, including four years in a full-time position at this particular university. Although I was clearly still an 'outsider' in not being Japanese myself, my growing familiarity with the context had given me certain 'insider' perceptions about students which served as a basis for the approach to be described. I was aware, for example, that: (i) most students in this particular university were well-motivated to study English, and already relatively proficient; (ii) however, they were generally worried that their abilities were in decline, since they only had two timetabled lessons per week of 'practical English', of which my own lesson was one; (iii) they tended to engage actively in and saw benefit in teacher-directed group work on relatively open-ended tasks and projects; and (iv) in common with other students I had taught in Japan, they were much more willing to express personal opinions and feelings via writing or private discussion than in open class discussion.

By this stage in my own development as a teacher in Japan I was actively seeking ways to make my teaching more appropriate to students' needs and concerns, and less dependent on methodological preconceptions and imported materials. In particular, I was conscious of a need to establish a connection between students' classroom learning and their lives outside the classroom, given that they themselves tended to see classroom learning as insufficient on its own even to maintain their current abilities in English (cf. (ii) above). I therefore hoped to build a connection with their out-of-class experience into my practice, initially by having students write about and share with each other their own goals and ideas for out-of-class English learning. On reading their reflections, I realized that students had various goals and preferences for improvement of their English and were far more active in attempting to learn English independently than I had expected (cf. Smith, 2001). This provided me with an initial rationale for then inviting students to make suggestions about classroom activities, again via writing, and then for provisionally suggesting that they could form groups around the different kinds of activity they had proposed.

Remembering this 'in tranquillity' at a remove of seven years, it is now quite difficult for me to recall the trepidation with which I took this first step towards student-directed classroom learning. I do remember that I spent a lot of time worrying initially about whether students' plans would work in practice. I frequently intervened to suggest materials, offer sometimes very directive advice and generally retain some control over what groups were planning. Having arranged for extra rooms to be available for students with special equipment requirements (VTR, for example), I requested a short written report from each student each week, aware that I would no longer be able to monitor what students were doing all the time. Over the following weeks I visited each group several times per session and was relieved to observe that students were actively engaged 'on task', implementing their plans. Despite my worries, they did not object to continuing with this kind of work; indeed it continued for the whole of this first year (interspersed with occasional whole-class sessions), gaining strong votes of overall approval each time I offered a return to more conventional arrangements. I was encouraged, then, to adopt the same basic approach with different classes over the following four years, with similarly positive overall votes of approval but some modifications, as I shall detail below.

Some details of practice

The following 'snapshot' of just one student-directed learning session (Figure 7.2), reconstructed from group plans and a video recording, can serve as an illustration of the variety of activities students in this context decided to engage in when allowed the freedom to plan activities for themselves (numbers of students in each group are in parentheses).

Over the five years during which I adopted this approach, groups of students engaged in a wide variety of types of activity, with a variety of goals. Activities ranged from the relatively product-oriented (such as transcribing taped radio broadcasts) to relatively process-focused (such as 'free conversation'). Sometimes students chose to focus on a particular skill using a particular type of material (for example, listening, using sitcoms they had recorded off air), sometimes they preferred to integrate skills (such as reading articles and discussing them, or interviewing international students around campus and subsequently writing a report). In 'receptive' work, students often chose to work with authentic materials and to devise their own tasks for using them, but they sometimes decided to engage in study using published learning materials (for instance, radio programmes recorded off-air, with accompanying purchased texts). In 'productive' mode, some students chose to engage in creative work such as individual fiction-writing combined with peer-response, writing poetry in groups or writing and

In the originally designated classroom:	
Topic discussion (4) (they'll discuss 'living alone')	**Free conversation** (5) (they'll talk about whatever comes into their heads)
Reading/discussion (7) (they copied articles from *Newsweek* last week, and will discuss them today)	**Business English** (5) (they'll improvise a sales negotiation)
In the empty classroom next door:	
Debate/discussion (3) (they'll debate the proposition 'Smoking should be banned')	**Watch TV drama** (7) (they'll help each other to understand an audio-recording one of them made of the video they watched together last week)
In an 'AV' room, some distance away:	*In my office (where there is a VTR):*
Movies (9) (they'll continue to watch the movie *Seven* and then will discuss it)	**TV drama (with skit)** (9) (they'll share new words and phrases they noted down individually while watching last week, and will write an original skit using these words and phrases).
In the library, or wherever else they want to work (they've arranged to see me at the end of the lesson):	
Individual writing activities (4)	

Figure 7.2 A 'snapshot' of student-directed classroom activities

subsequently performing rap songs; sometimes their work was more instrumentally focused, as in the 'Business English' group above. Thus, some activities which students found value in were what might be termed 'communicative', whereas others were relatively 'traditional'.

Classes met once a week over a total of about 28 weeks (about 14 weeks in each of the first and second semesters). This enabled the following cycle (Figure 7.3) related to out-of-class as well as inside-class learning to be repeated several – usually four to five – times in the course of a year.

This 'overall scheme' is an idealized and provisional one because it represents the end-point of five years of practice and was open to modification or indeed outright rejection during the course of each year with different groups of students, as I shall emphasize below. Although the basic overall approach was in fact supported by students over the course of five years, I introduced several modifications over time, in the light of

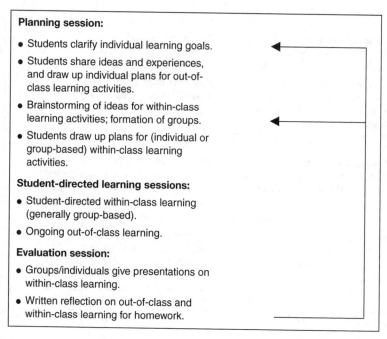

Planning session:

- Students clarify individual learning goals.
- Students share ideas and experiences, and draw up individual plans for out-of-class learning activities.
- Brainstorming of ideas for within-class learning activities; formation of groups.
- Students draw up plans for (individual or group-based) within-class learning activities.

Student-directed learning sessions:

- Student-directed within-class learning (generally group-based).
- Ongoing out-of-class learning.

Evaluation session:

- Groups/individuals give presentations on within-class learning.
- Written reflection on out-of-class and within-class learning for homework.

Figure 7.3   A 'student-directed learning cycle'

student feedback and my own developing sense of possibilities and needs in this context. Here are the most salient changes between the first and final years, in roughly chronological order. Some of these will be discussed further under the heading 'Becoming appropriate' below:

- increased initial explanation on my part of the rationale for and possible benefits of the approach;
- increased trust on my part that students could plan and learn for themselves, without my intervention;
- decreased recommendation on my part of particular 'communicative' learning materials or procedures; this led to an increased use of authentic materials (by some students) and 'traditional' procedures (by others), or a combination of the two (as in 'transcribing the news');
- relaxation of the requirement for individual student reports at the end of each session; instead, one member of the group wrote a short report each time;
- tightening of the planning–learning–evaluation cycle overall (i.e. increase in frequency of 'Planning' and 'Evaluation' sessions in

Figure 7.3, resulting in an average of three or four student-directed learning sessions between them);

- a more formalized structure for gathering evaluations as to the overall appropriateness of the approach (via end-of-semester assignments, and short reports at the end of each learning cycle, as indicated under 'Evaluation session' in Figure 7.3);
- increased activity on my part in 'interrogating' students as to what they were planning or doing and why, largely replacing advice to students as to what they 'should' do (particularly following the first learning cycle with each new class);
- a tightening of the planning–learning–evaluation cycle within groups (via a recommendation that groups should spend ten minutes at the end of each session collectively evaluating work that week and planning for the next session);
- relaxation of the requirement that groups needed to be formed: individual learning was also enabled (as shown in Figure 7.2);
- increased involvement of students in self-assessment for grades awarded at the end of the year.

In the light of concerns which I myself shared regarding the possible 'imposition' of a pedagogy for autonomy in this context, it is important to note that in the overall scheme (Figure 7.3), student-directed learning arrangements were open to rejection following initial experience of three or so sessions, and then, again, at the end of each subsequent learning cycle (the question mark in Figure 7.3 indicates that student-directed arrangements were always open to rejection at this stage). At the end of each learning cycle, I asked students to reflect on the experience in writing for homework, in response to the following questions: "Would you like to continue with similar [student-directed learning] arrangements in this class?", "If not, what kind of arrangements would you like to see?", and "If yes, how could arrangements be improved/ what kind of work would you like to do?" Apart from reading students' responses to these questions, I would confirm their opinions person-to-person as they wrote about and discussed individual learning goals and out-of-class learning plans at the beginning of the subsequent session (the 'Planning session' in Figure 7.3 above).

Although most students were always in favour of continuing with and improving on self-directed classroom work, two or three students in each class tended to be in favour of one form or another of whole-class instruction. With these students, I attempted to devote as much time as possible to understanding their objections to current arrangements.

Having talked to all students, I would then present my overall interpretation of the feedback I had received, making suggestions for improved arrangements on the basis of feedback received (without naming individuals). This was sometimes followed by more 'rounds' (during individual writing or pair/group discussion about issues relating to the organization of the class) where I consulted with students further about proposed arrangements, forming a view of the overall 'mood of the meeting', which I would then report back to all students. If it had been established that students – as a body – were content to continue with self-directed within-class learning, and once overall arrangements had been modified to take into account suggestions for improvement, students were invited to form (new) groups for the subsequent learning cycle. Thus, the overall scheme was both rejectable and modifiable, and all students' opinions were actively elicited and taken into account, not just those of the most vocal.

Becoming appropriate

I shall now broaden the discussion to consider the above approach in relation to general criteria for appropriate methodology, taking into account also possible objections to its feasibility in other contexts and illustrating my argument with extracts from student evaluations (in block quotations below).

From plausibility to appropriation

As Holliday (1994) has implied, and as my own experience has confirmed (cf. Smith, 2001), provisional local insights may need to be seen as an essential prerequisite for the initial development of interventions intended to be appropriate, in contrast with the potentially orientalist national or regional stereotypes which are so often appealed to in discussions of appropriate methodology. Thus, I could justify the strong version of pedagogy for autonomy which I adopted in this setting as appropriate in terms of my provisional 'insider' knowledge of the students and context, in other words in terms of my own initial sense of its 'plausibility' (Prabhu, 1987: 106) in a context with which I had become relatively familiar (cf. 'Background' above).

By themselves, however, prior local insights may not be sufficient to justify a particular approach as 'appropriate'. After all, such insights are generally based on what students have already shown of themselves in response to, that is, within the confines of existing classroom arrangements. When classroom arrangements are changed, so too are students' responses and behaviours, and this is one reason why a particular approach cannot be fixed in advance but must continue to 'become appropriate' (Holliday, 1994) in the light of students' and the teacher's changing perceptions of needs and possibilities.

For Holliday (1994), the role of continuing confirmation of appropriateness is taken on by ongoing 'ethnographic action research'. As I shall discuss below, this does seem to be an important principle. However, as Canagarajah (2002: 147) has implied, action research on the part of the teacher does not necessarily entail any transfer of 'ownership' of classroom work to students since opportunities for decision-making by students (enabling their 'appropriation' or, indeed, rejection of the approach) are not built-in. The teacher's perceptions of 'apparent suitability' remain the only, potentially fallible, measure of appropriateness in this case.

On the other hand, ongoing negotiation of classroom arrangements with students, where practicable, can provide valuable 'hard evidence' (or counter-evidence) of continuing appropriateness. Various connotations of the word 'appropriate' might be involved here, and highlighting these can show the need for 'appropriation' to be considered alongside 'apparent suitability' as a defining characteristic of appropriate methodology. In the above approach, as I have shown, students themselves determined the nature of classroom activities and had quite frequent opportunities, as a body, to reject or modify the overall scheme – in other words, it was *'given over'* to them. In practice it was also *'taken over'*, since students in this context wanted to work further to improve it rather than rejecting it entirely:

> For inside the class, I think we should keep doing the group work. At first, group work might not be effective, but I think that every time we get together, we think of different things to do and try to revise it to the better way, so I think the group work will eventually help us improve our English ability.

Each year, negotiation both of particular activities and of the overall scheme enabled classroom work to become appropriate in two further senses, in that activities were *'owned'* by and *'unique'* to the particular groups of students with whom the approach was implemented.[1]

In emphasizing the value of *appropriation* here, I would like to suggest that enhancement of student decision-making can be considered an important, hitherto relatively neglected principle in the development and subsequent justification of becoming-appropriate methodology, since only this can ensure that a new classroom culture is *jointly* created with students. From this point of view, a strong version of pedagogy for autonomy can, in contrast with concerns about the inappropriate 'imposition' of autonomy in non-Western contexts, be seen as a kind of becoming-appropriate methodology par excellence.

Learner development

The approach I have described appeared to be appropriate also in *effectively* improving students' English abilities and developing their autonomy. After an initial period of 'acculturation' (see "A 'cultural challenge'" below), students tended quite quickly to come to see the value of this approach, often expressing their appreciation of it in terms of its overall *efficiency* in coping with diverse needs and preferences in a large class context (cf. Smith, 2001):

> Personally, I very much liked the way we had our 'Advanced English classes'. As intermediate English students, we differ very much in what areas we want to improve our English, and a class in which the teacher decides what to do and what materials to use would not be effective.

On a basis of trial and error students became increasingly able to develop what they perceived as effective means for developing their English abilities:

> At first, we were puzzled what to do, but after a while, we could enjoy talking and tried to find better way to speak more and more. At first, I thought speaking was difficult and I was in tension, but recently, I can speak more relaxedly and I can enjoy speaking. I want to be able to speak more and more fluently, so I want to look for a better way to stimulate our talking.

In the light of some students' concerns as to whether they were really improving their abilities, one important overall modification in my practice was to place increasing emphasis on student self-evaluation, in the first instance by asking students to devote ten minutes at the end of each session to evaluating the session and planning the next one. I also began to feel less reluctant to interrupt student-directed work periodically to pose questions for reflection ("What have you been doing?", "Why?", "What has worked/not worked?", "Why/Why not?", "What are you planning to do?", "Why?", and so on). Finally, I began to ask students to suggest grades for their own work at the end of each semester.

These moves towards a greater degree of self-evaluation by students increased, I believe, the overall efficacy of the approach, enhancing student reflection and control and helping me to 'trouble-shoot' more effectively on the basis of data I gathered. By the end of each course, most students seemed to end up feeling they had made significant progress towards reaching their goals:

> We still have problems when expressing our thoughts in English, especially, when we began to talk in detail. However, I felt strongly that speaking ability has improved for everyone in the group. [...] I feel that I can do better in future, because now I see the problems of my English more clearly than the beginning of this course.

Just as importantly, perhaps, the approach did seem to be effective in developing students' overall ability to take charge of their learning. When asked what they had learned from the course, many students ended up expressing appreciation of this aspect in particular (cf. also Aoki and Smith, 1999: 25–6):

> What I realized and learned most was that there were many ways to study English and it is me who should decide which way to choose and study. Besides, I felt the importance of having clear goal in studying. Without any particular goal, it is difficult to choose which way to go. At this point, I really learned a lot from this class. This experience must have given me an important lesson.

> This way of class; thinking of the goal and the aim of studying English and making a study plan all by ourselves, gave us chance to consider what is need to be study each of us. And made us realize that learning English is our own desire and that the way of learning should be well considered by each of us.

To recap, in this section I have emphasized the apparent efficiency and effectiveness of the approach in meeting goals of improvement in English abilities and development of learner autonomy. After all, appropriate methodology – as with any educational intervention – must presumably be effective in 'moving students on' (in mutually approved directions), rather than simply 'remaining with' their prior abilities, thoughts and behaviours.

Teacher development

A final argument in support of the appropriateness of this approach might be that the initially unfamiliar teacher role of 'mediator' or 'negotiator' seems to bring with it a *requirement* for the kind of ethnographic action research which is viewed by Holliday (1994) as crucial to the development of becoming-appropriate methodology more generally. My own initial and ongoing uncertainties about the appropriateness of the approach led me to investigate students' responses more actively and systematically than I had ever done before. I needed to assume an identity as a kind of 'ethnographer' of the unfamiliar, developing classroom culture both in order to support students in their self-directed work and as a basis for negotiation of the overall scheme (in other words, to find out what they felt about it, as described above). This requirement was also identified by one of my students, who described it perceptively in the following terms:

> Teacher doesn't have to make the detailed lesson plan and talk during the whole lesson. It seems that it makes teacher easy to hold the class, but I don't really think so. As long as the teacher teaches in front of the whole class, he/she can expect what students are supposed to acquire through the lesson. It is because that the aim of the lesson is planned by teacher him/herself and students just follow it. But in this kind of class, aims are made by each student and they work separately according to their own aims. Grasping every student's aim and see how they are doing is rather difficult for teacher. He/she has to look students carefully to understand their ideas and give appropriate advice to them. I think it is important not to forget to make contact with students to see what they want to do next and how the plan improved.

Much of my time was spent in deliberately gathering data (from written student reports, ongoing observation, discussions with groups and individual students and final presentations), and my reflections on the insights I gained fed directly into suggestions I made for improvements in overall learning arrangements (making this 'ethnographic *action* research') as well as into more immediate interaction with groups and individual students. Thus, each cycle of student-directed learning in the overall scheme described above constituted at the same time a teacher action research cycle.

By engaging in the above approach, I gained a sense of being 'in control' of my own learning of teaching – in other words, I became less dependent than previously on external insights into how I 'should' be teaching, much more in touch with students' priorities. I also felt that I was developing appropriate methodology because what I was doing reflected the needs which they had articulated. Thus, teaching these classes became a positive source of teaching-related learning for me: a resource, in other words, for the development of my own autonomy as a teacher. This corresponds well with Vieira's (1999: 155) observations that, through engagement in this kind of pedagogy, "Teaching becomes a sort of research, and research becomes a way of teaching. Teachers, as learners, become involved in a process of autonomization, thus feeling more empowered to take charge of their own course of action." In other words, (ethnographic) action research needs to be engaged in when a strong version of pedagogy for autonomy is adopted. Adopting this kind of approach can, then, serve as a particularly convenient basis for developing appropriate methodology.

A 'cultural challenge'

Despite the positive arguments outlined above, there is no denying that the changes in teacher and student roles which accompany this kind of approach tend to counter conventional expectations, representing a challenge to established norms of classroom culture in most institutional learning contexts, Western or non-Western. It is necessary to recognize that in many settings students may appear reluctant, at least initially, to take on greater control over classroom learning. Additionally, when students *are* willing to engage in this kind of approach, teachers' freedom to innovate may itself be or appear to be constrained by a lack of autonomy with regard to institutional requirements and/or the expectations of stakeholders such as parents, other teachers or administrative authorities.

I have become more conscious of such constraints myself since moving back to the UK, where I now teach in a much more 'accountable' university setting. With hindsight I can see that a very important factor facilitating the approach I have described in this chapter was the relative freedom I had as a teacher in Japan to engage in experimentation involving student decision-making. As in many other Japanese universities, teachers in this setting have considerable freedom to design their own courses: apart from needing to specify overall objectives and contents in very general terms for a prospectus, teach at a particular time each week and submit overall grades for students at the end of the year, I had sole responsibility, and was therefore free to negotiate control with students, in many areas, including evaluation procedures, without being clearly accountable to 'stakeholders' other than the students themselves. This is not so clearly the case in my present teaching context (where there are various departmental and institutional constraints on course planning and evaluation) and is unlikely to be true in many settings.

Since I am still struggling to identify 'spaces of freedom' for the development of learner autonomy in my own current teaching situation (cf. Smith and Barfield, 2001), I wish to avoid suggesting that a strong version of pedagogy can or should be implemented to the same degree in more 'difficult' circumstances than those I have described above. However, in general terms, I would suggest on the basis of my experience in Japan that it is, perhaps, only by attempting to engage in negotiation, in other words by challenging previously accepted classroom norms, that individual teachers can identify what the 'real' external constraints on this kind of practice are, and what is in fact feasible and appropriate.

If teachers are willing to engage in innovation of this kind, negotiation is likely – on the one hand – to involve a requirement for 'cultural continuity', as recommended by Holliday (1997a). Viable negotiation strategies will vary in different settings, and an important role for the teacher engaged in this kind of practice is to develop workable local forms of classroom democracy, since, as Breen and Littlejohn (2000: 281) have emphasized, "Much [...] would appear to depend on *how* negotiated work is approached, rather than on a general factor of appropriacy or otherwise [of negotiated work] to specific cultural contexts." On the other hand, as I have already implied above, appropriateness cannot be seen just as a matter of 'fitting in' with established norms – education can only ever take students in new directions. A strong version of pedagogy for autonomy which is developed jointly by the teacher and students involves neither 'cultural imposition' nor complete 'cultural continuity'. Rather, it involves what might be termed a 'cultural challenge': negotiation inevitably takes the teacher, students and the emerging classroom culture in unaccustomed directions which are nevertheless appropriate because they are *jointly created* within the limits of what proves to be feasible and acceptable in a particular context.

Finally, if this kind of cultural challenge is to be managed in a context-sensitive manner it may be necessary for the teacher to provide "firm insurances of security" (Holliday, 1994: 187) even as the classroom becomes more decentralized. For example, an overall scheme comparable to the one I have described might reassure students that self-directed work is regularly open to rejection or renegotiation while allowing the teacher opportunities to re-establish a more familiar kind of authority if this seems necessary.

Conclusion

A strong version of pedagogy for autonomy, as exemplified in this chapter, is likely to challenge both the teacher's and students' preconceptions about classroom behaviour and, for this reason alone, may seem difficult to implement ('inappropriate' in one sense of the term) in many contexts. However, if culturally sensitive and 'secure' mechanisms for negotiation are evolved, this kind of approach can result in enhanced classroom participation and motivation, giving the lie to stereotypes about 'passive' learners. In such circumstances, far from autonomy being inappropriate for general cultural reasons, a strong version of pedagogy for autonomy, where practicable, offers opportunities to connect classroom learning with students' lives outside the classroom, enabling them to become more active in engaging and developing their own learning styles and strategies in ways which *they* find appropriate. Involving as it does an ongoing requirement for ethnographic action research on the part of the teacher, the approach can also help him/her to learn with and from students, and thus move beyond a priori stereotypes and attachments to 'method'.

Although there might be difficulties in implementing this kind of approach in other (including Western) contexts, it seems important to re-emphasize finally that it has proved feasible in one large class, non-Western setting. As Crabbe (1999: 7) remarks, "The fact that the autonomy of language learning is understood and accepted in a given cultural context is sufficient counter to any categorical claim of general cultural inappropriateness in that context." Beyond this, however, it is acceptance or rejection by students of a particular *approach* to developing autonomy which is the issue I have been emphasizing here. The approach I have described, being based on what students themselves brought to the classroom and offering them ample opportunities for rejection or modification, has proved to be popular and apparently successful in one 'Asian' setting. This suggests that it is important to look elsewhere than to national or regional cultural characteristics in the future (for example, to institutional constraints and opportunities, students' previous learning experiences, teachers' degree of readiness, and, importantly, the degree of control students have over the approach 'offered' to them) for explanations of the appropriateness or otherwise of different pedagogies for autonomy in classroom contexts around the world.

Acknowledgement

I'm very grateful to Andy Barfield, Sultan Erdoğan, Mike Nix and David Palfreyman for their helpful comments on previous drafts of this chapter.

Reflection/discussion questions

1. What might be 'appropriate' or 'inappropriate' about some approaches to developing learner autonomy you are familiar with, in a classroom context known to you?
2. To what extent do you agree or disagree with the argument above that 'a strong version of pedagogy for autonomy can [...] be seen as a kind of becoming-appropriate methodology par excellence'?
3. What factors might constrain the implementation of a relatively 'strong' version of pedagogy for autonomy, in a context with which you are familiar? How could some classroom arrangements nevertheless be negotiated with students, in a culturally sensitive fashion?

Note

1. The connotations of 'appropriate' identified here ('apparently suited (to)', 'given over (to)', 'taken over (by)', 'unique (to)' and 'owned (by)') are abstracted from definitions in the *Oxford English Dictionary*.

8
Autonomy in a Resource-Poor Setting: Enhancing the Carnivalesque

E.A. Gamini Fonseka

Introduction

This chapter focuses on the significance of developing autonomy in a resource-poor classroom environment and introduces one approach to doing so. Lack of exposure to English prevents most learners in resource-poor settings in countries such as Sri Lanka from meeting the challenges of globalisation. Nation-wide programmes to teach the language have so far failed, as they do not address the circumstances under which these learners carry out their studies. This is why it is imperative to promote autonomy as a rescue strategy. In this connection, songs have been found to be highly effective learning materials. They can introduce a carnivalesque element into children's learning efforts, helping to redefine the classroom as a place for recreation, harmonisation and socialisation, and attracting children to learning. In turn, this can help dispel frustration and learned helplessness, and children can develop optimal strategies for remembering, appropriating, and using without hesitation the new language they learn.

A problematic situation

English education in the post-colonial Third World

Inequality in English education continues to be a hindrance to the creation of cohesive communities in most post-colonial Third-World countries. As experienced in Sri Lanka during the British colonial period, the school system was divided into three – English schools, Anglo-vernacular schools, and Vernacular schools – based on the emphasis that each of these placed on English learning (De Silva, 1981: 239). The same division continues to prevail in the current educational system. The state and private schools that prepare students for public examinations are clearly divided into Vernacular and Anglo-vernacular, while the so-called 'international schools' emphasising British or American examinations are totally English-medium. All these schools function with the blessing of the Ministry of Education, but international, Anglo-vernacular and Vernacular schools produce three types of users of English: fully competent, fairly competent, and incompetent, respectively. The candidates classified as fairly competent or incompetent face the same discrimination in higher education and employment that their parents and grandparents used to face under colonialism. While English continues to be the lingua franca in Sri Lanka, only those who are competent in English are enabled to receive higher education. Likewise, all good jobs demand a certain proficiency level in English, and only the fully competent candidates are always selected. Thus the hegemony of the English-speaking minority over the non-English-speaking majority prevails in all spheres – cultural, educational, social, economic, and administrative (Fonseka, 1995: 82). Building up a strong community out of the two categories of users and non-users of English in order to tackle the challenges of national development remains forever a dream because the gap created by inequality in English education is such a hindrance.

Scarcities generally experienced

The physical evidence that can be statistically calculated and presented to measure Sri Lanka's progress in ELT during her years of independence includes: the increased number of English language teachers, the increased number of schools that have introduced English into their curriculum, the advances made in publishing English textbooks and educational material within the country itself, the increased number of English language teacher education programmes, the increased number of foreign-trained ELT experts operating within the educational system, and above all the increased number of learners who officially take English as a subject throughout the school system in the country. Thus Sri Lanka's national ELT programme looks strong enough to meet the challenge of providing a suitable environment for the propagation and use of the language (Fonseka, 2001: 126). Technically speaking, every school-going child in Sri Lanka is today provided with free textbooks and free instruction by teachers who have achieved at least a basic qualification in English.

Nevertheless, no Sri Lankan public school can match the facilities offered by private or international schools. These maintain standards recognised in advanced educational settings in highly industrialised 'First-World' countries. From newspaper advertisements, anniversary publications, brochures, and so on, it is clear that cosy classrooms, handy furniture, carefully selected textbooks and educational materials, thoughtfully established self-access learning systems, logically defined syllabi and learning programmes, reasonably small classes, and, above all, competent, friendly, and well-paid teachers are features of such schools. In contrast, most urban public schools today suffer from the problem of large classes consisting of more than 45 children, despite the ministerial rule that class sizes should not exceed forty. Although some rural schools have small classes they do not have English teachers with advanced qualifications, nor do they enjoy even the bare minimum of the facilities their private and international counterparts have. These logistical problems are compounded by the complacent and hypocritical attitude of the English-speaking elite with regard to the efforts of poverty-stricken learners.

National-level failures

As a result the pedagogical efforts made for satisfying the national requirement of teaching English to every schoolchild result in overall failure. Although the national education policy offers every schoolchild a teaching programme of ten years leading to a working knowledge of English, which is a compulsory subject at the GCE ('O' Level) Examination, most pupils in Sri Lanka do not achieve recognised standards of proficiency in the language. Table 8.1 shows representative final results of a ten-year ELT programme within the Sri Lankan educational system.

According to these statistics, only 31.09 per cent of all candidates passed the English GCE O Level Examination in 1995, and of these 67.7 per cent had only an Ordinary Pass, which is not recognised for further education or entry to most professions. Of the whole population of the English Language candidates, only 1.3 per cent offered English Literature at O level, and those who passed represented only 0.78 per cent of the overall total. Judging by the complexity levels of the respective examination formats, this latter group can be considered to represent candidates who can use English in a relatively creative way. Generally, these candidates attend international schools, take private tuition and/or speak English at home.

Table 8.1 English examination results of school candidates

Year	Exam	Subject	Distinction		Credit		Ordinary pass		Fail	
			No.	%	No.	%	No.	%	No.	%
1995	GCE O Level	English Language	8 263	2.65	27 809	9.11	58 855	19.28	210 412	68.91
1995	GCE O Level	English Literature	354	8.86	1 138	28.49	889	22.25	1 614	40.4

Year	Exam	Subject	Distinction		V. Good		Credit		Ordinary pass		Fail	
			No.	%	No.	%	No.	%	No.	%	No.	%
1998	GCE A Level	English	8	0.52	23	1.51	84	5.5	349	22.84	1 064	69.63

Source: Compiled from Sri Lanka Department of Examinations Register of Results.

Technically speaking, this cohort of candidates sat their GCE A Level Examination in 1998. The ratio of the candidates who succeeded in English at 'A' Level in 1998 to the 1995 O Level English Language group is 15 to 10 000. Sadly, this represents the output of a ten-year-long struggle to learn English within the school system of Sri Lanka operating under the direction of the Ministry of Education, and it is imperative that an alternative approach to the study of the language be developed.

Conditions for an alternative approach

Are we to blame the children who are the victims of this situation for the failures of the public school system? Many children who fail in English prove their abilities in other subjects in the curriculum whose medium of instruction is either Sinhala or Tamil. There are some candidates who earn Distinction Passes in all the subjects they take in their mother tongue but who fail in English. This is why it is clear that the present approach to the study of English has to be replaced by an approach which addresses the circumstances under which the children carry out their learning and which exploits the linguistic and cultural potentials they have within their own environment.

In deciding on a new approach, one has first to consider the circumstances under which the majority of children carry out their studies. It is obvious that they do not have the bare minimum of the facilities available in an advanced educational setting. Most learners in rural settings in Sri Lanka come from poor domestic environments, sometimes without a proper meal in the morning or a proper rest at night. Their school culture may totally differ from their home culture. The maintenance of exercise books, the execution of classroom projects, the preparation of study materials and the exploration of related materials from outside sources are not learning strategies workable with these learners. Even to keep them at school during classroom hours can be a challenge for the teacher.

While developing a methodology for teaching English in Sri Lanka, it is also important to take into consideration that the average Sri Lankan schoolchild does not need English for his/her immediate survival. Sinhala or Tamil inevitably play a much more important role in children's daily life than English. This does not mean that children have no need for English all their life. Of course, they will need it one day if they wish to start higher education or enter an occupation in a multicultural social milieu. Therefore it is the duty of teachers and parents to give the children a basic knowledge of English that can be of use when they need it for serious purposes. Serious needs for English do not arise until the children become adolescents. Until that time the knowledge of English they acquire should somehow be made to live with them.

However, the present official classroom textbooks contain ambitious types of material which make English look like an elitist and difficult pursuit to the average learner (cf. Canagarajah, 1999), and these have aggravated the problem of motivating pupils. Completing cloze-reading passages, answering questionnaires, working out the answers to puzzles, and presenting information provided in prose passages through diagrams or charts are not the kind of strategies that can make the language 'real' to these children. Of course, such tasks can be enjoyable when the children carry them out in the classroom, but how many times can a teacher expect the children to repeat or refer back to the same task outside class, and how often can they use such experiences for communication? Ultimately, pupils remain frustrated and unmotivated.

Aiming at the requirement to relate materials to pupils' lives outside the classroom, some textbook designers have included materials that can be incorporated into the rituals and games of children outside the classroom (see, for example, Dakin (1968), Papa and Iantorno (1979), Ward (1980), Fonseka (1993–94), Imbert and Rixon (1994)). These aim at helping children learn English to enhance their childhood rituals in a carnival atmosphere, at the same time as helping them become fluent speakers or writers of the language. As I shall discuss below, enhancing the carnivalesque elements in teaching and learning can be an effective strategy in motivating pupils to learn.

Just as importantly, however, a new approach should derive from a theory that does not demand such facilities as small classes, regular meetings with teachers, close monitoring of the progress of studies, contact with a target group of speakers, and so on. In the absence of a proper school environment equipped with these, first the learners have to be helped to achieve autonomy in their learning efforts – to face the challenges of poverty.

The importance of autonomy and the carnivalesque

Autonomy as a rescue strategy

Learner autonomy can be referred to as a governing principle for developing an alternative approach to second language teaching in a resource-poor situation such as that described above. Here I consider learner autonomy as a rescue strategy because the children concerned are in a precarious condition compared with the privileged minority in their own society. Their continuation in the present situation will destine them to be the underprivileged majority of their nation. On the other hand, by developing autonomy within them it is possible to empower them to take the initiative in relation to their own learning requirements and to build up their character to be resilient in the face of the numerous challenges they experience in their school and home life. Littlewood (1996a: 125), for one, regards autonomy as "a state of mind that permeates all aspects of a student's learning". Once pupils develop autonomy in the context of language learning they can apply it to all their learning efforts. They will find greater meaning in the instruction they receive from teachers and will attempt to carry out recommended tasks with greater diligence.

In a society without basic survival problems it may be relatively easy to establish autonomy and self-directed behaviour in learners. However, to be independent in one's thoughts, words, acts, dreams, and behaviour, one needs a strong backing from the environment. Therefore, however crucial a role autonomy can be seen to play in a resource-poor second language classroom, it is also important to understand that different procedures should be followed in fostering different levels of autonomy to suit different types of learners and settings. The teacher has to reflect on the home background of the children, the nature of the didactic support they receive from school, the children's general outlook resulting from their long years of living in their environment, and what may appeal to them as English in their daily life. It is only with an awareness of these aspects of their life that the teacher can develop an autonomous learning model for his/her own pupils.

Entertainment as a motivating force

Transforming a frustrated individual from a resource-poor setting into an autonomous second language learner can be a gigantic task. First the teacher has to find ways of introducing the language as something that satisfies an immediate requirement, because the standard integrative and instrumental needs of learning the language such as enjoying and mastering the target language culture, associating with the target language group, visiting countries where the target language is spoken, higher education, employment, and so on are remote from the interests of these learners, whose horizons are limited to home and school. With such learners, the most prominent requirement is entertainment. No matter what background the children come from, they like anything that entertains them. Because of the plainness of their horizons these learners can be drawn into the learning process through something that appeals to them, to a far greater extent than simply via reiterated pronouncements on the importance of English for educational and professional life. Made into a means of entertainment, then, English can be introduced to these learners in a more effective manner than otherwise. If the language is introduced through suitable material as a means of entertainment, it is quite possible for the children to adjust their behaviour to fulfill task requirements with regard to learning, and to develop autonomy and self-direction, because they obviously enjoy what they are doing and they feel the necessity of that enjoyment for the growth of their personalities. As Kirtikara (1996) emphasises with reference to the promotion of autonomy in Thailand, "Formal learning has become oppressive and we now need to find a way to make it sanuk (a learning process combined with fun)."

Songs as appropriate material

If the children are to feel that they learn English for entertainment, they need a suitable variety of staple material to work on. Prose texts, dialogues, and poems are not as effective as songs in the rural, resource-poor surroundings of countries like Sri Lanka, because the children find it difficult and uninteresting to engage in performance of written texts, which is an unusual form of entertainment in their own experience. They find such performances boring. In this sense the classroom textbooks freely distributed by the Ministry of Education are not very effective. Although the children feel the necessity to learn from the classroom textbooks, which are designed only with prose passages, dialogues, and poems, they do not enjoy them in their everyday life because they lack authenticity in the context of their lives. Therefore this chapter suggests the use of songs in a school curriculum as alternative material for motivating pupils on the basis of their relevance to the learners' lives.

Children clearly respond well to English children's songs. Songs enable their users to derive great aesthetic pleasure that harmonises them to the language and culture. The children react to the music of songs and even to their powerful rhetoric because of their rich poetic qualities. The use of songs is also supported by Sri Lankan children's liking for performing with peers. Within their own surroundings there are many examples of situations where songs are recited, sung, related, or dramatised by children in groups for pleasure. Once they learn the relevant texts they can use and enjoy them with their peers as part of their culture. They can repeat the same performance whenever they get together, just as they do with songs in their mother tongue.

In ELT terms, too, song texts are authentic. They are meant to entertain and educate people in their everyday life. Inasmuch as songs present a language close to the spoken idiom, the children can grasp the fundamental tools of expression by interacting with them. Songs also contribute to the expansion of their vocabulary. Children's songs display the use of many words in simple registers, and the understanding of their meanings is basic for the understanding of complete texts. Moreover, through various extension exercises, children's attention can be drawn to the synonyms, antonyms, inflections, genders, numbers, and definitions of the words they come across and their special usage in idiomatic expressions. The basic knowledge of pronunciation, intonation, vocabulary, syntax, and the denotative and connotative meanings of words that children gain from simple comprehension exercises on songs can motivate them to explore more complex areas such as the style of songs (Fonseka, 1997: 64–5).

A full semantic grasp of a song plus an oral memory of it enables children to personalise its contents (as I shall illustrate below). So, in the course of learning a series of songs they can personalise a complete language syllabus presented throughout an academic year. Extension exercises emphasising the use and usage of various language elements represented in the syllabus also help them become flexible in the application of the new language learnt. The resulting ability to personalise the whole syllabus and to manipulate its contents helps them experience autonomy as something more than an ideology and a device. With total control of the learning material, autonomy becomes a source of energy and intellectual strength.

Enhancing the carnivalesque

As described by Coleman (1987: 103) with reference to Indonesia, through promotion of the 'carnivalesque' a festival mood can be achieved in the classroom, where all participants can be made equally active throughout the lesson period, classroom activities can be made interactive and fun for both pupils and teacher, and the distinction between the teacher and the learners can be minimised. According to Fiske (1989: 83),

> Carnival is concerned with bodies, not the bodies of individuals, but with the body principle, the materiality of life that underlies and precedes individuality, spirituality, ideology, and society. It is [a representation] of society at the level of materiality on which all are equal, which suspends the hierarchical rank and privilege that normally grants some classes power over others.

If textbooks and methodology are developed by incorporating this carnival principle, learners can be rescued from the malignancies of diglossia, poverty, and the lack of exposure to English which have been major constraints in Sri Lanka's efforts to teach English, because pupils tend to react to the language with pleasure and with a sense of belonging. The long-established detrimental habit of worshipping English from afar (but not making it 'one's own') will also disappear when the children learn to treat it as an object of enjoyment and pleasure.

In fact, the aim of this chapter overall is to show how learner autonomy can be established in a carnivalesque spirit by turning the learning material into a means of entertainment, and from here on emphasis will be laid on the materials, methods, techniques, and practices involved. As I shall describe below, children can embark on serious autonomous learning projects when the medium is defined as song, and autonomy is developed 'in a carnivalesque spirit'.

Redefining the classroom environment in a carnivalesque spirit

An account of practice

To give first-hand evidence of how the use of songs can work in achieving autonomy with a set of learners who are from a typical Third World resource-poor setting, I would like to describe what I have noticed for over ten years as a community worker. Since 1989, I have been using English songs with rural learners in the village of Amunudowa where my home is situated. About forty children within the age group of 8 to 13 years have been visiting my house in Amunudowa where my wife and I have conducted weekend classes in English for over four years. Each lesson is based on a song that pupils have to learn by heart through close interaction with the text. I keep records of the children's progress each year in terms of the number of songs they can recite from memory and the language functions they know in English after each lesson. I also observe what they do during the free time in my home garden when they have gathered there before and after the lessons.

We conduct the lessons in several stages intended to establish learner autonomy throughout the children's effort. The children hear a recording of the song first and get used to its melody. After three or four hearings they learn to read the song text with correct pronunciation and intonation. While learning to produce the song in their own voices they get acquainted with its meaning through extensive exposure to an oral rendition by the teachers accompanied by appropriate gestures. Here the text is treated as a narrative or drama and each sentence or idea unit is considered a language function. Overall, each lesson appears as an episodic whole introducing several language functions. I have noticed that the children improve their oral skills very well and my faith in the application of the carnivalesque has grown every time I have observed their performance.

Let us look at part of one such song-oriented lesson in more detail, based on the following:

> Young Roger came tapping at Dolly's window, thumpaty, thumpaty, thump!
> He asked for admittance, she answered him, "No," stumpaty, stumpaty, stump!
> "O Dolly, my dear, your sweet heart is here," lumpaty, lumpaty, lump!
> "No, no, Roger, no, as you came, you may go," dumpaty, dumpaty, dump!

After the children finished hearing and learning to recite the song the teachers elicited the meanings from them. Then they handled the dialogue in the song. In pairs the children practised,

> "O Dolly, my dear, your sweet heart is here."
> "No, no, Roger, no, as you came, you may go."

Here they learnt how to request and deny admittance. Then they learnt the narrative part and developed an ability to sing the whole song with action. Later they dramatised the song with actions in pairs. Here I noticed that each pair acted with great commitment, with a hidden ambition of emulating others, as every performance was acknowledged with applause from the rest of the class. Thus there were ten performances at a stretch in the mood of a competition.

Familiarised with the song from an aesthetic perspective the children could be easily drawn into the language use part of the lesson. Here they were supposed to relate the story of Roger and Dolly. In their narration some confined themselves to the phrases used in the song and some had their own wording. One such creation was as follows:

> Roger loved Dolly but Dolly did not love him. One day he was hard up for Dolly and came to see her. He was thumping on the window to ask for admittance. Then Dolly was angry and shouted at him. Roger was shy and ran home after that.

This could be achieved within the first two hours with the song. After the lesson the children dispersed with the instruction to practise the song as well as the oral presentation of the story and entertain their families with their performance. Here learner autonomy was promoted by encouraging children's responsibility to master in their own domains what they had learnt in the lesson.

When the children came back the following weekend all of them had developed an ability to sing the song and present the narrative in their own ways. This was discovered by getting them to sing, dramatise, and narrate what happened between Roger and Dolly. On this basis, the teachers could draw their attention to the following language functions in the song:

- Enquiring about a person unseen in response to a knock on one's door: "Who is it?"
- Introducing oneself to a person unseen in response to such an enquiry: "It is Nimal."
- Reqesting admittance: "May I come in please?"
- Denying admittance: "No, no. Please go away."

After focusing on these main functions in the song a dialogue depicting a vivid situation could be created on the blackboard through contributions from the group. Here too autonomous learning was encouraged as the children were motivated to contribute, conscious of their responsibility to form a meaningful dialogue. Incorporating suggestions from the group the following text could be created:

Nimal: (Knocking on the door) Tuck, tuck, tuck!
Kaanthi: Who is it?
Nimal: It is Nimal.
Kaanthi: What do you want?
Nimal: May I come in?
Kaanthi: No, no.
Nimal: Oh, please, let me come in.
Kaanthi: No, no, no, as you came, you may go.

This was real fun. Children volunteered freely to perform this dialogue and enjoyed the others' presentations as well. The carnivalesque played a large role in the whole process of involving them all in the dialogic reproduction of the lesson material. More interesting and creative dialogues were presented in this session and I just would mention that they all manifested the children's enjoyment of the lesson.

Because these children had no exposure to English in their domestic environments the input given here figured prominently in their regular pursuits. Its contribution became strong in the long run. By the third week they came prepared with tremendous intertextual skills, presenting the song in the form of a narrative, a dialogue, and an impressive dramatisation. They could even express themselves in writing.

In becoming autonomous, as the children need to extend the learning materials from the classroom to their home life or social life, songs they easily commit to their memory serve them as a steady didactic tool. Songs that they can make use of in their gatherings outside the classroom help them to extend their learning and language use beyond the classroom, which they need to do in order to 'live' the target language. Here the memory of the songs concerned gives power to the person who performs them or shares them with others. The leader of the group is decided on the basis of ability to sing from memory. The others who are less fluent in singing the songs automatically rally round the one who is better. The self-esteem the fluent learner enjoys here is also conducive to his/her further internalisation of songs and continuation with the language. Yet a healthy competition for a bigger share of power develops among the other learners, which is solely determined by the ability to sing fluently. All learners try to do better the following day and all become equally fluent at the end. As the positions in their small ritual or entertainment milieux are open for all learners, they autonomously work for them.

In response to my offer to assist in promoting English as a link language for achieving ethnic harmony in Sri Lanka, I received in March 2002 an invitation from the National Integration Project Unit under the Sri Lanka Ministry of Justice to reintroduce my ideas to teachers from all ethnic communities. They are meant to meet their learners at venues outside the classroom and sing with groups of teachers and children from various ethnic groups. Reports from the teachers who work on these English singing campaigns have also helped to establish that song is an effective medium for achieving autonomy. In the type of situation created here the only way the learners can communicate with their counterparts coming from different linguistic groups is by singing, and as they feel a concrete necessity to communicate with them they try to improve their singing abilities by themselves. Here, too, then, autonomy has been shown to emerge through song, this time through children's efforts to develop friendships with speakers of other languages.

The pivotal role of the carnivalesque in achieving autonomy was experienced throughout the effort with the learners described above.

Learner autonomy with its multiple features such as sense of responsibility, self-direction, metacognition, and motivation came into operation in a carnivalesque spirit.

Autonomy in a carnivalesque spirit

Based on the above experiences, certain general points can be made about the development of autonomy in a carnivalesque spirit. Firstly, English language learning organised within a framework of song works with these children, for the reasons explained above. Such a learning process does not alienate them from their indigenous culture, since, according to the German Buddhist monk Bhikkhu Nanamoli (Nanamoli, 1991: xxiii–l), the Buddhist intellectual traditions established in Sri Lanka have led to the development of a strong oral culture where didactic practices with regard to advances in mental solace and spirituality are emphasised in daily life. Bhikkhu Nanamoli focuses here on the religious domain. But, with oral educative practices embedded in the local culture, it is clearly feasible to draw children's attention to the necessity of self-direction in developing English oral skills by means of song. They can recall and apply the words and structures they have learnt in situations similar to those that they come across in the songs and develop their own strategies to learn even other forms of texts in this way (Fonseka, 1997: 78).

Songs can, then, have a great impact on children's internalisation of the language. Although rote learning of material is often viewed as the antithesis of learner autonomy, this does not mean that material learned by heart cannot be subject to reflection by the learner, nor contribute to other kinds of learning. For example, Donato (2000, citing Takahashi, 1998) describes how Japanese schoolchildren supported a fellow pupil in recalling vocabulary by singing a class song. In this example, the song is used as a 'mediating object' (Vygotsky, 1978), which helps learners to go beyond what they are already familiar with and to venture into their 'zone of proximal development'. Donato claims that in this way "the children are not only learning Japanese from their teacher, but also, through her dynamic assistance [...] ways of mediating their own and each other's learning" (p. 39): that is, they are moving towards interdependent learning autonomy by using memorised material.

The style of children's songs has been influenced by the performers' necessity to enact them from an oral memory (see Buchan, 1972; Zumthor, 1990). The children learn them by heart without much difficulty because the songs abound with mnemonic devices. These devices, which appear in terms of metre, rhythm, rhyme, figures and tropes, imagery, pitch, tone, timbre, gesture, movement, dress, mask and so on, enable the children to learn songs and to reproduce them orally in natural settings. Once they have grasped the meanings and retained the texts of the songs in their memory, they find great support in what they have learnt while communicating in authentic situations. My own pupils have claimed that they find the songs they have learnt ringing in their ears, and, when they are faced with the requirement of expressing something, the pattern in which they should formulate their expression flashes back to their mind as a line from a song they have learnt. Mnemonically powerful song material, once embedded in their memory, can be referred to any time it is necessary or it resonates automatically when the learner is faced with a situation similar to that in a song learnt in the past.

When songs, a rich communicative modality, become the content for the children's daily oral interactive exercises, they contribute to a large repertoire of dramatic performances, which is always alive with them as part of their childhood rituals. With their newly learnt songs and newly cultivated expertise the children gather during their English hours not for formal classroom lessons but for enjoying English through the medium of song. In the terminology of Coleman (1987: 98), this is a type of 'risking fun' because of its apparent deviation from the conventional didactic framework. Under the compulsion of having an oral memory of the complete song texts they have learnt in their previous lessons, they develop optimal remembering strategies peculiar to each one of them and, in inventing their own strategies to remember the songs, they develop their autonomy.

Moreover, autonomy becomes the governing principle in the children's individual efforts when they start taking initiatives in decision-making with regard to objectives, material, methods, time, place, evaluation, and so on, for their 'carnivalesque' learning programme. When the children jointly decide with the teacher on a song for practice, they begin to define to the teacher the nature of assistance they require from him/her, eliciting from him/her the correct pronunciation of the new lexis, getting him/her to explain the meanings of the new words, and sometimes requesting him/her to give them a model recital of a line. Then they set their own objectives for learning the song. In this case, very often, they aim at amusing themselves, their parents, their friends, or the rest of the school. After they have received the primary instructions from the teacher they operate with the determination to commit the words to their memory and use their own methods to perform the songs. With a strong sense of responsibility they go on practising the songs as long as it is required. In other words, once the surface meaning of their effort is made to appear as entertainment, they act with enhanced diligence. They depend on the teacher only for controlling and upgrading the quality of their performance.

Thus in a carnivalesque spirit the children can embark on serious autonomous learning projects when the medium is defined as song. They even tend to consider the teacher one of themselves, overcoming hierarchical barriers and letting the carnivalesque dominate the classroom atmosphere. As stated by Handleman (1982: 172), in the atmosphere engendered by this type of festival, participants who are normally separated by social rules are brought together. This type of classroom atmosphere is crucial for these children from resource-poor third-world settings because carnivalesque-inspired autonomy is a route out of their suffering. It helps learners as an ideology, a strategy, a device, a remedy, and as an element of empowerment.

English becomes the medium of the whole process of entertainment and the children get rid of their inhibitions in using it. To survive in an atmosphere where all the activities are carried out in English the children have no other support than autonomy nurtured within them in a carnivalesque spirit. Here autonomy functions as an element of empowerment. The learner's inhibitions, insecurity, hesitancy, estrangement, and practical problems of memory, pronunciation, and vocal delivery, can all vanish under the influence of autonomy. Barriers between teacher and students can disappear when schoolchildren from resource-poor Third-World backgrounds are given the opportunity to carry out their learning in a carnivalesque atmosphere. Thus strategies promulgated by means of song can help to redefine the ELT classroom environment as a place for recreation, harmonisation, and socialisation. The friendly atmosphere developed in this way helps the children break through social, cultural, economic, and psychological barriers and interact with each other and the teacher without hesitation.

Conclusion

In Sri Lanka, and, I would argue, most developing countries, autonomy can be seen as a vital rescue strategy in ELT with regard to children coming from resource-poor backgrounds. Currently, however, it is difficult for the teacher to establish autonomy in schools for the rural poor because of some fundamental problems in the system. For example, the present official classroom textbooks, which contain ambitious types of material, make acquiring English seem an elitist pursuit. The English-speaking and the non-English-speaking sectors of society have come to a consensus that English is not for those who find it difficult to master, and this has aggravated the problem of motivating the learners. The introduction of song into the curriculum can reduce the effects of the complacent and hypocritical attitude of the English-speaking elite to the efforts of the poverty-stricken learners implied in the present ELT system. By means of song the children can be harmonised to learning, and their learning efforts can be transformed into a process of pleasure. The teacher can get children to be autonomous in their learning efforts, as the song texts which they carry in their heads enable them to organise their didactic interactions without excessively depending on the teacher. With a complete grasp of a song – semantic, syntactic, grammatical, pragmatic, semiotic, narrative, musical, dramaturgical – a child acquires the competence and confidence to carry out learning tasks, and this can transfer to more 'conventional' instructional situations. A series of interactive learning sessions where the children are encouraged to act as well-equipped decision-makers boosts their ego in a positive way and strengthens their attitudes to the language. When a learning process is established in this way through regular interactive sessions, quite unawares the children become autonomous learners. By means of song, a carnivalesque atmosphere can develop between the learners and the teacher and all participants in the learning events begin to act as a single body. This is the phenomenon that autonomy in a carnivalesque spirit can lead to when song is used as the energiser of the learning process. Childhood hours spent in learning English can reverberate in the learner's memory if autonomy is inculcated in a carnivalesque spirit through song.

Reflection/discussion questions

1. What are the most valuable resources for developing learner autonomy in your teaching/learning context, and why? Think not only about physical resources, but also more intangible ones such as Fonseka's students' liking for performing with peers.
2. How do you feel about the role of the 'carnivalesque' in promoting autonomy?
3. What means might you use to establish a carnivalesque atmosphere in the pursuit of autonomy?

9

Neither Here Nor There? Learner Autonomy and Intercultural Factors in CALL Environments

Klaus Schwienhorst

Introduction

The issue of cultural factors in the development of learner autonomy has in recent years become a focal point for discussion among researchers and theorists on the concept of learner autonomy. This issue has been explored from a variety of perspectives, but not, so far, in relation to the topic of this chapter – the development of cross-cultural understanding via computer-mediated communication.

I begin by presenting a three-tiered approach to conceptualising learner autonomy which I have found useful, and then move on to provide a short overview of how learner autonomy principles can be implemented in a CALL (Computer-assisted Language Learning) context, namely, via tandem learning in synchronous text-based environments (multi-user object-oriented domains, or 'MOOs'). Tandem learning is a learning partnership between language learners with complementary L1/L2 combinations, and is based on principles of learner autonomy, reciprocity, and bilingualism. A MOO provides 'chat' functions similar to other programs (such as Internet Relay Chat or ICQ), but goes far beyond them, in that it provides learners with additional communication and collaboration tools and a whole virtual environment that learners can contribute to and participate in. Tandem learning in MOOs can provide a completely different learning environment from the classroom and this can have important repercussions for the way in which learners encounter a target language culture and how they co-create, in Kramsch's words, "a third place" (Kramsch, 1993: 233–59).

I will therefore move on finally to look more closely at cross-cultural factors in a virtual environment like the MOO. In what ways does it differ from physical classroom environments? How is it co-created by learners and teachers? What are the factors that influence this environment? What are the possibilities and pitfalls of such environments, and how can we as teachers make them more effective tools for cross-cultural learning in a pedagogical framework based on learner autonomy?

Exploring learner autonomy: a three-tiered approach

In a recent article (Schwienhorst, 2002b), I have suggested three perspectives on learner autonomy: an individual-cognitive, a social-interactive, and an experimental-participatory view. This three-tiered approach is based on Little's (1996a: 203) summary of Legenhausen and Wolff's model (in Eck, Legenhausen and Wolff, 1994), where the learner is seen at once as:

> (1) communicator – continually using and gradually developing communicative skills [my "social-interactive view"]; (2) experimenter/ researcher – gradually developing an explicit analytical knowledge of the target language system and some of the sociocultural constraints that shape its use [my "experimental-participatory view"]; and (3) intentional learner – developing an explicit awareness of both affective and metacognitive aspects of learning [my "individual-cognitive view"].

I adopt a different order in presenting these perspectives from Legenhausen and Wolff, as I consider an experimental-participatory view to be in some ways a synthesis of the other two perspectives.

Firstly, then, an individual-cognitive view of learner autonomy takes Kelly's theory of personal constructs (Kelly, 1955/1991) as its starting point. In the context of language learning, learners need to be made aware of their underlying construct systems and be confronted with their attitudes to and beliefs about language, learning, and language learning. This represents an important step towards learner autonomy, as processes of detachment and language awareness (Little, 1997b) are crucial to planning, monitoring, and evaluating language learning processes and outcomes (cf. Dam, 1995: 80). Kelly's theory of personal constructs also has strong social-interactive elements. As we anticipate other people's behaviour, we also construct other people's anticipation of our own reaction, and this process of anticipation could be continued ad infinitum.

A social-interactive view of learner autonomy – the learner as communicator – is often associated with the work of the Soviet psychologist Vygotsky and the "zone of proximal development"(Vygotsky, 1978: 86). On the one hand, this view supports in a general sense the importance of collaborative or guided activities in the process of learning.

Vygotsky's view, however, is not exclusively social-interactive:

> The mechanism of social behavior and the mechanism of conscious-
> ness are the same [...]. We are aware of ourselves, for we are aware of
> others, and in the same way as we know others; and this is as it is
> because in relation to ourselves we are in the same [position] as
> others are to us. (Vygotsky, 1979: 29–30)

In the learner autonomy literature, the social-interactive view of learning is reflected in an emphasis on using the target language as the language of communication in the classroom (see, for example, Little,
1997a, 2001a); not only should it be used for personally meaningful and
authentic interpersonal activities between learners and their peers, native
speakers, and the teacher, but it should also be used for reflective intrapersonal activities such as the learner diaries promoted by Dam (1995).

An experimental-participatory view combines both of the above
views, but also adds a number of aspects. Kelly emphasised that
favourable environments are needed to effect changes to construct systems. These include the use of fresh elements, the ability to experiment
with new ideas in a safe environment, the idea of 'trying on for size',
and the availability of validating data (Kelly, 1955/1991: 112–16;
cf. also Dam, 1995: 5–6). Conversely, unfavourable environments are
preoccupied with old material and do not offer laboratory-like environments in which new constructs can be 'tried on' (cf. Dam, 1995: 5–6).
The idea of 'trying on for size' has been discussed in detail by Papert in
relation to his concept of constructionism (see Papert, 1991: 3).
Learners should be enabled to experiment with learning artefacts that
are external or shareable, producing – in the context of language
learner autonomy – artefacts in the target language that can be shared
and edited. These constitute what Clark (1998: 178) has called "cognitive tools": "a key resource by which we effectively redescribe our own
thoughts in a format which makes them available for a variety of new
operations and manipulations". I consider the availability of validating
data a central issue: if learners are to develop language or metacognitive
awareness, they need to be provided with easily available validating
data, such as records in various media of their performance in the target language, in comparison and interaction with native speakers and
peers, records of intrapersonal dialogues about language and language
learning, for example in the form of learner diaries (see Dam, 1995),
and records of experimentation with language in a laboratory-like
environment.

Bruner (1986: 127) has also emphasised the interactional nature of discovery learning: "the importance of negotiating and sharing – in a word, of joint culture creating as an object of schooling and as an appropriate step en route to becoming a member of the adult society in which one lives out one's life". The joint creation of culture is often not perceived as a feasible option in the harsh reality of institutionalised language learning, where the restraints of the physical classroom and the language curriculum rarely allow learners to participate in joint culture creation with their peers, native speakers, and teachers. (Dam's (1995, 2000) and Thomsen's (1991, 2000) reports on their language classrooms are notable exceptions; cf. also Smith, this volume.)

These views of learner autonomy and their associated demands can, then, pose various challenges for learners and teachers. First, in a foreign language context, direct access to a target language culture and its individual speakers is often mediated or filtered by textbooks, teachers, and other elements of the institutional context. Second, a separation between learning and using a language is still a reality in many language classrooms; in many cases language classrooms are still far from being communities of practice where language learners are enabled to develop an identity in the target language culture on an ongoing basis. Third, the demands of "learning in situ" (Carr et al., 1998: 6) are difficult to realize in physical classrooms; thus, in a recent paper, I have argued for CALL alternatives based on virtual reality solutions (Schwienhorst, 2002b).

It should nevertheless be clear from the above that I share Little's (1991) view that learner autonomy cannot be equated with self-access. If learners are simply left alone with CALL software or authentic materials, they will rarely, if ever, become autonomous; indeed, learners may find it painful to confront and restructure existing learning strategies (cf. Gao, this volume). They may also find it difficult to make decisions about their learning and stand by them. The role of the teacher is therefore crucial, and teacher autonomy needs to develop side by side with learner autonomy (cf. Schwienhorst, 1999; Little, 2001c; Vieira, this volume).

In this section, I have explored the concept of learner autonomy from three different perspectives. In short, learner autonomy principles strive to work towards:

- A learner who is able to plan, monitor, and evaluate his/her learning processes and outcomes and take and assume responsibility for his/her decisions;

- A learner who tries to communicate in the target language at every opportunity, making use of records, notes, diaries, and so on to evaluate target language interaction reflectively;
- A learner who experiments with language and participates actively in the learning environment. Only if the learner can determine the learning framework (in negotiation with the teacher) can s/he assume responsibility for his/her learning.

From an individual-cognitive perspective, learners need to be supported in becoming intentional learners. This involves the ability for detachment, the ability to plan, monitor, and evaluate their learning, and the ability to achieve a degree of language and metacognitive awareness. From a social-interactive perspective, learners need to be involved in communicative activities as far as possible in the target language with peers, native speakers, and the teacher. From an experimental-participatory perspective, learners need to be encouraged to participate in the learning process and learning environment at all levels. I have also argued that language learning should strive to embed learners in an authentic sociocultural context of ongoing and direct exchange with target language speakers in a stress-reduced environment that is conducive to experimentation. Finally, I have suggested that these demands might be met by CALL alternatives to physical classrooms.

Tandem learning in synchronous and asynchronous environments

In this section, I will first describe one implementation of learner autonomy principles in CALL, namely, tandem learning. Second, I will give a short overview of tandem projects at the Centre for Language and Communication Studies (CLCS), Trinity College Dublin, and the technologies that were used. Third, I will present details of the student groups that took part in the project, and the initial pedagogical set-up.

The concept of tandem learning involves a combination of three principles: bilingualism, reciprocity, and learner autonomy (Little and Brammerts, 1996). Two language learners with complementary L1/L2 combinations are paired up by a 'dating agency' (most typically, the E-Tandem Network – see below) or language learners select a partner themselves (our procedure at the CLCS). This means that, for example, an Irish learner of German selects a German learner of English to form a tandem pair. This pair then collaborates on a number of tasks and activities, either self-selected or in collaboration with teachers and peers.

The exchange should involve the same amount of use of both languages (the principle of bilingualism); however, there is a danger that the target language of the more proficient L2 user may take over. Both partners should, then, put a similar amount of effort into the exchange and provide similar support in error correction, input and interactional modifications, and so on (the principle of reciprocity). Finally, both partners should adhere to principles of learner autonomy: they should negotiate the framework of their collaboration, and take responsibility for the success of their own (and by extension their partner's) learning (Little, 2002: 25).

While initially tandem partnerships were restricted to face-to-face collaborations, the E-Tandem Network in Bochum, Germany, has facilitated e-mail exchanges since 1994. Apart from a 'dating agency' that provides language learning partners, it has also created bilingual e-mail mailing lists for a large variety of language combinations. Initially, we used the dating agency for our first tandem project at the CLCS in 1996 (Little et al., 1999). However, it soon became clear that this scheme has a number of drawbacks for class exchanges. Students did not feel responsible for the exchange, as their partner had been chosen for them by the agency. Different mail clients caused technical problems. It proved difficult for students and teachers/researchers to monitor and to keep track of exchanges. Nevertheless, this type of exchange, where both learners alternate between the roles of native speaker expert and target language learner, was often described as highly motivating (Ushioda, 2000).

In 1997, I decided to transfer tandem learning into the context of a synchronous environment (that is, where communication takes place 'in real time'), the object-oriented multiple-user domain (MOO). Though initially text-based, the MOO has now been developed into a hypertext and multimedia environment that provides a feasible and technically reliable platform for telecommunications projects on the Internet. The screen shot in Figure 9.1 shows some of the most important elements: at the top is the menu bar that provides access to the help system, to the list of people connected, to the creation of new objects, and so on. On the left students see their own and their partner's output as well as system messages that inform them of new users connecting, of available tools, and so on. At the bottom left learners find a white box where they can input their message, and where they can also communicate with the MOO via a command line language. Learners can move swiftly between tandem pair work, learner–teacher work, and peer collaboration, using either synchronous or asynchronous communication. On the right learners can see room descriptions and their contents in

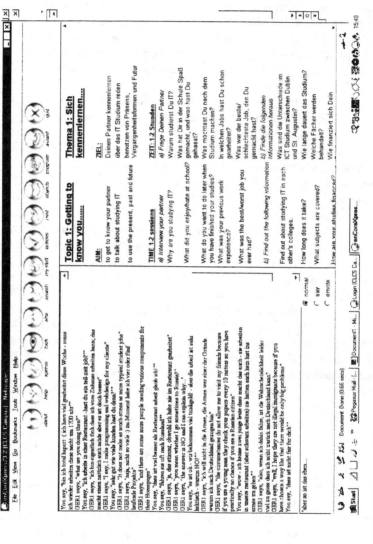

Figure 9.1 The MOO: general layout

hypertext. This right-hand panel appears the same to all participants. In Figure 9.1, the learner looks at an activity with bilingual help that includes links to other Internet resources (though these are not shown).

Primarily, then, the MOO is a tool for synchronous communication, but it goes far beyond that. It provides a virtual environment, where users or learners can assemble existing Internet learning tools and personally meaningful resources. Using the written language, they can even create tools or virtual objects that they can then use as 'cognitive tools' as defined by Clark (see above). For example, learners can author bots (programs that behave almost like real users, but which use pattern-matching and random phrases to simulate communication) and other objects on the basis of templates. With the help of bots, for example, learners can experiment with discourse structures ("What would be possible phrases that could trigger the replies 'thanks' and 'please', or 'danke' and 'bitte' in German?") by replacing existing trigger words and patterns in the template with new words and phrases. At this stage, the re-programming of bots is quite cumbersome; nevertheless, several learners in my tandem projects have experimented with these and other objects (Schwienhorst, 2000: 300–2), including their own virtual representation (which is customisable). In this sense, the MOO offers real participation at all levels in the design of the learning environment.

The MOO system itself provides a highly modular and flexible framework of programming. All the code can be made visible to users and the system can distinguish between all forms of input, which means that external Internet resources can be combined with MOO programming tools to support learning processes. One example may suffice to demonstrate this capability. The Bilingual Tandem Analyser is a tool that analyses learners' output and keeps statistics on levels of bilingualism. This tool, similar to the tools on the Electronic Tandem Resources web site developed by Christine Appel (cf. Appel and Mullen, 2000), can support balanced bilingual use by displaying statistics on the two languages used. Many more tools could be developed along the same lines, which can give learners support not only after the actual communication, but also during their communication with the partner. I have already implemented a mechanism that records every individual user's session and sends it automatically to their e-mail account for further analysis. This can present a valuable resource for off-line work, as learners can search for new vocabulary in context, analyse instances of miscommunication, and so on.

The MOO projects at CLCS have so far been conducted with Information and Communications Technology (ICT) students at Trinity

College Dublin who are studying either French or German for the first two years as part of a four-year degree course. They select partners from introductory e-mails distributed in class. Students taking French are paired up with Belgian Arts students from the University of Louvain, while students taking German collaborate with German ICT students at the Fachhochschule Rhein-Sieg near Bonn. Students meet for one hour a week over the course of 8–10 weeks (October–December). They can select between various activities that are listed in the MOO, from general activities involving getting to know one another (cf. Figure 9.1) to specialised tasks on computer science subjects. They can connect from home or computer labs on campus. They discover and share new resources, such as dictionaries; they discuss new web sites while looking at them with their partners; they discuss 'live' events, such as the first snow fall in Germany during one session, which triggered off a whole discussion on what snow means for Irish and German people, and how it relates to Christmas, sports, and so on. Half the session should be spent communicating in each language. At the end of each session, learners are reminded to enter into an online notebook what they have done, what went well or not so well, and how they want to proceed in the next session. Learners also need to complete offline tasks for the activities they choose, such as writing a CV based on their partner's information, a summary of a discussion, and so on. Teachers very rarely, if ever, interfere with tandem work during the MOO sessions. Learners ask their peers for help and are completely absorbed in their work.

In this section, I have described one implementation of learner autonomy principles, tandem learning, both in face-to-face and computer-mediated contexts. I have also described how tandem learning was integrated into language courses at CLCS, and how I created special software tools and pedagogical frameworks to make it a more successful learning experience, in particular by using a primarily synchronous environment, the MOO.

Virtual text-based environments and cross-cultural learning

From the above it should be clear that tandem learning provides a very different language-learning environment to the traditional language classroom. In this section, I will focus on how this affects cross-cultural learning. First, I will summarise some aspects that I consider unique to the pedagogical framework of tandem learning and the virtual environment of the MOO, and examine what kind of culture is being created via this combination; second, I will relate these features to theories of cross-cultural communication in the context of language learning; and third, I will look at the opportunities, and also pitfalls, that lie within such virtual environments for language learning.

There are several aspects of our MOO projects at CLCS that support learner autonomy: the complementary nature of tandem partnerships, the learner-centred nature of the environment, the use of the written medium for both communication and object creation, the relatively neutral position of the MOO between native and target culture, and the role of the teacher in MOO tandem projects. Tandem partners share the same goal, namely to improve their language skills in each other's L2. The complementary combination of their languages makes it easy for them to switch languages, and the alternation in roles between native speaker expert and target language learner is perceived as motivating and confidence-raising.

The environment and pedagogical framework are essentially learner-centred. Learners can modify almost all facets of the online environment and customise their online character. While initial tasks or activities are loosely framed by the teachers, learners soon branch off in their conversation to very current or even 'live' events in real life which no doubt enhance the experience of an immediate link to a target language culture. Both real and virtual environment determine their tandem work.

All communication and the primary representation of the environment are in text, in writing. Writing plays a major role in the development of language awareness, which is in turn one of the central issues in learner autonomy (cf. Little, 1997c, 1999b; Aase et al., 2000; Little, 2001b). Learners are enabled and even compelled (O'Rourke and Schwienhorst, 2003) to re-read their own and their partner's messages as they scroll up the screen. In principle, this should support processes of 'noticing' (cf. Schmidt, 1990; Ridley, 1997). As all transcripts are automatically recorded and sent to each participant, live communication becomes a valuable resource for future awareness-raising activities.

The MOO itself is for many learners, even ICT students, a new and unknown tool/environment. It does not have the same connotations as public chat programs (anonymity, obscene language, transience, non-committal nature of participation) nor does it share many similarities with text-messages or e-mails. As a new, unfamiliar, yet non-threatening environment it provides an ideal laboratory where learners are encouraged to experiment with language without being monitored and evaluated by the teacher. Many learners are also unfamiliar with being represented by a virtual character. While many have emphasised that they have tried to and feel able to describe their true personality, many learners have also reported that their online character is much more confident in using the target language, and much less threatened by signs of rejection from their partner (Schwienhorst, 2000: 313).

The teacher's role during the MOO exchanges is radically different from that in physical classroom sessions. Rarely, if ever, do learners ask the teacher for advice, although sometimes technical assistance may be needed. The main role of the teacher probably consists of bringing opportunities that are offered by the tandem set-up and/or the MOO environment into the view of the learner (see O'Rourke and Schwienhorst, 2003). Learners, for example, will not tend to exploit their own MOO transcripts without explicit tasks set by a teacher. I suspect that a tool that records one's own conversations in writing is simply too far removed from the learning (and life) experience of most learners to be considered a valuable learning resource without such intervention by the teacher.

How do these technological and pedagogical features relate to cross-cultural communication in language learning? In a previous paper (Schwienhorst, 1998) I argued that the MOO provides an ideal 'third place' for language learners, where they can experiment with language while communicating with native speakers. The same phrase has been used by Kramsch in the context of cross-cultural learning to describe the sociocultural aim of language study:

> [W]hat is at stake is the creation, in and through the classroom, of a social, linguistic reality that is born from the L1 speech environment of the learners and the social environment of the L2 native speakers, but is a third culture in its own right. (Kramsch, 1993: 9)

The culture created on the MOO, in these respects, is certainly born from both L1 speech environments of the tandem learners and thus contains elements of the social environment of both L2 cultures. In addition, elements of the tandem set-up itself – features of synchronous written discourse and computer-mediated communication in general – certainly contribute to the sociocultural context. Nevertheless, because culture is primarily created by learners, through the medium of writing, the 'white canvas' is only filled when learners communicate with each other or create new objects.

It is useful here to refer to Kramsch's first three principles for achieving the goal of cross-cultural awareness through language teaching:

1. "Establishing a 'sphere of interculturality' " (Kramsch, 1998: 205). The tandem partnership emphasises the use of both L1 and L2. Learners are always aware that their own L1 is their partner's L2 and vice versa. Even learners who conducted a large percentage of their exchange in the L1, for example English, reported that they had gained insights about the L2 (e.g. German) from their partner's use of English. In this respect, tandem learning supports reflection on both the target and the native language. This translates into the topics of discussion. Tandem partners discuss similar situations, events, traditions, and so on, from their own individual experience. Without the support of other members of their cultural group, it could be argued that they are much less likely to reproduce stereotypes and mainstream opinions and, rather, present a very personal view of their own culture in relation to their target culture. Thus, tandem learning supports reflection on the target and the native culture.

2. "Teaching culture as an interpersonal process" (Kramsch, 1998: 206). Kramsch argues against "the presentation/prescription of cultural facts and behaviors" and seeks to replace it with an emphasis on 'foreignness' and 'otherness'. In direct communication with their partners, tandem learners discuss cultural factors in context rather than merely presenting them as national traits. As individuals, tandem learners may feel less compelled to define themselves as 'insiders' against 'outsiders' (cf. Kramsch, 1998: 8). In the following example, we can see a typical exchange dealing with personal interests in music, linked to very personal experiences (IRL stands for the Irish, GER for the German student; spelling and punctuation are as in the original):

IRL28, "Do you know Fatboy Slim and Basement Jaxx"
GER21 says, "Not really. I heard the name Fatboy Slim but I can not imagine who it is."
IRL28, "He is an English DJ and he is playing at a party for the MTV awards tonight in Dublin and I am going"
GER21 says, "Well, that sounds interesting. Is he a famous DJ?"
IRL28, "Yes he is very famous at the moment have you not heard the songs 'Praise you' or 'Funksoul Brother' "
GER21 says, "What kind of music is it?"
IRL28, "Big Beat its called, its probably house music like the chemical brothers and i am going to get very drunk tonight"

GER21 says, "I do not know these songs. Perhaps because that is not the kind of music I am going for."
IRL28, "What do you liker"
GER21 says, "Well just as I already said. I like music from REM, Jamiroquai, Shania Twain, Alanis Morisette, and also rap-music, especially german rap like 'Die fantastischen Vier' oder 'Thomas D'."
GER21 says, "Ever heard of 'Die fantastischen Vier'?"
IRL28, "I heard 'Die fantastischen Vier' when I was in Germany in the Summer"

3. "Teaching culture as difference" (Kramsch, 1998: 206). Kramsch emphasises that "National traits are but one of the many aspects of a person's 'culture'" (ibid.). The fact that most tandem work is conducted in pairs emphasises the reality that learners are individuals who represent a specific cultural context, rather than a group with homogeneous attributes (the "one language, one culture" belief; see Kramsch, 1998: 67). In discussions with peers, students often report on their partner's individual traits rather than stereotypical clichés, leading to a much more individualised, differentiated perception of a target language culture (this can also be seen in the example above).

When Kramsch speculates on what the third place would be like, she mentions as one possibility the fostering, within a framework of critical language pedagogy, of "pedagogical exchanges of teachers and students across national boundaries" (Kramsch, 1993: 235), and this clearly applies to tandem learning. Additionally, several aspects of the critical view of culture she proposes (Kramsch, 1993: 244) seem close to learner autonomy principles, including the following: "awareness of global context", "awareness of local knowledge", knowing "why [learners from other cultures] talk the way they do, and why they remain silent", the "ability to listen [to] students' implicit assumptions and beliefs", the use of metatalk, an emphasis on "making do with words", on "resourcefulness", "imagination", and on "effective poaching", for example in the form of effective re-use of output (the notions of "making do" and poaching have often been reported by learners in MOO tandem projects), the dual concept of learners taking decisions and assuming responsibility for them, and finally an emphasis on lifelong learning, pointing to the fact that cross-cultural learning is a long and continual process of creating a new or 'third' place for oneself as a language learner between the L1 and the L2. This process requires personal engagement and flexibility to adapt to new situations of language use (cf. Aase et al.,

2000: 47), a position reflected in Pennycook's (1997: 48–9) argument that "to use language is not so much a question of mastering a system as it is a question of struggling to find means of articulation amid the cultures, discourses and ideologies within which we live our lives".

Nevertheless, in a recent article, Kramsch and Thorne (2002) have criticised the use of Internet communication media such as e-mail and the MOO for the development of cross-cultural communication: "Neither the French nor the American students [in their study] were aware that the global medium only exacerbated the discrepancies in social and cultural genres of communication" (p. 100). However, some of their conclusions/generalisations seem questionable. From my description of tandem learning above it should be clear that the organisational and pedagogical framework is as important as the communication medium that is used. Unfortunately, Kramsch and Thorne say very little about this. They state: "The course instructor has provided a brief description of the Ivry students as primarily of North African descent or recently immigrated to France. The American students have also been told that a number of the Ivry students live in HLM, or subsidized public housing" (p. 87). Thus, it appears that the (initial?) information that the American students received centred on group-based rather than individual cultural factors, and this approach seems to contradict Kramsch's (1998: 206) own three principles as summarised above. This can be contrasted with our own tandem projects, where students select their partner from individual introductory e-mails distributed by the teacher in class. The "blurring of institutional and personal domains" (p. 88) noted in MOO exchanges among the American students prior to engagement in the project does not seem unusual for any student–student interaction that happens "outside of class, and without the instructor as an intermediary" (p. 88). This effect has nothing to do with the medium of the MOO (and Kramsch and Thorne do not provide any data, for example, from a control group discussing the issues face-to-face), but rather indicates the lack of a clear pedagogical framework.

The framework behind the subsequent e-mail project they describe is equally unclear. Both French and American student groups had watched a French movie, *La Haine*, dealing with "racism, violence, gang culture, and the influence of American culture" (p. 91). Had the teachers chosen this film, or was it chosen by the learners themselves? Why was only a French movie chosen? In tandem projects, learners choose their own activities and materials, and both L1 and L2 artefacts are used as sources for activities. The paper does not make clear whether the e-mails were posted by individuals to individual e-mail accounts or whether a mailing list was used (it mentions that the French e-mails were sent through the teacher's account, but fails to consider this as a possible factor in explaining the different "genres" used by American and French students).

Kramsch and Thorne's emphasis on the way genre can be a "major source of misunderstanding in global communicative practice" (p. 99) is certainly a valuable contribution to computer-mediated communication (CMC) research, but in my view only for a limited context. They transfer the results from their asynchronous (e-mail) project to all Internet communication media. However, only the e-mail project showed the importance of genre as "the concrete repository of [a community's] common history, of the way it conceives of language, communication and interpersonal relations, and of the way it envisages its future" (ibid.). It appears that rather than individual exchanges, there were groups exchanging e-mails; is it then surprising that they resorted to genres rather than style (that is, "individual choice in discourse" (ibid.))? In my view, it is difficult to argue that Internet communication tools alone are responsible for an exacerbation of "discrepancies in social and cultural genres of communication" (p. 100). Instead, I would argue that any communication mode, whether Internet-based, phone-based, face-to-face, or otherwise, certainly has built-in features that make it more or less valuable for certain areas of language learning. For instance, text-based modes can do very little to improve pronunciation, while audio- and video-based communication lacks the reflective potential that written language can provide. However, and most importantly, the use of a communication mode always needs to go hand in hand with a pedagogical framework based on learner autonomy.

What, then, are the opportunities and pitfalls of the MOO as a technology and tandem learning as a pedagogical framework? Kramsch (1998: 10) defines culture as

> membership in a discourse community that shares a common social space and history, and common imaginings. Even when they have left that community, its members may retain, wherever they are, a common system of standards for perceiving, believing, evaluating, and acting.

This certainly holds true for the MOO tandem learning partnerships, but there are vital differences between classroom settings and native/non-native speaker encounters. The MOO provides a space in which language learners collaborate individually with other language learners. In our experience, this means that learners are likely to bring their own individual cultural background to bear on the exchange to a much greater extent than socially determined aspects of their culture. Finally, the MOO itself is not culture-free, but does not, in principle, represent a clear native or target language culture. (It remains to be seen whether text-based environments should be monolingual, bilingual, or multilingual, and what the impact of new 3D environments will be on tandem partnerships (see Schwienhorst, 2002a).)

MOO tandem partnerships are not without pitfalls. Organising synchronous communication sessions demands close co-operation between institutions. Finding tandem partners with similar proficiency levels is a problem, as the bilingual balance of the exchange may suffer otherwise. Teachers need to make sure that learners exploit the vast potential of learner transcripts for offline work. Designers are only just starting to incorporate new features such as shared whiteboard tools that enable collaborative writing and editing, analysis tools that detect misspellings and make suggestions, easily available online dictionaries with sample sentences of various contexts of use, and so on. Nevertheless, I consider that the combination of the MOO environment and tandem learning already constitutes an excellent laboratory for the language learner to experiment with language and culture.

Conclusion

In this chapter, I have first explored the concept of learner autonomy from three different perspectives: an individual-cognitive, a social-interactive, and an experimental-participatory view. Secondly, I have outlined one possible implementation of learner autonomy in telecommunications, tandem learning, especially in the context of the synchronous MOO environment. Finally, I have related the combination of tandem learning and MOO environments to cross-cultural issues. In terms of culture, the MOO is neither 'here' (a native culture) nor 'there' (a target culture), but drops learners into an unfamiliar, challenging, yet highly motivating environment that is largely created by the learners themselves as they communicate and participate. In this sense, it becomes a linguistic and cultural space where a 'third place' – the learner's position between the native language culture and the target language culture – can be created.

Reflection/discussion questions

1. Can technologies by themselves produce autonomous learners? If not, what else is needed?
2. The MOO has been categorised as a form of 'virtual reality'. Which MOO aspects are virtual, and which are real, and how can they contribute to learner autonomy?
3. What would you expect to be the major advantages and pitfalls of tandem projects conducted via MOOs, via audio conferencing, via video conferencing and via non-synchronous media such as traditional 'snail mail'?

Part IV
Institutions and Teachers

10
The Representation of Learner Autonomy and Learner Independence in Organizational Culture

David Palfreyman

Introduction

My focus in this chapter is on how learner autonomy is *interpreted* by people involved in language education; and in particular how it is *represented* within the culture of a particular ELT organization which has made a concerted attempt to promote learner autonomy through its curriculum. Wright (1994) notes that the concept of culture has been used in the field of organizational studies to analyse not only ethnic differences within an organization (for example by Hofstede, 1990), but also *organizational* cultures, including "informal concepts, attitudes and values" (p. 2; cf. Morgan, 1986) and "formal organizational values and practices imposed by management" (ibid.; cf. Peters and Waterman, 1986). These interpretations of culture share the characteristics established in the introduction to this volume (*systems of meaning* which are *communal* to some extent); but they also share a concern with *managing* these meanings in some way.

In this chapter I will analyse the ways in which autonomy is interpreted in managing the curriculum of an organization which I will call the University School of English (USE): a large section of a private, English-medium university in Turkey. After introducing some concepts relating to organizational culture, I will analyse the informal interpretations of learner autonomy and independence expressed in interviews with key figures in USE. I will then relate these to the ways these concepts are represented in official USE documents such as the syllabus and the Student Handbook, and consider how these concepts came to play a part in the organization's curriculum. I will argue that organizational factors have been predominant in shaping the curriculum according to a 'training' model of autonomy, and I will conclude with some comments about how organizational culture relates to the wider cultural picture.

Discourses, cultures and representations

Learner autonomy is of course not simply (nor perhaps even primarily) something which *learners* do; it is also a reference point and subject of debate for language education professionals (as in this volume). Attempts to define learner autonomy in a more or less objective way – to say what it is, what it is not, and what it can encompass – include those reviewed by Oxford (this volume), as well as Littlewood's (1996a) distinction between 'proactive' and 'reactive' autonomy, which relates autonomy more directly to an organizational setting: the former term refers to full individual autonomy, and the latter to an ability to fulfil the responsibilities put on one by an organization (either directly or through the teacher). These different interpretations of autonomy do not simply represent academic positions. They also have practical implications, and are of some importance to teachers and policy-makers who wish to have a sound base for practical decisions. However, putting them into practice can be problematic: Benson (2001) notes that a concern for conceptual clarity should be balanced with the need to recognize that autonomy may be realized in different ways in different settings; while Benson and Voller (1997b: 2) point out that

> whenever autonomy and independence figure in concrete language education projects, there is always a risk that underlying conceptual differences will emerge in the form of conflicts over the practical steps to be taken.

It is important to note that all the parties involved in such a language education project may agree that 'learner autonomy' (or 'learner independence') is a 'good thing'. However, this apparent consensus may make it difficult to resolve disagreement in practice. There is an old story about a number of blind people who encountered an elephant for the first time. One person felt the elephant's trunk, and said that an elephant seemed to resemble a snake; another felt its tail and declared that an elephant was like a piece of rope; another felt its ear and maintained that an elephant resembled a large leaf; and so on. This group of people had all experienced touching an elephant; but if, without further clarifying their perceptions, they had set about a practical task such as making a house for an elephant, they would probably not have been impressed by each others' efforts! Similarly, an educational organization which attempts to promote learner autonomy without facilitating discussion about what this means to different participants may well run into practical difficulties, which are all the more baffling if those concerned appear to share a common goal.

Differences in interpretations do not exist only between individuals or between groups: interpretations may also vary according to the context. Ribbins et al. (1988), for example, note how teachers and headteachers tended to describe their goals and methods in terms of *pupil-centredness* when they were speaking in an 'educationist' context (such as in a public meeting); but more in terms of *discipline* when in a 'teacher' context (e.g. in a chat in the staffroom). These different ways of talking and thinking about students and teaching constitute different 'discourses' (Foucault, 1977; Fairclough, 1992). A discourse about learning or teaching is a way of interpreting and describing learning or teaching which has some consistency across contexts (Salaman, 1997): the discourse of pupil-centredness, for example, may be observed in various meetings or school documents; and the discourse of discipline may occur in different staffroom conversations and other settings.

The discourses referred to by Ribbins et al. were perceptible, then, in the way school staff talked and wrote about their work: they *represented* education in particular ways. A discourse represents the world in two senses: it

> claims both to grasp the nature of [reality], and literally to 're-present' it in a form amenable to [...] deliberation, argument and scheming. (Miller and Rose, 1990: 6)

More specifically, a discourse about 'learner autonomy' aims both to describe learning, and to render it at least potentially *manageable*: we talk about 'learner autonomy' in the hope that it will guide us in dealing with learners so as to reach certain goals – hence the practical implications referred to earlier (for one discussion of the implications of representation in EFL and ESL settings, see Harklau, 2000).

Legitimacy is another key concept in the interplay of discourses. Although there are likely to be competing discourses about education in a given setting (as in Ribbins et al., cited above), each discourse will tend to represent itself as the 'obvious' or 'natural' way of looking at things (Fairclough, 1992; Holliday, this volume), thus giving itself legitimacy at the expense of other possible discourses. Another possible source of legitimacy is the authority of the person using the discourse (Bourdieu, 1982), such as a headteacher or an influential author. A further source of legitimacy is association or alignment with another commonly accepted discourse, such as that of 'technology' or 'development' (Pennycook, 1994; Crewe and Harrison, 1998): if 'learner autonomy' is represented as a more 'developed' state, or if it is associated with technology (Benson, 1997, 2001), this will be a point in its favour for many people. Efforts to (re)construct indigenous antecedents for learner autonomy (e.g. Kirtikara, 1996; Pierson, 1996) are equally examples of claims to legitimacy.

Drawing together the points made above, we can say that any given discourse will involve the following related elements (adapted from Rose (1996) and Hall (1997)). All of these elements are largely constructed through language (Pennycook, 1994; Riley, this volume), often bringing with them a specific terminology associated with the discourse in question:

(a) underlying *assumptions* which either condone or problematize certain ways of thinking or talking about learning. For example, discourses of autonomy in language education may assume that self-determination is an important part of learning; or may problematize 'teacher-dependence'.

(b) *roles, identities* or *'subject positions'* for learners and teachers, which are constructed by these assumptions. Again, these roles may be positively or negatively viewed. Riley (1999) and Ellis (2001) analyse metaphors for the learner (e.g. 'flowering plant', 'negotiator') used within different discourses about learning; while Voller (1997), Riley (1997) and Oxford (2001) discuss some identities (e.g. 'facilitator', 'guru' and 'catalyst') which are constructed for and by teachers.

(c) *practices* or *'technologies'* of learning and teaching. In the case of learner autonomy, these include learning strategy training, peer evaluation, self-access materials and self-evaluation activities (Palfreyman, 1999).

(d) *authorities* and *other discourses* (e.g. applied linguistics; 'development') which legitimate the discourse.

The legitimacy of promoting learner autonomy is sometimes seen as compromised by the need for order and structure inherent in organizations. Wenden (2002: 39), for example, describes self-direction as "in potential opposition to the culture of the classroom", and notes that "in a school setting, very often even the teacher cannot autonomously decide what is to be learned, as language syllabi may be pre-set". In response to this apparent contradiction Wenden cites the examples of Huttunen (1988) and Dam (1995) to show that learner autonomy is *possible* within organizations (cf. Vieira, this volume). In contrast, I will argue that certain interpretations of autonomy can in fact *serve* established organizational discourses of structure and control.

An organizational or professional *culture* is a broader concept than a discourse; but discourses are associated in different ways with these cultures (Holliday, 1994, 1996b; Wright, 1994; Milton, 1996). A headteacher and teachers in the same school may draw on similar discourses, constructing a common organizational culture of 'quality assurance', for example; the teachers may also share a common discourse with teachers in other schools, orienting to a shared professional culture. However, different groups of teachers may also form subcultures, taking relatively 'pupil-centred' or 'disciplinary' approaches; and of course the same teacher may draw more on one discourse in one situation and more on a different discourse in another.

In studying how learner autonomy is interpreted in an actual "concrete language education project" (Benson and Voller, 1997b: 2) we must be aware of the variety (or otherwise) of interpretations circulating in the organization; of the relations between these interpretations in the particular setting; and of the connections between different aspects of the project (assumptions, roles and practices). In this chapter I will focus primarily on the representation of learner autonomy and learner independence by 'organizational' sources (curriculum developers and managers).

USE, the context for this research, is responsible for providing English language preparation for students before they enter their University departments; but it has also taken on responsibility for promoting learner autonomy. One of the aims stated in USE's mission statement is to "develop [students'] potential as independent 'autonomous' learners". There is some equivocation here between the terms 'independent' and (in scare quotes) " 'autonomous' " – and between 'student' and 'learner' – and it is the tensions in organizational culture underlying the differential use of these terms which I shall explore in this chapter.

I shall now provide more details of the research context, and how I went about studying the interpretations of learner autonomy and independence there; then I shall present an analysis of the different discourses and cultures which appear to be influential in this setting.

The organizational context and the research methodology

USE forms part of a private university, one of the first to be established in Turkey. While several Turkish universities had, at least until the 1980s, a reputation for student unrest and political violence, the university in question is a product of the 'bourgeois revolution' following the 1980 coup, and the university and its students tend to be commercially rather than politically oriented. However, USE is influenced by a widespread discourse in Turkish middle-class society that social order is fragile, and that one must be on guard against the forces of disorder (Stokes, 1994). USE also has a certain concern with consumer satisfaction: as one manager put it in an interview, the University authorities "don't want problems, they don't want lots of parents [...] or students going to them complaining about things. [...] They want to feel that things are running smoothly in the school."

A few years prior to the time of the research reported here (just before my own arrival in USE), some significant changes had occurred in USE. The university had taken on an expatriate (mainly British) management team, which had instituted a student needs analysis and replaced the fairly traditional grammar-based curriculum with a new curriculum aiming to develop language skills and learner independence. The new management team also encouraged an ethos of accountability and a 'role culture' (Handy, 1993), developing a formal organizational structure within which individuals occupy predefined positions such as 'Curriculum Level Co-ordinator' or 'Head of Teaching'.

Various elements of the new curriculum seem to form what Cotterall (1995) calls a "course strategy for learner autonomy". These include:

- a skills-based syllabus including learning and study skills;
- "Independent Study Assignments", including library research projects;
- self-access provision, including a language lab and CALL lab;
- encouragement of a learner-centred teaching methodology, including a process writing approach and groupwork;
- dissemination of curriculum information to students, e.g. student course outlines – week-by-week summaries of course content posted on classroom walls for students' attention;
- student evaluation of learning and teaching;
- student representation in certain meetings with curriculum developers, middle managers and and others.

In terms of the official culture of the organization, this suggests an influential discourse of learner autonomy (the term more widely used in

USE was 'learner independence'). I will discuss below the ways in which this was confirmed by a closer examination of the organization.

My own role in USE was that of Teacher Trainer; this position offered me insights into the culture of the organization at a management level, while allowing me some critical distance from this culture. The data drawn on here was collected in 1996–9 as part of a study of teacher, student and manager perceptions (Palfreyman, 2001), but for the purposes of this chapter I will restrict my discussion to views expressed by managers and curriculum developers in the school, since these clearly shape the 'official' culture of the organization. I will discuss two kinds of data. The first derives from a series of semi-structured interviews in which I explicitly asked certain key informants to talk about their interpretations of learner autonomy/independence and its place in the curriculum. All the interviewees except Curriculum Head E2 (the expatriate Head of Curriculum) had been involved in developing the new curriculum since its inception. The second kind of data which I will use here is organizational texts, which embody more implicit representations of autonomy: USE syllabus documents, the USE Student Handbook, and materials for the USE Student Orientation Programme. For the purposes of this chapter I will focus on representative examples from both these data types which illustrate key themes in the official culture of the school.

Learner autonomy and independence are represented in a variety of ways in this data, but overall a distinction emerges between two discourses which potentially conflict in their assumptions and in their implications for practice. One I will call an 'educationist discourse', oriented to broad educational goals, freedom and the realization of individual potential; the other is a 'training discourse', oriented to organizational considerations: the curriculum, order, and developing skills for a tightly defined study context. This distinction resembles Littlewood's (1996a) distinction between proactive and reactive autonomy; and some of the informants identified it as a distinction between 'autonomy' and 'independence', although the interview questions were not phrased in these terms. However, I want to emphasize that I am not referring to objectively identifiable kinds of autonomy, but to discourses *about* autonomy which are grounded in the social setting of USE, and which indirectly shape perceptions, policies and documents.

Representations of autonomy in the interviews

I shall now discuss the representations of learner autonomy and independence in the interviews with key informants. In quoting from specific interviews I shall refer to the informants using pseudonyms such as 'Director E1' to refer to the expatriate Director, and 'Head of Teaching T1' to refer to the Turkish Head of Teaching, thus indicating the key variables of ethnicity and organizational role; the (arbitrarily assigned) number simply distinguishes different members of each group.

Assumptions about autonomy/independence

In the educationist discourse, autonomy is seen as relating to attitudes and capacities in learners, for example:

> having the ability to choose, and then making that choice and know-ing that choice is the most effective one. (Director E1)

This corresponds more or less to Benson's (1997) 'psychological' inter-pretation of autonomy, or Wenden's (2002) 'self-direction'. Curriculum Head E2, on the other hand, emphasizes a 'training' ('technical') inter-pretation, focusing on what learners should be able to *do*:

> It comes down to the basics of [...] doing homework, and seeing the value of it, and being able to check their own work; [...] and good habits like [...] keeping records of your work, organizing your work, that sort of thing.

Some of the interviewees made an explicit distinction between 'autonomy' (the more psychological interpretation) and 'independence' (the more technical one). In these cases, they consistently evaluated the former more highly than the latter, for example:

> I think learner autonomy involves many more things than indepen-dence does. I think we're aiming for independence rather than auton-omy. It's sort of down a peg from autonomy. (Materials Developer E3)

Similarly, Director E1 portrays the 'independent' learner as less 'competent':

> You would have to refer to other people to help you make choices, because you really wouldn't be a competent person in terms of know-ing what those best choices were. (Director E1)

These informants also tended to represent 'autonomy' as an ideal, and 'independence' as a more realistic compromise (as in Materials

Developer E3's remark above). That is, they tended to see the education-ist discourse as more desirable but less practical.

Positioning of students

A distinction emerged in the interviews between different views of the students and their role. Again with reference to the terms 'autonomy' and 'independence', Curriculum Developer E4 distinguished their roles as follows:

> An *autonomous* learner monitors his learning, identifies problems, goes to get help and so on. [...] An *independent* learner can fill in the timetable himself, choose elective courses, decide when to take an exam, manage his time on a daily or weekly basis.

Again, this recalls Littlewood's (1996a) proactive/reactive distinction: the former represents the students as 'learners': independent agents who pursue their own agenda; the latter represents them as members of an organization, who function in interaction with organizational frame-works.

Qualities to be developed in students similarly differ. In the educa-tionist discourse, the students are expected to develop initiative and creativity, to

> develop an internal sense of independence; so becoming an original thinker, becoming an independent person. (Materials Developer E3)

In other cases, however, students are seen as being trained to fit into an organization. Director E1 gave the example of teaching students about time management, to prepare them for their future working life.

Conversely, other qualities of students were cited as problematic for autonomy or independence. Materials Developer E3 draws on the educationist discourse, criticizing students' inarticulacy and lack of creativity:

> They can't discuss things, they can't generate ideas in an interest-ing way.

The training discourse, on the other hand, problematizes students' 'dependence' on teacher instructions and other input, and the inability to "operate on your own" (Director E1).

Pedagogy for autonomy

The contrast between the different discourses about autonomy is particularly apparent in relation to pedagogy. The educationist discourse often
represents autonomy as ultimately outside the domain of teachability:
Director E1 describes autonomous students as 'bright' and 'gifted',
suggesting that autonomy is a personal characteristic rather than something to be taught; while Materials Developer E3 similarly refers to
autonomy as

> an internal development, rather than something that can be imposed
> from the outside, or encouraged from the outside.

In so far as pedagogy is seen as effective in the educationist view, however, it is seen as *allowing* the learner to express autonomy through
choice, for example:

> [students] doing extensive reading in the class, for example. [...] they
> choose their own thing. Or even pairwork, speaking activities in
> groups, [...] if they're doing different group activities, whatever.
> (Curriculum Head E2)

> [teachers] letting go and being facilitative rather than upfront and
> directing. (Materials Developer E3)

The training discourse, on the other hand, takes a more instrumental
orientation, representing pedagogy for autonomy as instilling appropriate skills through practice, notably in the Independent Study
Assignments:

> we give them a task which has definite stages, and you ask them to go
> out and follow these stages in the hope that going through these
> stages they will be able to reproduce these stages in similar tasks in
> future contexts that they may find themselves in the faculties.
> (Director E1)

This contrast between approaches to developing autonomy, and the
greater ease with which the training discourse deals with the issue of
pedagogy, will become even more apparent in the discussion of official
documents below.

Alignment with wider discourses

Representations of autonomy tend to be linked by the interviewees
to other discourses. The educationist conception of autonomy is linked

to humanistic discourses of self-fulfilment (letting students develop their potential); and also to entrepreneurial economic discourses:

> [The Head of the University] wants creativity; he wants people who are self-starters, who can set things up, who can help develop the economy, from a liberal perspective. (Director E1)

Notice how this positions the individual 'self-starting' learner as 'human capital' for the nation, in the interest of economic development.

The more locally focused training discourse, however, links independence with concerns of social order in USE, related by Teaching Head T1 to maturity and the transition from high school to university:

> They were really rule-bound in high school, and when they come to university they think they can do anything they want. So we have to help them again in that aspect of the transition: i.e. [show them that] being able to do anything you want is not being disruptive, but making your own decisions, being more mature.

A 'crack' in the system?

Running through the interview extracts above is a tension between educationist and training discourses of autonomy: learner autonomy is associated both with a liberating individual capacity, and with responsible compliance with organizational requirements; freedom is represented both as key to autonomy, and as an impractical luxury in the USE context. Berg and Östergren (1979) refer to this type of discordance as a 'crack' in the organizational system, which holds the potential for change of some kind. We will see in discussing official USE documents below that this tension is being resolved in the direction of a particular version of autonomy, based on the training discourse.

Representations of autonomy in organizational documents

The tension referred to above is visible also in the discourse of organizational documents. Fairclough (1992: 219) notes that "the potential student who is constructed as a consumer [by a university prospectus] may find herself constructed on arrival [at university] as an 'autonomous learner' ". In this section I will examine this latter process, by analysing representations of learner autonomy and assumptions about students in successive versions of the USE syllabus documents, the Student Handbook, and the Student Orientation Programme.

Comparing the introductions to the USE syllabus documents for 1994–5 and 1998–2000, we find that the importance of independent learning is mentioned explicitly in both. However, as I will explain, learner independence is represented somewhat differently in the two documents. Two key concepts in these documents are 'needs' and 'skills'. These terms became much more widely used in USE as part of the changes in the curriculum; and are closely linked to the representation of learner autonomy in the organizational culture. Although the terms 'needs' and 'skills' are part and parcel of the ELT professional culture, Edwards (1991) reminds us that they are in fact discursive constructions. Needs and skills are not givens, but are determined by those reflecting on a learner's situation; and different people may well see different needs and skills, according to how they approach the situation. Indeed, choosing to use the discourse of 'needs' and 'skills' in itself represents one particular view of the world, and tends to highlight deficiencies in the *individual learner*, as opposed to the social context within which they learn.

The introduction to the 1994–5 syllabus, however, represents skills and needs in a straightforward, utilitarian way: it stresses throughout that the syllabus is intended to "identif[y] the areas of proficiency required by the students" (p. 1) and "is based on the findings of the Student Needs Analysis which undertook to identify the needs of the students in the faculties in terms of language and study skills" (ibid.). Much of the document refers to language skills; and learning strategies are included in the sections relating to language skills, for example in the section on vocabulary: "students must keep a permanent and organized record of words as they are encountered" (p. 4).

The word 'must' in the preceding sentence could have two interpretations. The context at this point in the document implies that students 'must' do various things *if they are to be successful students in their future university departments*. However, later in the introduction independence becomes clearly a 'must' of *organizational obligation* by USE, for example in the section on the Independent Study Assignments (ISAs): "students must complete a prescribed number of assignments which focus on appropriate syllabus objectives" (p. 5). The obligations of the ISAs are in turn justified with a preamble referring to the "demands" of the university context: "At university, students are exposed to an unfamiliar learning situation which often demands that students work independently outside the classroom" (p. 3). Thus, *needs* are identified with *demands* of the university context, which are translated into *skills*, which in turn become *obligations* in USE; and independent learning is one of these organizational demands/obligations/needs/skills.

A later edition of the syllabus (1998–2000), shows a more ambivalent positioning of the students, compared with the 1994–5 version. A section on 'learner training' takes a more tentative stance, talking in terms of "introducing the students to various strategies which they may choose to utilize and adopt to enhance their learning" (p. 3). This suggests a lesser degree of confidence in the aim of developing autonomy than in that of developing language; it also shifts the terminology from 'skills' (demanded by the context and acquired by the student within an organizational setting) to 'strategies' (used with discrimination by the responsible learner, but without organizational requirement). This shift in emphasis from bald imposition (in the 1994–5 document) to suggestion (1998–2000) reflects a tension underlying the organization's attempt to bring individual learning processes under the control of the curriculum. Note that the later syllabus document still positions the learner as responsible for coping with the organization; but in this case as a *responsible learner*, rather than as an obedient student. In doing so, however, it constructs a position (that of " 'self-policing' individual" (Edwards, 1991: 92), which students are seen as ignoring or rejecting at their own cost.

The Student Handbook and the Student Orientation Programme booklet, prepared by management in conjunction with the Curriculum and Self-access Units, appeal to learner independence as a key construct in students' official induction into USE. In the 1997 Student Handbook a section entitled "Education at USE" includes the following explanation of teachers' and students' roles: "Teachers will help the students to organize their learning efficiently out of class time, and students will be expected to be hard working and assiduous in tasks and self-study" (p. 4). The handbook goes on to recommend that students spend at least 15 hours per week on "self study", that is, "working on [Independent Study Assignments (ISAs)], doing homework, and using the self-access facilities" (ibid.). The representation of learner independence here is again one of "reactive autonomy" (Littlewood, 1996a), whereby students cooperate to the best of their abilities with the system in which they find themselves, by taking responsibility for continuing organizationally regulated learning activities outside the scheduled, supervised class hours. ISA tasks are specifically presented as "an integral part of the USE educational programme" (p. 3) – although on p. 11 they are described as being done "in [students'] own time". This highlights another potential tension in the promotion of learner independence in USE: the fact that the organization constructs itself as an authority over students' time outside class.

Other elements of the USE learner autonomy strategy mentioned in the Handbook include the Student Representation Scheme, one of whose aims is "to increase student autonomy". This use of the word 'autonomy' (as opposed to 'independence') is rare in USE documents; here it perhaps reflects the fact that the Student Representation scheme seems to offer some input by students into organizational processes, in contrast to their reactive role elsewhere.

The Student Orientation Programme booklet (addressed to teachers) largely concentrates on the need to make clear to students the demands entailed by being a student in USE (and in their future University departments). The 1996, 1997 and 1998 versions of the booklet all include sections on course requirements, students' rights (for example, the right to "receive quality tuition" and to "make complaints and write petitions" (1997 booklet)) and rules governing students (for example, not to "behave inappropriately" or "disrupt [the] teaching and learning atmosphere" (ibid.)). In terms of learner autonomy/independence, the impression given is again one of learner independence as reactive and conformist; and successive versions of the booklet seem to move further in this direction. Whereas the 1996 booklet suggests beginning with a humanistically oriented lesson in which students tell the new group about their own good qualities, and then reflect on their past experiences as students, the 1997 edition suggests looking at the Student Handbook, rules, and course requirements, with the latter part of the material focusing on organizational facilities such as the (largely administrative) Student Services Unit and the Self-access Centre. The 1997 edition subsumes the 'sharing' lesson referred to above into a section entitled "Familiarizing students with academic demands". This section includes for the first time a bare, bilingual sheet of injunctions to students, headed "Strategies for success in USE", and including imperatives such as "Learn to use the library!" and "Check the noticeboards regularly". In the 1998 booklet this sheet is presented and expanded upon as the core of this section of the Student Orientation Programme, the humanistic activities being appended without comment.

Through these examples, we can see how learner autonomy plays a part in the USE curriculum not simply as a rational "course strategy" (Cotterall, 1995), but as a discourse, running through various organizational documents and aligning learner independence with organizational concerns of student conformity. This training discourse constructs over time an increasingly technical version of autonomy (Benson, 1997), emphasizing the individual student's utilitarian 'skills' and 'needs' (as opposed to 'capacities' or 'attitudes'). These are linked to and aligned with 'demands' and obligations of organizational order, constructing a student position of active conformity and co-operation with the organization, its aims and its representatives. Educationist concepts such as 'choice' and 'original thinking' which were referred to in the interviews are generally absent in these documents. What hints there are of other, more humanistically oriented discourses (for example, in the mission statement) have become even less prominent in successive editions of the documents. When they do appear, they tend to be used (paradoxically) in alignment with the prevailing discourse of conformity and regulation (as in the 1998–2000 syllabus document, which uses the idea of 'choosing strategies' to construct the position of the 'responsible learner').

For some informants, the highly structured Independent Study Assignments had become an epitome of this interpretation of autonomy, for example:

> We are using a very limited definition of learner autonomy. It's nearly become equal with ISA's [...], and that disturbs me [...]: how about other things they could do, like [...] reading English books not because they have to, but because it will help them? (Teaching Head T1)

The reader might agree with this informant, and feel that the organization has a distorted or confused idea about what learner autonomy or independence is. However, my point here is that the organizational documents make a clear (though paradoxical) *link* between a discourse of the independent learner on the one hand, and a position of conformity on the part of the students on the other.

Organizational culture and the wider context

As well as the variety of interpretations of learner autonomy in USE (and indeed the variety of interpretations used by any one individual), I have tried to convey a sense of the organization's tendency to implement the interpretation which was *easiest to administer* and which was *most aligned with other organizational concerns*. Since most of these interviewees had been involved in the planning of the new curriculum, in this final section I will consider where they perceived the original emphasis on learner autonomy and independence to have come from. Their answers to this question highlighted two organizational factors:

1. Constraints of classroom time on skills such as reading long texts (recalling economic arguments for autonomy mentioned by Benson, 2001), for example:

   I remember highlighting the objectives we thought would take a long time, and that they really had to do outside of the classroom, and that's how Independent Study Assignments came about. (Teaching Head T1)

2. Pressure from the University management, for example:

   A lot of dissatisfaction was being expressed with the quality and standard of the learners who were coming out of USE [...]. Students were not independent when they went into the faculties: they didn't have ability to use the library properly; they didn't have the ability to function independently out of their courses; [...] they didn't have all of the general skills one associates with somebody who is competent and self-starting. (Director E1)

Remedying the quality of students was thus seen as the responsibility of USE and its new management team; and this was to be achieved by changing the USE curriculum to give the students what they needed in order to fit into the University.

Two other factors, however, relate to the professional culture of ELT:

3. The 1992 Student Needs Analysis process:

   The people who worked on [the needs analysis] also thought that the ability to be an independent learner was important. (Director E1)

Note that the comment in point 3 does not say what part the needs analysis survey *data* played in the decision to promote learner independence. Other data suggest that certain skills (such as reading periodicals) were included in the new curriculum because they were felt by the writers to be useful, and despite not being mentioned by lecturers or students in the survey. The needs analysis seems to have been not so much the *origin* of the ideas embodied in the curriculum, as an *instrument* of the discoursal current in USE which led to them, linked in turn to:

4. Discourses of the ELT profession:

> maybe because it is talked about in the profession as being something important as well. (Director E1)

Although I have focused on organizational rather than ethnic culture, the two are in fact interlinked: for one thing, at the time I collected this data, the management (of USE, though not of the University as a whole) was almost exclusively British. Although one of the interviewees cited here was Turkish, she in general concurred with the views of other management informants: position in the organization seemed to be more significant than ethnicity in this case. On the whole, the informants did not refer to 'Western' culture in accounting for the changes. They *did* refer to a 'Turkish high school' culture of dependence as an obstacle to promoting autonomy; but this was represented in opposition not to Western values, but to 'rational', 'professional' norms, as in Director E1's references to "general skills one associates with somebody who is competent", and to "the profession" (see points 2 and 4 above).

Judging from the comments above, the technical version of autonomy seems to have become influential in USE for several reasons, rooted in macro- and micro-level sociocultural contexts. The 'new broom' approach to managing USE in the early 1990s can be seen in the wider context of a drive for 'modernization' in Turkey as in other developing countries. The *choice* of 'broom' was not random, but followed a tradition dating back to the late Ottoman period (Lewis, 1982): expertise and validation were sought from 'Western' sources, and specifically from the internationally influential profession of ELT, which contributed to the focus on learner autonomy as a key goal. The later predominance of the *technical* version of autonomy in particular may be linked to a concern with rationality and bureaucratic accountability (cf. Miller, 1988; Dobbin, 1994). The new management in USE was obliged to *show* that it was addressing perceived problems; and a focus on students' subskills is one way of making this observable and quantifiable – a pattern also noticeable in the parallel development of USE's very structured Teacher Appraisal System.

The naturalization of Western practice, as in many domains (Said, 1978; Scollon and Scollon, 1995), was rarely questioned by the informants in this study; but I would like to end with a comment from

Curriculum Developer E4 which raises further issues: a comment that the new curriculum was

> influenced by foreigners, who maybe concluded that the Turkish education system makes students too dependent. But even in Western countries the transition from school to university is a big jump, and there is a big drop-off in the first year.

This comment highlights the issue of representation of other cultures vis-à-vis one's own; and it points to the need for further research which compares Western with non-Western learners, and which construes it as multiple and negotiated, rather than taking the notion of a starting point.

Acknowledgement

I am grateful to Phil Benson and Richard Smith for their comments on previous drafts of this chapter.

Reflection/discussion questions

1. What different discourses about learning and/or autonomy can you notice in your organizational context? Where do they come from?
2. Would you say there is any tension between these discourses?
3. Who tends to espouse which discourse, in which situations?
4. How does your organization deal with any differences of interpretation?

11
Learning Cultures and Counselling: Teacher/Learner Interaction within a Self-Directed Scheme

María de los Angeles Clemente

> *In order to do our jobs better we need to know what the learners mean, and not just what they say.*

> (Roger, a counsellor in Oaxaca)

Introduction

Counselling in language learning can be defined broadly as one-to-one interaction between a teacher and a learner in order to "support students in their language learning and help them find the most effective and efficient way of [learning] in a variety of learning environments" (Mozzon-McPherson, n.d.). With the emergence of self-directed learning schemes and the current emphasis on learner-centred pedagogies, classroom teachers as well as those working in self-access centres are increasingly expected to play a counselling role (Tudor, 1997). The teacher's main role when counselling is that of "helping the student to discover for himself" (Hargreaves, 1975: 116), although other roles such as advisor, motivator or resource person also play a part (ibid.). This chapter will show, however, that as well as being pedagogical events, counselling sessions are, like any other interaction, social events where participants negotiate different agendas and interpretations.

Relatively little has been written about this type of interaction in the field of language teaching (however, see Gremmo et al. (1985); Hatch (1992)). As Riley (1997: 115) points out, "we have no discourse in which to discuss or 'do' counselling". Within the learner autonomy literature, there have been many reports of schemes for learning to learn, but only a few have focused on the role of the teacher as language learning counsellor (Kelly, 1996; Riley, 1997; Voller, 1997; Clemente, 2001), and there has been little research into the interaction between teachers and individual language learners within a counselling context.

The rationale for this chapter is that developing learner autonomy and self-direction schemes means working with particular *learning cultures*: considering, in other words, the ways in which the participants in counselling discourse negotiate the parameters of their learning encounter. This involves negotiation between the learning authority of the counsellor and the learning aspirations of the student. The idea of a learning culture is congruent to Holliday's (1999a) concept of a "small culture", which can be used as an "interpretative device for understanding emergent behaviour" (p. 237), although we should bear in mind that such behaviour takes place within a broader, multidimensional context.

In the case studied here, the overall sociocultural patterns of Oaxaca, Mexico, of the university's academic culture and of conventions relating to teacher–student interactions provide 'learning spaces' within which teachers and learners express their own agency as they construct the learning cultures of particular counselling sessions. The nature of these learning cultures can range from traditional transmission patterns to attempts at more egalitarian forms of interaction. Ideally, by becoming more aware of these cultural dynamics, teachers and learners can develop clearer understandings of their own learning concerns and needs.

In this chapter I will present my analysis of a set of counselling sessions and of learners' and counsellors' retrospective comments about these interactions, inspired by Erickson and Schultz's (1982) analysis of school counselling. I will look first at two important learner outcomes from counselling sessions: the degree of *satisfaction* expressed by the learner, and the extent to which the learner feels that his/her expectations of the session were met. I will then discuss an aspect of counselling style which is particularly related to the development of autonomy: the attitude which counsellors expressed toward their own *power* in the sessions. After this I will examine some interactional processes which characterized the counselling sessions: *control of turn-taking, development of records*, and *flouting of the co-operative principle*. In conclusion, I will argue that these processes are of particular importance in the way learning cultures are constructed.

Methodology

This chapter presents an analysis of counselling sessions that took place in teacher/learner dyads within the context of a self-access centre (SAC) in a state university in Oaxaca, Mexico. The University of Oaxaca's SAC was set up in 1992 and so far more than 2,000 people have registered to use it. Before studying a foreign language in the SAC, learners attend obligatory sessions to give them information about the organization and resources of the SAC and to help clarify their needs, goals and learning styles. These encounters are usually intercultural interactions involving a counsellor (typically a non-Mexican teacher who had experience of teaching but not specialized training for a counselling role) and a Mexican university student.

The counselling sessions in this study (see Table 11.1) were about half an hour long and (with the exception of session 1) were conducted in Spanish. They were pre-scheduled and took place in a cubicle in the SAC. The purpose of these obligatory sessions was to give some guidance to the learner, who had enrolled and taken an introductory session two weeks before. During these two weeks learners were supposed to have worked by themselves on an orientation task (to get familiar with the nature and location of materials and equipment) and in the elaboration of a study plan (taking into account their personal objectives). I analysed five different counselling sessions (involving five learners and four counsellors) and their respective verbal protocols. In this study, verbal protocols consist of retrospective verbal interactions with the researcher in which the participant talked about the session s/he took part in (Ericsson and Simon, 1984).

Table 11.1   Details of the sessions (CS = counselling session)

Session	Language used	Role	Age	Gender	Ethnicity (origin)
CS1	English	Counsellor (C1)	59	M	Anglo (USA)
		Learner (L1)	30	M	mestizo (Oaxacan)
CS2	Spanish	*Counsellor (C2)	56	M	Anglo (USA)
		Learner (L2)	26	M	mestizo (Oaxacan)
CS3	Spanish	Counsellor (C3)	44	F	Anglo (Scottish)
		Learner (L3)	20	F	Zapotec Oaxacan)
CS4	Spanish	Counsellor (C4)	62	M	Anglo (USA)
		Learner (L4)	16	F	mestiza (Oaxacan)
CS5	Spanish	*Counsellor (C5)	56	M	Anglo (USA)
		Learner (L5)	18	M	Zapotec (Oaxacan)

* Same counsellor.

The procedure for gathering data was as follows: the sessions were video recorded and transcribed, and each participant was asked for a separate interview. All the interviews were carried out in the participants' first language (either Spanish or English). I assured the participants that the information was confidential, emphasizing that the purpose of the study was to understand the sessions and not to judge them or their deeds. I asked general questions (for example, "How did you like the session?") about the participants' feelings towards the sessions and towards the other participant. Then we watched the video together and I stopped it to ask specific questions or allow the participant to make comments. Finally, I asked some more general questions (e.g. "What are your overall feelings about the session?") to elicit a summary of the participant's attitudes and to gather any afterthoughts.

Data

In order to illustrate what the discourse of counselling is like and the kind of information obtained from the protocols, I include in Appendixes 11.1 and 11.2 some extracts relating to one of the sessions. (The participants have been given pseudonyms; and throughout this chapter transcriptions from sessions 2, 3, 4 and 5 and all student comments have been translated from Spanish.)

In Appendix 11.1, the left-hand column represents the session itself, while the right-hand column contains the most relevant comments from the protocols. If we consider only the left-hand column, focusing on the session itself, there could be several possible readings. On the one hand, one could say that there are good signs of cooperation and communication. On the other hand, the reader may perceive a lack of commitment by both participants to carrying out a useful conversation.

However, it is the participants' comments (Appendix 11.1 right-hand column and Appendix 11.2) which make us realize how far the two participants were from agreement. It becomes very clear that neither the learner nor the counsellor was eager to collaborate for mutual negotiation.

Analysis and discussion of data

In analysing the data I focused on the following aspects of the interactions and protocols: *learners' degree of satisfaction, counselors' attitudes to power, control of turn-taking, development of records* (Erickson and Schultz, 1982), and *flouting of the co-operative principle*. The way in which these aspects interact illustrates how the participants are constructing a learning culture. Because of the variation between the participants' interpretations, my analysis will move back and forth between the views of counsellors and learners.

Learner satisfaction

One measurable outcome of the sessions is the degree of satisfaction and feeling of achievement (or otherwise) of expectations on the part of the learners. Four levels were identified (Table 11.2).

"Degree of satisfaction" was assessed by the frequency and wording of the learners' comments about this aspect. Thus, L1 and L2 expressed more often and with more emphasis their positive attitude towards the sessions than L3; L4 was very dissatisfied and L5 was overtly negative about the session. The overall degree of satisfaction is linked to the learners' perceptions of whether their expectations were achieved in the session (summarized in the right-hand column of Table 11.2). Assuming that counselling sessions should address the learner's expectations, this is a key aspect in the negotiation of the learning culture.

Counsellors' attitudes to power

Because of the institutional setting in which the counselling took place, a power difference in favour of the counsellor was almost inevitable. However, the counsellors' attitudes to exercising this power varied (see Table 11.3), as illustrated in extracts from the verbal protocols.

Firstly (Possibility 1), the counsellor may use power implicitly:

C4: If she had another thing wrong, she would have to do it over again.

Secondly (Possibility 2), the counsellor may show awareness of the

Table 11.2 Degree of satisfaction expressed by the learners

Session no.	Degree of satisfaction	Achievement of expectations (summarized from learner comments)
1	+ +	learner got what s/he needed
2	+ +	learner just needed confirmation and s/he got it
3	+	learner needed a lot and got something
4	−	learner needed a lot and got nothing
5	− −	learner did not need counselling

Table 11.3 Counsellors' attitudes to power

Condition	Possibility 1 (e.g. CS4)	Possibility 2 (e.g. CS5)	Possibility 3 (e.g. CS1, CS3)
Explicit awareness of power position	NO	YES	YES
Imposition of power	YES	YES	NO

power s/he has, and use it for his/her own purposes:

> C5: I wanted to put her on the spot a bit.
> C5: I know, I was using my power position to let her know that I was impressed.

Thirdly (Possibility 3), the counsellor may try to avoid situations in which s/he plays a powerful role:

> C1: To correct his English would have meant putting more pressure on him and more power on me.
> C3: According to our philosophy here counsellor and learner should use mutual tú [Spanish informal pronoun].

In the first case, the power of position is taken for granted in the discourse of the counsellor. The second case is very different: although the counsellor is still using his/her power, s/he is making explicit decisions about when and how to do so. The third case is similar to the second in that the counsellor is able to talk about his/her power position. However, s/he tries not to impose this power, in order to offer the learner some space for empowerment. This gives the encounter a sense of perceived 'equality' (although it is hard to imagine a truly equal encounter in any dyad where a teacher and a learner are involved). The perceived 'equality' in the third case is intended explicitly to build a learning culture favouring learner autonomy.

Although power can take many forms, I proceeded to look at the counsellors' attitudes to power in these sessions particularly in terms of who had the means and the authority to direct the content and form of the interaction, through the control of turn-taking. As the next section will show, the use of power by counsellors had more consequences in directing these sessions than the power of the learner.

Control of turn-taking

Discourse control is one way in which power is displayed or used between participants. In terms of discourse analysis, controlling the

Table 11.4   Types of conversational move in two sessions

Participant	Total moves	Openings (%)	Replies (%)	Closings (%)
C5	77	30 (39%)	0 (0%)	47 (61%)
L5	43	0 (0%)	30 (70%)	13 (30%)
C2	72	10 (14%)	2 (3%)	60 (83%)
L2	53	2 (4%)	10 (19%)	41 (77%)

opening of an exchange means that "the speaker imposes on one or more other participants the right/duty to reply" (Gremmo et al., 1985: 41). In the sessions analysed, most often the counsellor controlled the openings of the interactions. Hence, s/he also controlled the communicative situation, exhibiting "a form of control over the learner's behaviour" (ibid.: 45). A comparison between Session 5 and Session 2 (involving the same counsellor) shows the way language was controlled by one of the participants (Table 11.4). In Session 5 the learner's moves are mainly replies (not free contributions but elicited responses – 70 per cent); and he opens no exchanges. Moreover, the exchanges in this session generally consisted of the classic adjacency pair that occurs in the classroom, where the teacher is in charge of the questions, and the student responsible for the answers (McCarthy, 1991). The fact that the counsellor is the only person making openings means that s/he also holds the right to change the topic, which involves a specific "relationship of communicative rights and obligations among speakers" (Erickson and Schultz, 1982: 82). Thus the counsellor has control of the structure of the session, and also makes more interactional moves overall. In Session 2 (which ended with the learner feeling more satisfied) the situation is somewhat different. The learner opens some exchanges; and less than 20 per cent of the moves are openings by the counsellor. This leaves more room for the learner to negotiate in the communicative event, not just answering questions or giving replies but also making closing turns, that is, non-elicited contributions "in which no duty to reply is imposed" (ibid: 142). Thus discourse control contributes to the communication style of the emerging learning culture.

Developing records

In terms of my analysis, if a participant in an interaction "develops a record" (Erickson and Schultz, 1982), s/he does something which contributes to a positive or negative impression of him/herself in the other person's mind. Here, I will focus mainly on the development of the *student's* record with the counsellor (that is, the opinion the counsellor has of the student) because in institutional contexts "if a student develops a record during the interview, the consequences of it are immediate and potentially serious" (Erickson and Schultz, 1982: 26). However, learners also form impressions about counsellors: for example, the consequences of Session 5 (see Appendix 11.1) were that the counsellor never heard from the learner again, even though they had agreed on an appointment. Within these sessions there were three emergent features that helped to develop a record: *comembership, institutional identity* and *universalistic attributes*.

Establishing comembership

Comembership is "an aspect of performed social identity that involves particularistic attributes of status shared by the counsellor and the student" (Erickson and Schultz, 1982: 8); it concerns, in other words, how the actors make some kind of personal connection by finding out what they have in common. Anything that is "locally produced" (ibid.) within the frame of a session and serves the purpose of establishing comembership may develop a good record. Although in this specific situation the participants clearly did *not* have ethnic or institutional comembership, they relied on other ways of constructing comembership. I found that *sharing the same interests* was one of the factors that helped to develop the learners' good record:

> (CS = counselling session; VP = verbal protocol).
>
> CS2   C2 (Reading the written task): Aha! *Howard's End!* Did you understand something of *Howard's End?*
>
> VP2   C2: I like to talk about movies.
>
> CS2   C2 (later, still reading): Tracy Chapman ... yes ... I love her.
>
> VP2   C2: I was letting him know that he had good taste.

Another way to establish comembership was *sharing the same problems*:

> CS3   C3: And the computers? What's that? [meaning "what do you think?"].
>
>   L3: No (laughter) [meaning "I can't understand how to work with them"].
>
>   C3: Neither can I (laughter).
>
>   L3: (laughter).
>
> VP3   L3: You identify with the counsellor. It feels good when you know that there is someone that has gone through the same problems.

Establishing institutional identity

'Institutional identity' means the degree of agreement learners show with institutional procedures and situations. When the learners are positive about the way the SAC works, and agree to do what they are told, they tend to develop a good record:

VP3   C3: She is really enthusiastic, she likes the task.

But if the learner shows disagreement with this, she may develop a bad record:

VP5   C5 [referring to the learner's negative attitude towards the task]: I was expecting something positive.
C5 [later, referring to the learner's lack of a written study plan and his preference for using videos and songs]: The learner isn't well organized ... I want him to be more prepared, to have more structure ... He is using us as an amusement centre.

Identifying universalistic attributes

Universalistic attributes which contribute to a good record are "those which potentially could be achieved by any individual, given the requisite motivation, talent, opportunity and perseverance" (Erickson and Schultz, 1982: 15), that is to say, more general attributes of learners. In the present case, these features include past academic experience related to learning languages, and general and specific experience in the SAC. L1 and L2 developed good records because they showed a fairly good command of English and completed the two activities they were supposed to do very well, whereas L4 and L5 developed bad records. L4 had problems in the task, while L5 did not show interest in the activities and did not have the study plan; both of them were beginners in English. The situation with Session 3 is rather different. The participants hardly talked about the task and the learner did not have the study plan with her. Nevertheless, the information the learner provided about past and present experience developed a good record.

VP3   C3 [expressed at different points during the protocol]: The learner knew what she wanted [...] She was quite clear [...] She was responding very well [...] She wanted to take responsibility [...] She was quite positive.

Table 11.5   Comparative table of factors related to students' good/bad records
(0 = 'neutral')

Session No.	Learner's degree of satisfaction	Comembership	Institutional identity	Universalistic attributes
CS1	+ +	+ +	+ +	+ +
CS2	+ +	+ +	+ +	+ +
CS3	+	+ +	+	+
CS4	−	0	0	+
CS5	− −	0	− −	−

Table 11.5 shows the overall pattern of these features of the different counselling sessions (as summarized from explicit indications in verbal protocols). Note that the sessions which favoured establishment of a good record also seemed to end with greater learner satisfaction; this suggests that how records are developed is a vital factor in the configuration of emerging learning cultures.

Flouting the Co-operative Principle

The Co-operative Principle (Grice, 1975) suggests some general assumptions about everyday discourse: the maxims of quality, quantity, relevance and manner, whereby participants are assumed to make truthful, concise, pertinent contributions to an interaction. However, when these maxims are purposely violated or flouted, they provide insights beyond "the semantic content of the sentence" (Levinson, 1983: 103). In the present case, flouting of the Co-operative Principle reveals some of the processes which may contribute to the learning culture of the counselling session.

Wanting to talk

From the counsellor's point of view, the maxim of quantity was flouted by the learner in Session 1. Unlike learners in the other sessions, L1 took long turns when he was asked questions. The counsellor remarked on this during the protocol and even commented on his own failure to finish the session in the time intended. However, the learner's intention was different: he was taking long turns on purpose. The session was held in English because the learner wanted it to be an opportunity to practise his English, so the more he talked the better. They obviously had different interpretations of the function of the session. For the counsellor, counselling serves to guide and help the learner; in fact, according to him, this learner "does not need counselling [...] he is already independent [...] confident, mature". For the learner, on the other hand, counselling has to serve his own purposes. He felt satisfied with the session despite the fact that the counsellor felt that he was "inadequately prepared" for this kind of learner.

Engaging in small talk

Another maxim that was violated for interactional purposes was relevance, through the introduction of topics that were strictly irrelevant to the purpose of counselling:

CS1   L1: Are you from the United States?
       C1: I am from the United States.
       L1: How many times do you have here? [*sic*]
       C1: I've been here almost four years.
       L1: Four years and ... Do you teach in the school that is near here?
       C1: Yeah, I also teach.

However, there is no divergence in the points of view of the participants. Both agreed that this kind of digression was necessary to build up a working relationship. When I asked participants about this, almost all of them said that it was important to get to know each other and to develop a good relationship. If the counsellor wants to engage in a meaningful interaction, s/he needs to understand the importance of small talk, a useful device s/he can use to move towards a more informal and relaxed situation, thus diminishing social distance (Wright, 1987). Small talk can also serve to establish comembership between the participants, thus encouraging the emergence of good records (Erickson and Schultz, 1982).

Avoiding rudeness

When the counsellors were asked about the procedures they think they should follow in advising learners, almost all of them answered that they would prefer to suggest rather than direct, not because of politeness but because, as C2 said, "those are the rules of self-learning". In contrast, the learners showed a concern for politeness: they behaved in specific ways mainly because they wanted the counsellor to feel good:

VP4   L4: A lot of times we don't clarify misunderstandings just because of politeness ... I didn't clarify anything because it would have been very abrupt, very strong. I decided that it was better to let it go or to wait for a clarification on the part of the counsellor.

In being polite learners sometimes flouted the maxim of *quality*. This became evident through the protocols, which revealed that many uses of 'neutral' adjectives and hedges were actually euphemisms:

(CS5)   L5: Well, it was interesting.

But he actually thought:

(VP5)   L5: it is only an obligation, a requirement.

And the same learner clearly lied for the sake of politeness on several occasions:

(CS5)   C5: Really? Do you think that, now, you know what ... what the SAC is like, what ... where the materials are, and how to use the equipment ...?
          L5: Yes
(VP5)   L5: No, it isn't enough to know the SAC. It was very limited.
(CS5)   C5 [continued from above]: ... and all that?
          L5: Yes ... more or less
(VP5)   L5: It was neither a good experience, nor useful ... I didn't say what I really thought because it would have sounded very strong, very impolite. It is not the right thing to do.

These processes of interaction illustrate the subjective dynamics of these learning cultures, which may work either with or against peda-gogical aims of learner autonomy.

Conclusion

This study has analysed the discourse of counselling in order to explore how it creates a learning culture. The analysis has considered various lin-guistic and nonlinguistic features of the sessions: degree of satisfaction, control of turn-taking, counsellors' attitudes to power, development of records, and flouting of the Co-operative Principle. Through the interre-lationship of these processes we have seen how the contours of a learn-ing culture emerge and how this might affect the process of self-directed learning.

The construction of a learning culture can be seen as a means by which counsellors and learners attempt to bridge their divergent perceptions of counselling sessions. Because of their social histories, counsellors and learners have different expectations about counselling (Swales, 1990), which are built on their personal backgrounds. Counsellors draw upon academic and institutional procedures, whereas learners have built their assumptions on their understanding of the "classroom script" (Hatch, 1992: 92). What seems to be missing is a mutual understanding of the "script of the student–teacher tutorial" (ibid.).

This script would have to deal with the diversity of roles found in autonomy schemes. It is often assumed that the goal of counsellors is to play 'equal' with the learner. However, it is a fallacy to think that there is equality between the counsellor and learner. There is a difference of power and it is that difference that makes guidance and assessment possible (Bloor and Bloor, 1988; Pugsley, 1988). However, counsellors should remember Widdowson's (1990: 187) distinction between being 'authoritative' (using one's knowledge and expertise) and being 'authoritarian' (using one's power to control the situation). We have seen that the counsellors' attitudes to power play an important role in the counselling interaction. In this study, some counsellors seemed to be authoritarian, rather than using their power in an authoritative manner, adapting their knowledge and experience to the learner to allow for flexible decision-making and negotiation.

Riley (1988) sees *joint culture-creation* as a process of creating an "intersubjective world" among the participants in an interaction. This process is one of negotiation, which is "not a bargaining process but a joint exploration of possibilities and targets [...], a process of reaching agreement through discussion" (Bloor and Bloor, 1988: 63). At two different levels, institutional and individual, this negotiation should be at the core of counselling.

Institutional adaptation would involve an attempt to find convergence between external factors within the institutional context and the internal factors that the learner brings with him/her. Thus, institutional procedures need to be flexible. Flexibility would be reflected in the structure of the sessions, their content and goals, but, above all, in the way the institution interprets counselling. If counselling is prescribed, if authorities dictate the rules, and if sessions are perceived as gatekeeping (see Erickson and Schultz, 1982) into self-access learning, then sessions are more likely to be an obstacle than a support for learners. I strongly believe that counsellors and learners, *together*, should decide the conditions under which they want to work.

Individual adaptation should take into account the diversity of the social actors within the learning cultural context: the counsellor has to be aware of the differences between his/her culture(s) and those of the learners. The learners and counsellors in this study rarely referred to the social and cultural factors of gender, ethnicity or social class; moreover, the aim of this study was to reveal details of interaction which seemed typical of these counselling sessions, rather than to make generalizations about the wider sociocultural context. Indeed, with a small sample such as this it is impossible to separate out the influences of ethnicity, gender and institutional identity, but like Riley and others (this volume) I feel that these parameters should be particularly noted. It seems likely that these factors affect the style and dynamics of the interaction and negotiation that take place during counselling. It is risky to take these elements for granted, for they can strongly influence the understandings of the participants. Although it is beyond the scope of this chapter to make prescriptive recommendations, a first stage in defining these problems would be to explore which elements seem to contribute to misunderstanding and patterns of social distance (Wright, 1987: 20). Table 11.1 shows some of these diverse factors, and further research into the creation of learning cultures should attempt to explore these factors in connection with the features of interaction considered here.

Learning cultures are forms of creative adaptation between individuals (the counsellor and the learner) and between these individuals and the institutional context of their learning. Learning cultures provide space for counsellors and learners to negotiate their own respective teaching and learning styles and to locate each other within their respective sociocultural histories. In preparing language educators to take on a counselling role, it is crucial to raise awareness of the dynamics of learning cultures, and of how counsellors' and learners' actions are framed by their broader social and cultural context.

Reflection/discussion questions

Think of a teaching/learning interaction which you have experienced recently (this could be in class, in an independent learning centre, or outside any formal setting).

1. What was your attitude to *power* in the interaction?
2. What were the individual/contextual factors that helped to *develop records* of participants?
3. What were the means to *control discourse*?
4. How have you allowed or could you allow for adaptation in order to foster the development of a new learning culture?

Appendix 11.1: Transcript from session 5 with corresponding comments from both participants

(C = counsellor, L = learner)

COUNSELLING SESSION (CS5)	VERBAL PROTOCOLS (VP5)
1. C: ... I am John. Maestro John ... Did you do the task? ... Have you finished?	1. C: I told him the title with no intention, maybe I was being formal ... or it was ... nerves ... I use Maestro John for formal situations.
2. L: Yes.	
3. C: Good. How did you like it?	
4. L: Well ... It was interesting.	4. L: It wasn't. The task is only an obligation, a requirement.
5. C: Really? Do you think that, now, you know what ... what the SAC is like, what ... where the materials are, and how to use the equipment ...?	
6. L: Yes.	6. L: No, the task wasn't enough to know the SAC. It was very limited.
7. C: And all that?	
8. L: Yes ... more or less.	8. L: It was neither a learning experience nor useful.
9. C: More or less? (laughs).	9. C: I was expecting a positive answer because before he said it had been "interesting". Maybe it was a nervous laugh.
10. L: A bit of practice.	
11. C: Was the task useful?	
12. L: A little.	
13. C: Very little. Why?	13. C: I guess I wanted to put him on the spot a bit. I thought every-thing was going to be fine and then I see that everything is getting worse and worse, so I wanted him to explain it. This is my way of giving him a bit of a hard time, I know I was doing that ... These unexpected answers changed the tone of the whole CS, I took them a little negatively.
14. L: Well, the truth is that I don't know what it's for ... It helps to find materials and all that stuff, but only that ... I think that practice is enough.	
15. C: Yes. The truth is that the purpose of the task is for the students to know where the materials are, how to use the equipment ... Aha. Okay. What are your long-term objectives?	15. C: I was justifying that he hadn't been wasting his time, that he actually knows more now how to use the SAC.
16. L: Long term? Hmmm ... I want to start to learn as much English	

(Contd.)

as I can. I've told you that it is
going to be very useful for my
career, for my studies.

17. C: Yes, ... but you are only going
to concentrate on reading
comprehension?

18. L: Ehh? Above all listening
comprehension.

18. L: This is what I really need.

19. C: Huh?

20. L: I understand reading better
than listening.

19. C: I was taken by surprise. A
couple of times he said things
I didn't expect.

21. C: ... Then, the task had to be
useful for you because it is
based on listening comprehension,
(laughs) yes, no? I think so.
And ... ah ... okay, and specifically,
have you elaborated your
study plan?

21. C: I know exactly what I was
doing: this was to give him
again a bit of a hard time.

22. L: No.

22. L: I don't need one.

23. C: No? Okay, no it is all right,
it is all right. But, have you
thought about the material you
are going to use?

23. C: He wasn't prepared for the
session. He did the task but he
didn't have any study plan. I
didn't lose my cool with him. I
was nice with him. For some
people two weeks are not
enough time to finish their
study plan and the task.

24. L: Ehh ... In fact I am using
authentic materials, songs,
videos ... to improve my listening
performance. Grammar, I forgot
a bit ... I would like to do
something about that ... work
with grammar and authentic
materials.

24. L: This is my opportunity to
recall what I learned before ...
I am taking advantage of the
SAC: I listen to a song, try to
recognize the words. If there is
something I don't know, I look it
up in the dictionary and
sometimes I realized that it was
something I already knew. This
helps me a lot.

25. C: Yes, They are good, aha.
I think that it is a good idea but
when you find ... ah ... problems ...
problems ... ah ... you may need
to go to didactic materials in
listening comprehension ... to
develop this ability more and

25. C: He is using us as an
amusement centre. I don't think
he is well organized. I want him
to be more prepared, to have
more structure.

(Contd.)

understand what you hear,
okay? So, I would suggest not only
to use authentic materials, but
combine them with didactic
materials from the listening
comprehension section ... and ...
ahh ... How do you like
studying here?

26. L: I like it ...
27. C: Really? Do you like it?
28. L: Yes, because I'm not in the
school now so I need to start
studying in order to get a good
study rhythm when I enter the
university. That is the way, little
by little.
29. C: Yes, exactly.
30. L: I am working basically in
listening comprehension.

31. C: Aha. Yes, it is important to
concentrate on an area, ...
(laughs) Do you have some
doubts or ...? ... Do you have
any suggestions for us?
32. L: I consider that everything
is okay, okay, everything is okay.

33. C: And ... ah ... ah ... suggestions
for you, for yourself? (laughs).

34. L: Study more.
35. C: Do you come everyday?
36. L: Yes, I'm coming everyday.
...
37. C: Oh, oh, okay. Hmmm..
I would like to talk to you maybe
in two weeks, to see how it is
going, okay? ... So ... How do you
like if we talk, more or less ... the
seventeenth, no? ... (laughs)
Okay, maybe you should
write it down.

---

26. L: I agree, I know that I have to
study grammar. I know that I
have to study more, but later.
Maybe it is important to have a
certain order or something like
that, but I've never been very
organized, for anything. It is
difficult for me. Besides, I think
that wouldn't help me now ...
According to my experience,
authentic materials are better
for me than didactic ones.
31. C: I was running out of steam. I
thought that I did want to give
him a chance to make a
suggestion or so.

32. L: I didn't ask anything because
I didn't have questions to ask.
I didn't ask for this session. I still
don't have problems.
33. C: He didn't seem as prepared as
[Learner 2]; he was willing to
talk but needed to be asked.

35. C: It was maybe a good answer.

37. C: Maybe I shouldn't have done
this. I wasn't giving him too
much leeway but I was basically
insisting on another session
because we needed to talk
again. He wasn't prepared, so I
did that on purpose. I was being
demanding, I know. But if we are

(Contd.)

...

38. C: At nine (writing it down) (laughs) And it is only to see if you have a more specific study plan. Okay?

39. L: Yes.
40. C: Yes, Okay, Anything else?
41. L: No, ... Thank you.
42. C: (laughs).
43. L: So long.
44. C: So long.

making a date and nobody writes it down, we'll never have another session, so, yeah, I was being demanding.

39. L: No, I don't agree to have to do a written study plan ... I am not going to use it, maybe for other people it works ... I already have my plan: recall, learn my own way with songs, practise, listen in order to not to forget the English I already know. I am leaving in six months, so I would not have time to accomplish anything. The only thing I can do is practice and learn some new vocabulary with songs and movies.

Appendix 11.2: final comments about session 5 from both participants

C: The boy wasn't prepared. That's the way I read it ... He needs more support, more help ... He hasn't talked to me. We certainly didn't establish much of a relationship. I think he doesn't want sessions with me ... I over-reacted, I did make things difficult for him ... He is not independent. He will learn English because he seems to have a genuine interest, but would need more support ... I didn't like this session, I don't know. I didn't do much. I felt I was kind of useless.

L: Sessions shouldn't be compulsory. Sessions should be requested not imposed ... This session didn't help me. It didn't have an objective ... I didn't say what I really thought because it would have sounded very strong, very impolite. It is not the right thing to do ... I had the opportunity to talk; if I didn't say some things it was because I didn't want to say them or because I didn't have the courage to say them John overawes people.

(Contd.)

He seems very harsh … very big, very strong, very severe. He speaks with a very loud voice and makes one feel very small. He is okay when you ask him a question, I go and ask him when I don't understand something, but for a session, no; he really frightens me. Actually, I prefer to talk to someone who speaks Spanish. I don't feel secure with foreigners … John was polite, within his own personality … I am not going to follow all the pieces of advice he gave me. I like it when people suggest things. Any suggestion is good, but I always decide what is convenient.

12
Addressing Constraints on Autonomy in School Contexts: Lessons from Working with Teachers

Flávia Vieira

Introduction

Working with teachers on learner autonomy has largely determined my history as a teacher educator and researcher of language pedagogy. In presenting overall and particular 'lessons' from my experience in this chapter, I wish to underline the potential value of teachers positively and collaboratively addressing constraints as a springboard for improvement, thus counteracting dominant educational practices. In this view, addressing constraints can be seen as integral to learner and teacher development, with benefits for wider research on autonomy.

I start with a brief introduction to the Portuguese educational context as the sociocultural background to a practical theory about developing language pedagogy. This theory will be illustrated with reference to a particular case of school–university partnership, the GT-PA ('Grupo de Trabalho – Pedagogia para a Autonomia' (Working Group on Pedagogy for Autonomy)), a small network of in-service school teachers and university researchers/teacher educators whose common interest in pedagogy for autonomy has underpinned efforts to understand and foster it through collaborative inquiry. I will finish with reflections on the feasibility of our work, pointing out obstacles and limitations that are probably common to other projects with a commitment to emancipatory education.

Although the actions described in this chapter are discipline-bound and local, with a focus on teaching and learning English as a foreign language in particular settings within the Portuguese educational system,

I believe that they may have broader significance in that they represent a case of counteracting dominant educational practices that are also characteristic of other cultural contexts around the world.

The Portuguese educational context as the sociocultural background to pedagogy for autonomy

Several changes have taken place in education in Portugal since 1986, when a new Education Law set the basis for ongoing reforms whose main goal has been to build a better education for all, promoting the ideal of democratic citizenship. I will focus briefly on some aspects of schooling, teacher education and pedagogical research that are relevant for understanding the extent to which the development of learner autonomy is plausible in the Portuguese context.

At the level of schooling, a major effect of the reforms has been a continuous restructuring of the national curriculum towards greater valuing of learner autonomy on ethical and pedagogical grounds. In the field of foreign language teaching, according to official pedagogical discourse, pedagogy for autonomy seems to be both desired and expected. A progressive decentralisation of school management, which has given schools a considerable degree of autonomy to adapt the national curriculum to local contexts, can also be seen as a measure that supports and facilitates pedagogy for autonomy.

However, most school practices are not learning-centred, as has been demonstrated in a large body of descriptive research. The weight of a transmissive and individualistic pedagogical tradition, the lack of appropriate teacher development programmes, and the contradictions between reform principles and the demands of the system (national examinations, pressure to cover the syllabus, and so on), discourage many teachers from experimenting with alternative approaches and seem to promote a generalised attitude of resistance to change, reinforced by the government's top-down approach to innovation. Moreover, decentralisation has brought with it a need for greater accountability, thereby increasing the amount of bureaucracy and distracting teachers from pedagogical concerns.

In the Portuguese educational arena, promising local projects have been carried out, but mostly in isolation from one another, and without being given proper recognition. On the whole we might say that the culture of schooling in Portugal is fraught with tensions and conflicting rationalities. Innovation is cherished as an educational priority by some and resisted by others, while the development of learner autonomy is supported in theory, but is hardly a common reality in practice. The recent creation of a new area in compulsory education called 'Estudo Acompanhado' (Supported Study), where students are supposed to "learn how to learn", is an example of how governmental policies are dealing with deficiencies within the system by creating 'supplements' to "regular practices", the risk being that teachers do not feel obliged to develop learning competence in their own classes.

Teacher education has also become a priority of the educational agenda in the last two decades. The policies adopted have placed an increased emphasis on pre-service and in-service teacher qualification and on teacher research. The international movement towards reflective teacher education has had a visible impact upon academic discourses, and teacher education institutions have contributed to an increase of postgraduate courses intended to equip schools with better-qualified teachers.

The question is, to what extent is teacher education in general contributing to improvement of schooling in ways that facilitate the development of learner autonomy? How far is it preparing teachers to transform rather than reproduce dominant practices, to challenge rather than conform to given situational constraints? The impact of a reflective stance depends largely on *what* is questioned (Tom, 1985; Zeichner and Tabachnick, 1991), so teacher reflection needs to involve a consideration of justifications and implications of pedagogical choices, and of the historical and structural forces that tend to determine them. A conception of teaching as a moral and political activity (Smyth, 1997) presupposes that teachers are both willing and able to exert some control over educational settings by mediating between constraints and ideals, while this requires a collaborative culture of schooling. In my view, and also according to recent reviews of research (Estrela et al., 2002; Canário, 2002), initial teacher education in Portugal is far from fulfilling these goals in a satisfactory way. Curricula are largely theoretical and detached from professional settings, assuming an 'applicationist' conception of pedagogical experience and perpetuating a technical approach to teaching which may, in turn, reinforce established pedagogical practices. Investment in the qualification of supervisors has been scarce, and the potential for school–university collaboration is often wasted. On the other hand, most in-service teacher development programmes seem to ignore the idea that professional competence emerges from professional experience and assume a cause–effect relationship between decontextualised formal training and situated practice. In sum, if pedagogy for autonomy demands teachers who are ready to mediate between constraints and ideals, then teacher education practices in Portugal are hardly favourable to learner autonomy.

Pedagogical research has increased rapidly as a consequence of the recent reform movement. However, research on learner autonomy in the field of language didactics is still scarce in Portugal, which helps to explain why it is not a priority of most teacher education programmes. There has been a move from a research focus on 'textual' didactics (e.g. how to teach/learn reading and writing) to a focus on classroom dynamics and on broader views of language education (Andrade, 2002), but teachers are often objects rather than partners of inquiry (except in teacher-conducted research for academic purposes), and most studies do not seem to have a visible impact upon school practices (Canha, 2001). To a large extent, pedagogical research suffers from the problems of educational theory and research in general (that is, in all contexts), as pointed out by van Manen (1990: 135):

(1) confusing pedagogical theorising with other discipline-based forms of discourse; (2) tending to abstraction and thus losing touch with the lifeworld of living with children; and (3) failing to see the general erosion of pedagogic meaning from the lifeworld.

If, as van Manen (ibid.) cogently argues, the original mandate of educational theory is the need to educate people in a pedagogically responsible manner, then its scientific status must necessarily integrate 'social significance' as a validation criterion. Defending autonomy on ethical and theoretical grounds is important, but practical justifications are needed to legitimate it, and this clearly implies the direct involvement of teachers in pedagogical inquiry. The need for a school-based approach to research on learner autonomy has been acknowledged in the specialised literature, but Benson's recent (2001) review of research in this domain shows that we are still far from assigning to teachers a dignified role in efforts to understand and transform pedagogy.

From what has been said so far, we can conclude that several constraints on autonomy emerge from the cultures of schooling, teacher education and pedagogical research in Portugal. At the same time, a number of teachers, teacher educators and educational researchers are showing clear signs of dissatisfaction and are struggling to explore spaces of freedom within the system, or to find spaces for manoeuvre where constraints exist. The two following sections refer to one endeavour – the GT-PA – where the struggle for autonomy has taken the form of collaborative inquiry by a group of academic researchers/ teacher educators and in-service school language teachers. Although it is not representative of common practices in Portugal, it is an example of the possibilities of moving in a more liberating direction.

The working definition of 'pedagogy for autonomy' adopted in my work with teachers stresses opposite goals to those of a (still dominant) 'pedagogy of dependence' and can be summarised as follows:

> A pedagogy for autonomy in the school context seeks to move the learner closer to the learning process and content, by enhancing conditions which increase motivation to learn, interdependence relationships, discourse power, ability to learn and to manage learning, and a critical attitude towards teaching and learning.

The basis for this general definition was originally developed within a school-based research project that involved my collaborating with one school teacher in promoting her students' learning competence (Vieira, 1998). Its feasibility has been validated by teachers in other formal educational settings, not least within the GT-PA (see below), where teacher empowerment means, first of all, willingness and ability to manage constraints within a vision of education with hope. If "to hope is to believe in possibilities" (van Manen, 1990: 123), then I believe that it is possible to create teaching and learning conditions that improve the quality of teachers' and students' lives; I have also found that it is possible for academics and school teachers to engage in collaborative inquiry, here defined as "a process consisting of repeated episodes of reflection and action through which a group of peers strive to answer a question of importance to them" (Bray et al., 2000: 6).

The GT-PA: a case of school–university partnership for developing autonomy in the school context

In this section, I introduce the GT-PA and present principles for learner and teacher development that have emerged from this and other (previous and ongoing) projects involving the participation of teachers. An example of these principles in action will then be presented.

A brief introduction to the GT-PA

The GT-PA was set up in October 1997 as an extension of a previous in-service teacher development project (1993–6) whose outcomes highlighted the value of collaborative inquiry in promoting reflective teaching towards learner autonomy (see Vieira, 1997, 1999a). The results of this project were the main incentive for setting up the GT-PA and opening it to other teachers.

At present, the group includes about fifty voluntary EFL teacher participants from different schools, with diverse background experiences, all sharing a basic concern – pedagogy for autonomy – and a basic wish – professional growth. Three colleagues from my department at the University of Minho, Braga – Methodologies of Education – help me to coordinate the group: Maria Alfredo Moreira, Isabel Barbosa and Madalena Paiva. Three colleagues from the Languages department and also two external collaborators (Richard Smith from the University of Warwick, England, and Leslie Bobb-Wolff from the University of La Laguna, Tenerife) joined us in 2001.

The group's activities are funded by the Centre for Research into Education of our university's Institute of Education and Psychology and accredited by a national agency as a "teacher development workshop", so that teachers can gain credits for their work. We run joint sessions (about five a year) at the university and most of our actual research work is carried out in school settings. Since some of the group's members are school or university supervisors of trainees in the final year (practicum) of initial teacher education programmes run by the university, student teachers often participate in our action plans, as is the case in the example presented below.

Our goals as a 'learning community' can be summarised as: (i) understanding how learner autonomy and teacher development interact; and (ii) inventing pedagogical and teacher education strategies that help us address constraints. We have accomplished multiple tasks that involve some form of inquiry into professional contexts. Inquiry 'about/for' contexts is aimed at understanding situational variables that affect pedagogy and includes analysing EFL syllabi and published materials, surveying teacher and learner beliefs, and investigating teacher development processes; inquiry 'in' contexts concerns improving pedagogy and includes materials design and pedagogical or teacher development experiences.

Dissemination has been achieved mainly through the bi-annual publication of an in-house journal, *Cadernos* (Vieira, 1999b, 2001a), and participation in professional meetings on campus and outside, including a local conference organised by the group in March 2001 (Vieira et al., 2002). Supervising pre-service teachers in training has also contributed to disseminating, trying out and developing new ideas.

Diversity within a common direction, freedom of choice and context-sensitiveness are basic characteristics of our work. Agendas for action are negotiated at the beginning of each school year, and the participants' roles depend on what they decide to do, along a research–learning continuum ranging from 'researchers' to 'active listeners' trying to learn from others' experience. My role as the coordinator, with the help of my colleagues, is to promote reflective dialogue and inquiry, be responsive and supportive to needs and action plans, theorise from the group's experience, and participate actively in some of the group's tasks.

In Table 12.1 I present some global action principles which indicate how 'autonomous learner development' and 'reflective teacher development' can be promoted in tandem (Vieira, 2001b, c, 2002). These principles counteract the dominant practices described above and represent a practical theory in progress, clearly influenced by past and current developments in the fields of learner autonomy and reflective teacher education. However, the principles have also emerged from working with

Table 12.1 Action principles in a common framework for learner and teacher development

Action principles to promote autonomous learner development	*Action principles to promote reflective teacher development*
Reflection: Developing language/ learning awareness	*Developing a critical understanding of language education*, with a particular emphasis on a pedagogy for autonomy in the school context: assumptions, facilitating conditions, constraints, methodological approaches, research.
• Developing awareness of language (formal and pragmatic properties; sociocultural dimension).	
• Developing awareness of learning (sense of agency; attitudes, representations, beliefs; preferences and styles; aims and priorities; strategies: cognitive, metacognitive, strategic, socio-affective; tasks: focus, purpose, rationale, demands; instructional/ didactic process: objectives, activities, materials, evaluation, roles, ...).	*Inquiring into theories, practices and contexts* as a necessary condition for self-regulated thought and action. *Developing action (research) plans* whereby the 'paralysing' effect of situational constraints is counteracted, the limits on freedom are challenged, and 'spaces for manoeuvre' are explored.
Experimentation: Experiencing learning strategies	*Taking the initiative and making decisions*, thus realising the importance of making choices and
• Discovering and trying out learning strategies (in class and outside class).	assuming responsibility, taking risks and being creative, managing tensions and dilemmas, dealing with ambiguity and uncertainty, negotiating and compromising.

Table 12.1 (cont'd)

Action principles to promote autonomous learner development	Action principles to promote reflective teacher development
• Exploring resource materials (pedagogical and non-pedagogical). *Regulation*: Regulating learning experiences • Identifying learning problems or needs. • Setting learning goals. • Planning learning strategies. • Monitoring/evaluating attitudes, representations, beliefs, strategic knowledge and ability. • Assessing learning outcomes and progress. • Evaluating the instructional/ didactic process. *Negotiation*: Co-constructing learning experiences • Working in collaboration (with peers and the teacher). • Taking the initiative, choosing and deciding.	*Engaging in contingent communication with others*, within an atmosphere of mutual trust and respect, thus reducing asymmetries and democratising relationships. *Engaging in self-/co-evaluation of professional development processes and outcomes*, according to negotiated, context-sensitive criteria that are both locally/personally relevant and socially significant. *Disseminating experiences and confronting one's voice with other voices within the professional community*, so as to contribute to the emergence of collective knowledge, language and practice.

teachers within and beyond the GT-PA, through a combination of two strategies – 'theorising from practice' (reflection upon action) and 'authentication through practice' (action upon reflection) – in a process where ideas are developed, worked through and validated within practice.

The pedagogical principles of reflection, experimentation, regulation and negotiation (Table 12.1) indicate major learner roles that bring the language learner closer to the learning content and process, thus providing criteria for regulating the quality of instructional tasks. Action principles for the promotion of reflective teacher development include criticality, inquiry, managing constraints, initiative and decision-making, communication with others, self-/co-evaluation and dissemination of experiences (Table 12.1). A view of teaching as technical rationality is rejected in favour of a view of teaching as "a form of debate or struggle over important ideas and ideals" (Smyth, 1997: 1102).

Although there is a consensus within GT-PA about the value of the above principles, particular tasks always involve some kind of prioritisation, selection and adaptation to unique educational settings. One of these settings is the supervision of trainees, within an ongoing institutional project in which my colleagues and I try to foster the interplay of reflective teaching and learner-centred pedagogy through supported teacher-initiated action research (see Moreira et al., 1999). This is conceived as a way to counteract prevalent supervisory practices that tend to reproduce the dominant culture of schooling. The example presented below derives from this project and involves two members of the GT-PA as supervisors of a group of four trainees in a local secondary school. The reason for choosing this case as an example is that it illustrates how teaching, teacher education and pedagogical inquiry can work in synchrony, and shows how the principles that have guided the GT-PA also orient our work with beginning teachers, thereby building bridges between in-service and pre-service teacher development contexts.

An example: analysing and developing materials to foster learner (and teacher) autonomy

Although learner autonomy is a goal of the national syllabus for EFL teaching, didactic proposals in published materials are still very limited. Course books are compulsory, but they are chosen at the local level and teachers may supplement them when necessary, provided that they are aware of insufficiencies and know-how to deal with these. The report that follows shows how informed analysis and design of learning materials can be a powerful way to address this constraint on learner autonomy.

The experience reported on below involved two members of the GT-PA – Maria Alfredo Moreira and Paula Ferreira – in their role as supervisors of a group of four EFL trainees – Sandra, Susana, Alzira and Lurdes – in a local secondary school, in 1999–2000. During the practicum, trainees are supervised by a university teacher and a school teacher. My colleague Maria Alfredo (the university supervisor) and Paula (the school supervisor) were supposed to help this group of trainees develop small-scale action research projects in EFL classes. As mentioned above, action research is a supervisory/teacher development strategy we have used (since 1995) in order to promote reflective teaching towards learner-centred pedagogy. The topic chosen by this group was 'pedagogy for autonomy', which is a major content area of an ELT Methodology Course we run in the fourth year of the undergraduate programme. In fact, most of our students enter their practicum endorsing a view of their role which is favourable to the development of learner

autonomy, as becomes evident in their answers to an initial questionnaire about why they want to be teachers. In one of the questions,
we ask them to write a 'maxim' that sums up their professional stance.
Here is what these four prospective teachers wrote in October 1999
(translated from the original Portuguese):

> To teach is to be continuously learning with others. (Sandra)
> To be a teacher is to be able to learn daily, with a spirit of openness,
> critical reflection and construction. (Susana)
> As a teacher, I am attentive to the students' needs and interests,
> always keeping in mind that I will be able to make things better each
> time. (Alzira)
> Being a reflective teacher and educating autonomous learners. (Lurdes)

However, the shock of reality and the inability to address constraints
often inhibit trainees from exploring their intentions in practice.
The role of supervisors as 'diagnosers' of situational constraints and
'counsellors' in regard to alternative practices is therefore crucial in
determining a transformative rather than a conformist stance towards
the profession. In a joint paper presented at the GT-PA Conference,
Maria Alfredo and Paula described the problem that gave origin to the
experience reported here:

> As supervisors of that group of teachers [...], the authors diagnosed
> some problems with the course book materials being used, namely an
> overwhelming focus on the development of grammatical compe-
> tence (disregarding other competences) and a strong structural
> approach to language teaching, which tended to limit both teaching
> and learning approaches. (Moreira and Ferreira, 2002: 110)

The perceived gap between the prescribed approach and the trainees'
intention to develop learner autonomy motivated the supervisors to
develop two descriptive instruments that could help the trainees deal
with this gap: the 'Grid for the Analysis of Foreign Language Learning
Tasks' and the 'Observation Schedule for the Implementation of Foreign
Language Learning Tasks' presented in Appendixes 1 and 2, respectively.
Their use was intended to foster experience and reflection with regard to
quality criteria for learning materials and tasks:

> The grid should integrate some criteria regarded as essential for the
> promotion of learner-centred learning towards the development of

learner autonomy. It should also make explicit some critical criteria for implementing a communicative approach to language learning, for the course books did not take this into account either. The grid was then tested by the student teachers, who initially used it to analyse and evaluate the tasks in the course book or other materials in use, and later to improve the tasks, by adding, deleting or reformulating activities. An observation schedule was designed to help us reflect on the implementation of the approach. [...] Both the grid [...] and the observation schedule feature eight criteria that integrate a communicative approach and a pedagogy for autonomy: Focus, Purpose, Explicitness, Contextualization, Motivation, Interaction, Self-direction, and Monitoring. When filling in the grid, the user should point out the presence or absence of these criteria. (ibid.)

The path taken was, then, then from task analysis (inquiry 'about/ for' the context) to task design and experimentation (inquiry 'in' the context), that is, from 'understanding' to 'transforming' pedagogy. This is a summary of the supervisors' definitions of the eight criteria, which were largely based on previous work of the GT-PA on course book analysis:

Focus: communicative competence (CC) and/or learning competence (LC), in their various sub-components (linguistic, sociolinguistic, discourse, strategic, interpersonal, intrapersonal, etc.).

Purpose: reflection and/or practice (regarding language and/or learning strategies).

Explicitness: of purpose and/or task demands (what does the learner learn, how should the task be carried out in order to fulfil its purpose, and what strategies and resource materials should be used?).

Contextualisation: 'authenticity' of communication and/or learning process (whether the task responds to the learner's personal characteristics, interests and needs; whether it promotes relevant learning according to his/her level, age, sociocultural background; whether it involves capacities that can be transferred to other learning situations).

Motivation: expected learner willingness and readiness to carry out the task (whether it allows for the expression of opinions, ideas, feelings and personal experiences, whether it provides enjoyment and pleasure, whether it is appropriate to learners' level of achievement).

Interaction: cooperation and peer support (student–student inter-action) or the sharing of information/ideas with the teacher (student–teacher interaction).

Self-direction: learner choice, initiative or decision (for example, regarding content, way of implementing the task, use of other resource materials, learning strategies).

Monitoring: learner self-assessment (of attitudes, representations, knowledge, strategies, progress and outcomes), self-/co-correction, or assessment of the didactic process (aims, activities, materials, evaluation, roles). (Moreira and Ferreira, 2002: 111, 113)

In their report to the 2001 GT-PA conference, the two supervisors indi-cated how the use of the grid and observation schedule had enabled trainees to develop a series of tasks whereby the students' learning com-petence was promoted through raising their awareness of what is involved in the learning process and providing opportunities for trying out and monitoring learning strategies, including self-evaluation and evaluation of the instructional process. Some of the materials produced by this group of trainees were presented by them at the same Conference and published in *Cadernos* 2 (Pereira et al., 2001).

The outcome of the whole experience is synthesised by the super-visors as follows:

Both instruments proved valuable for our teacher development pur-poses: by requiring the student teachers to develop a more critical view of material in and beyond the course book, these instruments helped promote their autonomy as language teachers. They became increasingly more capable of designing their own material to fit their own pedagogical purposes.

In their EFL methodology classes before the teaching practice year, the student teachers had learnt the theory for developing a pedagogy for autonomy, had seen some sample materials, and were even will-ing to try out the approach. By making them analyse and reflect upon language learning tasks, the material we developed helped them con-ceptualize and implement it, with a growing sense of self-direction and self-fulfilment. (Moreira and Ferreira, 2002: 115)

Although, as pointed out by the supervisors, these trainees were ini-tially willing to promote learner autonomy on the basis of former train-ing, it was only through supported experience and reflection guided by theoretical and ethical assumptions that they were able to validate their belief in autonomy as a pedagogical goal. This kind of evolution from 'espoused beliefs' to 'belief-informed action' is well documented in their research journals, especially in final evaluation records where they reflect about the impact of their action research project upon themselves and their students. To illustrate the potential value of helping beginning teachers develop reflective practice towards learner-centredness, particularly in terms of how it may encourage the personal construction of what Holliday (1994: 164) describes as a 'culture-sensitive' and 'becoming-appropriate' methodology, I will quote from one of the trainees' reports (translated from the original Portuguese):

> At the beginning of the year I was very concerned about my own position in the English classes. I was very self-centred, trying to understand and improve what I was doing. With this project, the focus of my action changed. Whereas initially I was centred on me and my problems, I gradually started to centre my attention on the students and on how to help them solve their difficulties. This change of focus brought about many other changes. Practices and materials now emerged from the classroom context, that is, from perceived needs and motivations.

> This new critical stance leads to a continuous process of questioning and inquiring into knowledge and experience. Now it is not enough to apply a given strategy. It is necessary to apply it, question its effectiveness, and make changes if needed. In other words, it is necessary to be attentive before, during and after the lesson. Practice is no longer routine-based and definite. The task of being a teacher became more difficult.

> [...]

> The project allowed me to establish an integral relationship between theory and practice. I can now see that the barriers between them are practically non-existent, as I resort to theory to reformulate practice and vice-versa.

> The project expanded my perspectives as a teacher. Today, instead of paying attention only to the final product, I am also attentive to processes. The quality of the process influences the final product a lot, as I could confirm several times.

> Questioning, inquiry, awareness and autonomy are now fundamental attitudes in my stance towards teaching. Today I assume a much

more intervening position, where re-adjustments to contexts are permanent. (Lurdes, final entry in action research journal, June 2000)

As is evident from this quotation, the experiences described in Moreira and Ferreira (2002) helped the student-teachers reconstruct their professional theories and practices by assuming a critical position towards conventional pedagogy. For experienced professionals like Maria Alfredo and Paula, also, the experiences they describe represented an invaluable opportunity to develop their expertise through collaborative inquiry into the social significance of idea(l)s in local contexts of practice.

On the feasibility of collaborative inquiry into pedagogy for autonomy

Although educational discourses and policies in Portugal appear to encourage the development of autonomous learning, reflective teacher education and even school–university partnerships, there is still a long way to go before dominant educational practices address these goals. How, then, does our work take into account sociocultural constraints on learner autonomy? In sum, by (i) valuing school–university collaboration in the reconstruction of pedagogical knowledge and action, (ii) recognising that teachers play a crucial role in pedagogical understandings and innovation, and (iii) adopting a transformative orientation towards professional contexts. However, obstacles and limitations cannot be ignored.

Most obstacles can be summed up as involving 'institutional resistance' to change. In schools, this is quite evident in the difficulties experienced by GT-PA teachers when they try to share their work with others, look for partners to join them, or propose structural changes that challenge established routines. At the university, resistance is less visible but still present when our work is ignored by peers or dismissed as unscientific. A good example is the fact that the Research Centre from which we receive a small subsidy does not acknowledge our publication, *Cadernos*, as a 'research product' in the yearly evaluation of the Centre's research activity. In a nutshell, 'pedagogical relevance' seems to be considered incompatible with 'scientific rigour'. To adopt Schön's (1987: 3) topographical metaphor of professional practice, where "there is a high, hard ground overlooking a swamp", we might say that a lot of pedagogical inquiry has been operating on the high ground according to "prevailing standards of rigor", refusing to "descend to the swamp of important problems and nonrigorous inquiry" (ibid.). When this descent is attempted through the creation of a higher degree of intimacy between research and teaching, and between researchers and teachers, suspicions emerge as to the scientific status of their work.

Institutional resistance decreases the possibility for sustained change, which is a major limitation of our work. Innovation has been mostly local, and dissemination has been our main strategy for moving in a more collective direction. There are a few situations where GT-PA members have managed to involve large sectors of their school communities in collective projects supported by the school administration. However, we feel that there is a long way to go, and we are not sure about how to achieve wider change in a manageable and sustainable way. One cannot overlook the fact that groups like ours run the risk of isolating themselves (and their members) from their contexts of origin, namely the schools where participants come from. Our desire to be a learning community is cherished, and many teachers state that the main reason they join us is the need to meet people with whom they can share their concerns and interests freely, without feeling that they are looked upon with mistrust, condescension or envy. This socio-affective aspect has certainly contributed to group cohesion, but it should not prevent us from realising that if schools themselves functioned better as 'learning organizations', groups like the GT-PA might have a more prominent role in assisting school development through dissemination and joint projects.

Other limitations are inherent to our effort to accommodate diversity within a common direction. Firstly, methodological flexibility allows for different degrees of structure and rigour, and as some experiences are evaluated in very fuzzy ways, it becomes difficult to assess their outcomes. Secondly, strategies have to be developed to avoid a fragmented view of our work, as it involves different contexts and foci of inquiry. In my role as coordinator, I have prepared syntheses of studies and experiences (see Vieira, 2001c), but time constraints prevent me from doing this as often as seems necessary. Diversity also raises the need for reviews whose aim would be to have a clearer idea of how studies and experiences account for similar or different phenomena, with similar or different outcomes. This is especially difficult given a generalized resistance to writing extensive reports, and also because of time constraints. Although a certain amount of lack of structure can be beneficial in projects with no time limit like this one, I sometimes feel that more structure would avoid loose ends and lost possibilities, but that would require more meetings and more commitment from participants than has been possible. Finally, the heterogeneity of the group in terms of background knowledge and expertise in the field of learner autonomy may induce passive attitudes and lack of confidence to take initiatives on the part of less experienced teachers. Creating a relaxed atmosphere and encouraging the exchange of experiences among peers have been crucial ways to foster collegiality, but one still feels sometimes that it is difficult to develop collaborative relationships among and with teachers, even when there is a concern with democratising the construction of pedagogical knowledge, with implications for who decides what matters in educational settings.

In spite of the above constraints, we have learned that school–university partnerships can be valuable when they are grounded in the belief that collaboration will make inquiry relevant to both parties, on behalf of learner development. Emerging from our experience, the action principles below have facilitated the process of collaborative inquiry with regard to scope, direction, development, validity, and dissemination, and they may be equally relevant in other contexts:

- Developing and exploring, through action and dialogic reflection, principles that promote an *integral relationship of teacher and learner development processes* (Table 12.1);
- Working from a *negotiated agenda* that accommodates the participants' diverse background knowledge and experience in complementary ways, within *a shared view of education* as a transformative, empowering process;
- Allowing for *a variety of tasks and roles* within a research–learning continuum, with *different gains for different people*;
- Allowing for *flexibility* at the levels of working paces, methodologies, discourse, and types of emerging knowledge (empirical propositions, conceptual schemata, practical proposals, ethical and moral considerations, etc.);
- Evaluating experience according to criteria that attest to its *local relevance and social significance*;
- Encouraging *dissemination by participants*, in various ways and to various audiences, through documented descriptions that encourage and facilitate transferability of practices to similar contexts.

Collaborative inquiry undertaken within the GT-PA has promoted a shared understanding of conditions that hamper and facilitate learner autonomy, enabling us to explore possibilities that challenge dominant pedagogical practices. A sense of direction (within a plurality of voices) and pedagogical hope are perhaps the most important gains of our work, and also major sources of sustained motivation, energy, joy and inspiration to struggle for education that is (more) liberating.

Final words

As a teacher educator and researcher of pedagogy, I have learned many lessons from working with teachers, as I hope I have made clear throughout this text. If I wanted to sum them up in a couple of statements, this is what I might say: I have learned to be wary of educational discourses that are built on the margin of teachers' and students' experience, just as I have learned to trust discourses that are built upon the exploration and validation of ideals through collaborative inquiry with teachers, with reference to their working contexts; I have also learned the value of addressing constraints as a way to counteract dominant educational practices and recover hope in education; and I have learned that innovative local experiences may reveal plausible conditions of possibility that can inspire people in other contexts, especially because they highlight the fact that change needs to be a culture-sensitive experience; finally, I have learned that what emancipates us as professionals is not to do as we would like, but rather to narrow the distance between that and what is feasible at a given moment of our professional history.

Acknowledgement

I wish to thank the reviewers of the first version of this chapter – María de los Angeles Clemente, David Palfreyman and Richard Smith – for having stimulated me to increase the 'trustworthiness' of my discourse and for raising my awareness of how difficult it is to write from experience without becoming too detached from it, especially for an academic like myself.

Reflection/discussion questions

1. How do educational discourses and practices in your context encourage the development of learner autonomy? What constraints have to be faced at the levels of schooling, teacher education and pedagogical inquiry?

2. How do you see the integration of teacher and learner development into a common framework for developing pedagogy for autonomy in school contexts? In what ways could the action principles presented in Table 12.1 apply in your working context?
3. How do you feel about collaborative inquiry involving school teachers and academic researchers/teacher educators in efforts to understand and transform pedagogy? In what ways might the action principles for collaborative inquiry presented just before the "Final words" above apply in your working context?

Appendix 12.1: Grid for the analysis of foreign language learning tasks

Teacher: _____ Material: _____ SchoolYear: _____

Indicate the presence (√) or absence (X) of the criteria

Task	Focus		Purpose		Explicitness		Context-ualization	Motiv-ation	Interaction		Self-direction	Monitoring		Notes
	CC	LC	Reflec-tion	Practice	Purpose	Task demands			St-St	St-T		CC	LC	
1.														
2.														
3.														
4.														

Note: the number of rows depends on the number of tasks.

Appendix 12.2: Observation schedule for the implementation of foreign language learning tasks

OBSERVING FL LEARNING TASKS		
Teacher:_____ Date:_____ Observer: _____		
Scale (circle the relevant option):		
√ – Criterion present　　　　　　**X** – Criterion absent		
CRITERIA	**SCALE**	**NOTES**
• The task focuses on the development of communicative competence	√ **X**	
• The task focuses on the development of learning competence	√ **X**	
• The task aims at reflecting on learning the language / learning to learn the language	√ **X**	
• The task aims at practising the language/ learning to learn the language	√ **X**	
• The pedagogical purpose of the task is explicit for the learner	√ **X**	
• The task demands are explicit for the learner	√ **X**	
• The task is 'authentic' from both a communicative and a learning point of view	√ **X**	
• The task motivates the learner	√ **X**	
• The task promotes collaboration among learners	√ **X**	
• The task promotes collaboration with the teacher	√ **X**	
• The task allows the learners to take initiatives and make decisions	√ **X**	
• The task involves the learner in self-assessment	√ **X**	

Note: the schedule is replicated for each task observed.

13

Asserting Our Culture: Teacher Autonomy from a Feminist Perspective

Naoko Aoki with Yukiyo Hamakawa

Introduction

Reports of teacher education practice specifically focused on learner autonomy have only recently started appearing in publication in any substantial number (for example, Huttunen, 1997; Riley, 1997; Serrano-Sampedro, 1997; Moreira, Vieira and Marques, 1999; Vieira, 1999a, 2000; Thavenius, 1999; Lamb, 2000; McGrath, 2000). Many of these reports share the view that learner autonomy and teacher autonomy are two sides of the same coin and reflect the current trend in second language teacher education which emphasizes the value of reflection in teacher development and the role action research can play in stimulating reflection. Teacher autonomy, however, is a multifaceted concept (Aoki, 2002a) and teacher development is a long, complex process which involves teachers' personal as well as professional lives (Butt et al., 1992; Knowles and Cole, 1994). The schematic understanding, underlying much literature on teacher development, that action research stimulates reflection which helps teacher autonomy to develop is too simplistic a view. Particularly problematic is its assumed gender neutrality. In this chapter I shall discuss how the gender-blind nature of assumptions about reflective teacher education and action research which are widely accepted among second language teacher educators can undermine teacher autonomy as freedom; and I share a story of struggle for professional and personal autonomy by a novice female Japanese as a second language (JSL) teacher whom I worked with. In concluding I shall claim that asserting feminist values in teacher education can support developing teacher autonomy. Although I shall develop my argument from a feminist perspective, I do not claim that the argument applies to all women and no men. I do not endorse any essentialist arguments, whether they are about a culture of a nation or of an ethnic group or of a social group defined by such features as profession and gender. The title of this chapter, "Asserting Our Culture", should be understood as female teachers asserting their own culture, but it does not imply that all female teachers share one and the same culture, nor do I intend it to exclude all male counterparts.

Reflection and alternative ways of knowing

Schön (1983), whose work has been instrumental in fostering the current interest in reflective practice in second language teacher education, argues that the dominant positivist epistemology of practice is unable to deal with the uncertainty, complexity, instability, uniqueness and value conflict which professionals face in their daily practice. Professional practice is, rather, largely based on tacit knowledge, or knowing-in-action; and practitioners reflect on their tacit knowledge mostly when they encounter some surprise, be it an unwanted result or an unexpected success. Schön calls this latter behaviour reflection-in-action. The recognition of reflection-in-action frees practitioners from the traditional hierarchy in the academy where 'basic science' comes at the top, 'applied science' in the middle, and "concrete problem solving" (p. 24) at the bottom. In contexts where academic theorists are mostly men and practicing professionals are predominantly women, of which the field of teaching JSL in Japan is an instance,[1] the idea of reflective practice appears to have the potential to sponsor female practitioners' autonomy as freedom from the patriarchal hegemony of academism. In reality, though, the idea of reflective practice seems to have been hijacked by academic theorists as the popularity of the term has increased. Goodman (1992: 184), writing about pre-service teacher education in North America, observes that "professors define exactly what reflection means by stipulating different 'levels' of it that often reflect masculine concepts of cognition such as the ability to 'think logically', then we 'test' to see what level pre-service teachers 'are at' when they enter and leave a given program." Equating reflection with logical thinking excludes other types of knowing. Teachers' practical knowledge and women's ways of knowing most often fall into these unacknowledged types.

In the field of second language teacher education Wallace (1991) was the first to devote an entire volume to teachers' reflective practice.

The reflective model, Wallace contends, can integrate in teachers' practical competence knowledge received from academic disciplines and knowledge gained through experience, thus enabling teachers to update their expertise according to changes in the field and their environment. This view has been widely accepted by second language teacher educators (Richards and Lockhart, 1994; Roberts, 1998; Trappes-Lomax and McGrath, 1999). However, reference to the form of teachers' practical knowledge and women's ways of knowing is mostly absent from second language teacher education literature.

One type of knowing which was seldom referred to in the second language teacher education literature until recently is narrative knowing. Bruner (1986) recognizes two modes of cognition: paradigmatic and narrative. The paradigmatic mode of knowing uses a formal mathematical system of description and explanation. It attempts to categorize particulars and establish relationships among the categories in order to extract general propositions. In other words, it is the mode in which logical thinking takes place. The narrative mode operates in a completely different way. It deals with particulars and configures human actions and events into a believable story. Whereas a cause–effect relationship in the paradigmatic mode is derived by logical argument, the concept of cause in the narrative mode is based on a likely connection between two events. Schön (1991) notes the narrative nature common to case reports of reflective practice from a variety of fields; and in fact teachers' knowledge is mostly narrative embedded in context (Carter, 1993; Clandinin and Connelly, 2000; Johnson and Golombek, 2002). By telling and retelling stories teachers make sense of their experience and reshape their knowledge about their work and about themselves as teachers. This is no less a form of reflection than logical thinking is.

Another type of knowing that is missing from most gender-neutral teacher education literature is connected knowing. Connected knowing is one of the types of knowing identified by Belenky et al. (1986) among a large number of women they interviewed. The book has not been free of criticism and I myself do not entirely agree with the authors, but the concept of connected knowing remains a valuable tool for thinking about problems women face in education. Ruddick (1996: 261–2) summarizes the characteristics of connected knowing as follows:

> Knowing is not separated from feeling; emotion is not only a spur but often a test of knowledge. Knowers attend to particulars – particular persons, relationships, or objects; [...] Knowing involves a capacity to appreciate, subtly and accurately, that is as productive of truth and

knowledge as the ability to criticize. [...] Knowers present their evidence and construct understandings through contextual and open-ended narratives [....]. Knowers take disagreement as an occasion for collaborative deliberation and communication rather than for debate.

Connected knowers[2] do not enjoy or value arguing, attacking, and defending positions (ibid.), which is likely to make them vulnerable to criticisms from (often male) separate knowers who have recourse to impersonal logic and objectivity in their debates. Separate knowers can silence connected knowers and they often do. Some women may object, as Ruddick's students did, that "appeals to connectedness and relationships had been used to inhibit them, to 'keep them home'" (p. 259). I would not disagree with them. But teaching is not only helping learners to construct their own knowledge of subject matter, but also a moral act motivated by longing for caring (Noddings, 1984). A teacher needs to go inside a learner's mind and see the world from his/her perspective in order to understand and care about him/her. I quite agree with Ruddick (1996: 267) when she writes that "I evaluate ways of knowing and the knowledge they produce in 'the light' of the good to which they lead and that they yield." The value of connected knowing in the teaching profession must be recognized. This means that connected knowers should not be discouraged and separate knowers should be encouraged to develop a capacity for connected knowing.

A regime of pedagogy

Teacher educators tend to take it for granted that teachers should articulate the content of their reflection and share it with their peers and teacher educators. Richert (1992: 190), for example, claims that "[t]eachers who talk about what they do and why are able to know what they do and why, and to question themselves as well" and that novice teachers need to be drawn into conversations within themselves and with others in speaking and in writing about their points of view. Although I do not deny the role language plays in our thinking and the facilitating function of talking and being heard, Richert's position seems to overlook some issues related with voice. One such issue is power in a classroom. Ellsworth's (1992: 105) rather famous claim goes: "What they/we say, to whom, in what context, depending on the energy they/we have for the struggle on a particular day, is the result of conscious and unconscious assessments of the power relations and safety of the situation." Teacher educators may try hard to create a warm caring atmosphere in their classroom, but it is after all individual teachers (or student teachers) who judge the security level of the group for themselves. To make sharing a requirement runs the risk of reflective pedagogy becoming a regime (Gore, 1993).

Another issue is that women often separate themselves from their feelings and knowledge gained through experience in the process of growing up (Brown and Gilligan, 1992). This is a persistent problem which education seldom addresses. So some teachers may need to reclaim their authentic voice before sharing their reflection with others. Teacher educators have to facilitate the process if they are to encourage reflection, but this is a difficult task which sometimes has to be left with specialists. Perhaps the most important thing for teacher educators is to try to understand why particular teachers or student teachers are experiencing difficulty with sharing their reflection, rather than to draw them into a conversation.

Problems with action research

The popularity of reflective practice in second language education is linked to that of action research. Wallace (1998: 4), for example, defines action research as "a way of reflecting on your teaching [...] by systematically collecting data on your everyday practice and analysing it in order to come to some decisions about what your future practice should be". However, action research is only one of many ways to stimulate reflection (Bailey et al., 2001). Teacher educators should recognize the drawbacks as well as the merits of action research, and consider when it is appropriate to encourage teachers to engage in it. Unselectively advocating action research runs the risk of creating another regime.

From a feminist point of view, arguably the biggest problem with promoting action research among teachers is that many teachers are simply too busy to carry out even small-scale action research following the procedure suggested in books like Wallace's. 86.7 per cent of JSL teachers teaching in Japan are part-timers and volunteers, 78.9 per cent of whom are women (Bunkacho Bunkabu Kokugoka, 1998).[3] Part-time teachers often teach at several different schools scattered across a city. Female teachers are also often primary care-givers at home. In her critique of gender neutrality in staff development practice, Robertson (1992: 48) claims:

> Perhaps the greatest injustice inherent in using an 'activity index' as a teacher evaluation tool is its denial and dismissal of the multiple

roles of contemporary women. [...] No one who has held a role greater than 'helper' in the complex exercise of family management could see failure to sign up for voluntary week-end in-service or a reluctance to attend after-hours staff meetings as evidence of inactivity, or of personality deviation. To be assumed to be uninterested rather than overextended is grossly unfair.

Replacing 'activity index' with 'action research' in the above quotation would make Robertson's argument hold true in our current situation where collaborative action research seems to be regarded as the ideal. Teachers' knowledge, however, develops as they teach, in many cases without formally collecting any data. The assumption that teachers' knowledge does not develop without formally collecting data or that the knowledge thus developed is inferior to that derived from action research is unjust.

The second problem is that most literature on action research in second language teacher education is in fact ambivalent in its stance towards the positivist paradigm. Although action research is meant to be an alternative to traditional research, the procedure which proponents of action research often recommend for data collection, analysis and presentation is very much positivist. This tendency is observed not only in second language teacher education but also in other fields. Carr (1995) argues that the nineteenth-century positivists developed the methodological strategies of systematically collecting data and analysing them in order to prevent ideology intruding upon social life, but that positivism has since assumed "a central ideological role in maintaining dominant forms of social life" (p. 105). He claims that action researchers' willingness to accept the methodological strategies designed to serve the positivists' original intention to exclude ideology from research can be attributed to their false assumption that "there can be a philosophically uncontested, ahistorical concept of 'research'" (p. 106). Indeed the traditional concept of 'research' has developed in the male-dominated academy with little room for women's voice. Positivistic action research can undermine teachers' knowledge (which is often narrative and connected) and so become a serious constraint on teacher autonomy.

A further problem with action research is that many of the research topic examples offered in the literature focus on the solution of classroom problems. Zeichner (1994) claims that focusing on classroom problems precludes teachers' attention from being directed towards structural problems; however, in my experience of working with JSL teachers, teachers are often very aware of such problems. A real danger of focusing on classroom problems seems to be, rather, that it sends a message to teachers that they are supposed to solve all problems – which is, of course, an impossible task. I suspect that teachers' prevailing pessimism that there is nothing they can do about structural problems comes from this unreasonable expectation. Teacher education should focus more on teachers' successes, small as they may be. A success, as well as a problem, can trigger reflection. Celebrating successes could nurture realistic, constructive optimism among teachers.

Yukiyo's story

Yukiyo participated in a teacher conversation group (Clark, 2001) which I organized as a course in a Japanese as a second language teacher education programme. In this course each of the students wrote a story of a memorable event in their teaching or learning experience. During the class we brainstormed themes in each story and discussed them. The discussion often involved more stories from other members of the group, but those students who preferred a paradigmatic style of talk participated in the conversation with their own style. The ground rules we agreed on were: do not interpret or make judgmental comments on the story; do not ask questions about the written story; do not criticize other members' views. As a facilitator I tried to prevent any possibly harmful development and keep our talk on track. I also tried to provide alternative views and frames which might broaden the students' perspectives and facilitate reinterpretation and/or reorganization of their own experience. After each class meeting the students wrote a reflection on the discussion and these written reflections were e-mailed to the rest of the members before the next class meeting. The rationales I originally had in mind in choosing the procedure described here were not necessarily derived from feminist thinking. For a detailed description of the course, readers are referred to Aoki (2002b).

The following story is based on Yukiyo's written feedback (handed in at the end of the course), a three-hour interview in which she elaborated on the feedback, and an e-mail message to supplement the interview. At the time of the interview Yukiyo had just finished her MA studies and was about to leave for Thailand to teach there. I was her supervisor at the graduate school and had known her for a little over two years. The original data is in Japanese and I have translated the quotations in the story into English.

Yukiyo was very good at English in junior high school, which made her want an 'international' career. So she went to a senior high school which offered an international studies programme. Many of her classmates had lived abroad or were from a family of international marriage. Yukiyo's English was not as good as those classmates' English and it did not improve as much as she had hoped, but English remained her favourite subject. The inspiration to teach Japanese in the future came from two different sources. One was a native speaker teacher of German, which Yukiyo chose as her second foreign language. She realized that teaching one's language to foreigners could be a career. The other source was an exchange student from Ecuador whom Yukiyo made friends with. She had difficulty in understanding this student's feelings, but she suspected that he might be lonely and wanted to take care of him. So she was very glad to hear him say Yukiyo had been the kindest to him when he was returning to Ecuador. Teaching JSL in Japan seemed to her to be a very good option. It was an 'international' career, but she would not have to live abroad, which her parents would never allow. So she planned to go to a university which offered a JSL teacher preparation programme. She was not able to make it to the university of her first choice and ended up in one which only offered JSL-related courses as a minor subject. Yukiyo looked for learners by placing classified ads in free papers and magazines for foreigners and started teaching on a one-to-one basis. This seems to have been a satisfying experience. She said:

(Interview)
Yukiyo: I was lucky to start with one-to-one lessons. Seeing just one person from start to finish makes you understand their feelings. They may not make dramatic progress, but you are delighted when they say something they weren't able to say in a previous lesson or when they make a phone call after three months. You don't only see the person as a learner, but other aspects too. That was a merit of starting with one-to-one lessons. I sometimes feel those people who started teaching in a school are very much teachers. I wonder if they should try some other part-time jobs [one-to-one lessons] too. The experience was so helpful for me that I [would like to] impose it on others.

Yukiyo wrote a BA dissertation based on her experience of tutoring an American student on campus, spent a year as an auditor of a huge JSL teacher education programme at another university and came to Osaka for her MA studies. Six months later she started teaching part-time at a local language school. She had a difficult entry to the job:

(Written feedback)
I don't enjoy myself so much these days although I can think of a lot of fun things I did if I try hard to remember. Talking about my anxiety and problems about teaching reminded me of the obvious.

If I had a bad-natured class the cause may be with that class; but considering my current situation, my difficulty seems to lie outside the classroom. I'm a teacher. And I'm surrounded by other teachers. I always compare myself with other people with the same attribute. I have little experience. I don't know grammar very well. A couple of my classmates are also teaching at the same school.

Yukiyo attributes her tendency to compare herself with others to her upbringing. She said:

(Interview)
Yukiyo: I was never praised in my childhood. That may be the reason. I feel uncomfortable when I'm praised. I suspect that the person has some [hidden] intention. When a teacher praises me I wonder if they're going to use me for their purpose. And I convince myself it's OK if they use me as long as I can grow at the same time. My family always put the word 'idiot' at the end of what they say to me, like "What are you doing, idiot?". I was raised in such a family. I was never praised and I never am. I've always been put down. So I believe I'm…
Naoko: No good?
Yukiyo: Yeah.
Naoko: I had an impression that you were loved and well taken care of at home.
Yukiyo: Now I know I am. But I didn't think that way till I went to university. I felt my parents didn't take care of me at all and were detached although I knew they'd let me do what I wanted if I insisted. I don't think they respect me. They still tell me indirectly I don't have the ability to do what I want because I have their genes. They are so intent that I start thinking they may be right. I get down in the dumps when I go home.

Yukiyo's self-perception is basically that she is not smart but keeps up with other people by putting in a lot of effort. She probably compares herself with others to check if she is keeping up. She had not been unaware of this tendency, and she had known that such a tendency does not help much. She would actually advise her friends with the same tendency not to worry about others. But talking about her experience in the conversation group led her to another level of understanding that she is insecure in everything and often compares herself with others.

(Interview)
Naoko: You'd thought about it but you'd only been thinking? I don't quite get it. Could you explain the difference between only thinking and understanding?

Yukiyo: Well, what could it be... I might have been able to think in more concrete terms. I've settled in my job to some extent of course. I remained silent in last year's class. So I was able to spend the time only in thinking. But I was determined to talk this year. As I talked I realized everything I talked about was about the same thing. I had many thoughts and feelings and they formed a concrete picture or something like that. I can't tell a story of my experience in an easy-to-follow manner as other students can. I just tell things as they come up in my mind. The order I think of things is the flow of my talk. And bits and pieces gradually form a whole. I think I wrote in one of my reflections or feedback that I'm bad at reflecting on myself. I do have thoughts and feelings but they have evaporated when I try to reflect. Perhaps it's because I don't want to remember. It's easier to forget and start again. So my experiences are scattered somewhere in my memory. I had a chance to talk and those experiences were recovered. That was probably how I came to understand my tendency.

[...]

Naoko: Did it do you any good?

Yukiyo: Good? Good... Well, I even learned talking relieves stress.

Naoko: Even? What does that mean?

Yukiyo: I'd known that. Yeah I'd known that. Talking relieves. Talk to the right person. They'll understand. I learned that. I learned it was true.

Yukiyo is interested in action research, but her inability to reflect becomes an obstacle. She says that she cannot even keep a diary. She can describe what happened. She can write about how she feels as she writes. But she does not remember her feelings and thoughts at the time of events that are being described. She thinks that her inability to reflect also has its origin in her family background.

(Interview)

Yukiyo: Well, I wonder why... Perhaps because I haven't had many chances to talk about my feelings. I never appeal to my parents to understand my feeling. I don't have a means to convince my grandmother that I need to go to Thailand when she tries to stop me. I would choose an option to avoid a clash when there is such a possibility with someone. I have always avoided situations where I have to show my feelings or to talk my thinking through. And there are situations where you'd be looked down on if you honestly talk about your feelings.

Naoko: With 'idiot' at the end?

Yukiyo: Yeah. So I'd choose a way to win rather than to talk about my feelings honestly when I talked with my parents in my childhood. It didn't matter if it was a lie as long as I won. That was the only option. So I've never had a habit of honestly telling what I'm thinking. I never needed to remember my feelings to talk about them later. So they are just scattered all over in my memory.

It seems that Yukiyo's habit of 'putting a lid on her emotions' has been shaped by her family's communication style and has been made use of by Yukiyo as a strategy to avoid pains at the same time. A parallel mechanism seems to have been working in her professional life too. A teacher, for example, attributed Yukiyo's sickness to her supposedly unhealthy diet and equated it to lack of professionalism. Why does being unable to eat raw vegetables have to undermine her quality as a teacher? Yukiyo was deeply hurt. She would not tell her colleagues about her classroom experience even when she was delighted with having shared a feeling with her students. She was afraid that colleagues might say that they had had numerous such experiences. Her shaky confidence would be seriously affected if that happened.

Choosing the right person to talk to seems to be very important for Yukiyo. It has to be someone who she can trust would never position her negatively. The person also has to be a patient, supportive listener.

(Interview)
Yukiyo: I've gradually learned what I can talk about with whom. But even with a member of the class I wouldn't be able to talk in a one-to-one situation. Friends can remain silent without feeling awkward, can't they? So I needed a setting where we're supposed to talk. And they were the people who would understand my situation. They would be patient with my slow pace of talking. They would ask me questions if I left out anything. I don't have a story line, so answering their questions was also a process of putting things together in me.
Naoko: You can tell a story because they ask you questions.
Yukiyo: Yeah.

Apart from an increased understanding of her own tendency to compare herself with other teachers, the deepest insight Yukiyo gained in the conversation group meetings was that her view of classroom events differs between when she is a teacher and when she is a learner.

(Interview)

Yukiyo: I've always thought about it, but the thought has recently become very salient. Listening to other teachers made me feel they were teachers. Yukiyo as a teacher sympathized with them, but Yukiyo as a graduate student didn't. My uneasiness bottled up and gushed out ... The first time I told about my uneasiness their response was very positive. But I thought of the same thing next time I listened to them. I don't think that way when I'm a learner. So I said it because I knew it was OK. Then the next week again. I started worrying about repeating the same comment over and over again. I was relieved when some people started referring to their learning experience too.

Naoko: I thought that was very good. I think it's important to look at things from both angles. Contrasting our teaching experience with learning experience became a kind of trend, didn't it? That was a very good remedy for those of us who have been teaching for a long time. The more you stay in the profession the more you tend to forget about that perspective.

Yukiyo: That was why I started taking English lessons. But becoming a language learner again put me in a dilemma ... I don't know what to say to my students any more. There are so many things I would do if I were a learner, but I don't want my students to do. I confessed to my students I'd cheated in exams on an examination day. Perhaps it was because I talked about my learning experience in the conversation group. It was my favourite class too. Anyway the students were very surprised and said "You're a nice person. You're OK."

Naoko: What was OK?

Yukiyo: I told them I'd thought teachers wouldn't know if I only moved my eyes. All we had to do was collaborate and not tell the teacher. But when I became a teacher I found out a teacher could see the movement of students' eyes. So I knew I'd failed in cheating. I spent part of the time for calling the roll to tell the story. No one cheated on that day. The seating arrangement was certainly a contributing factor, but I felt my story had sunk deep in the students. I felt good about having talked about my experience honestly. ... I would have told my students what they shouldn't do instead of telling them about my personal feelings if I hadn't talked about my learning experiences in the conversation group. So that was probably a change in my teaching.

To the question "How do you think your awarenesses might benefit your future teaching?" in the final feedback form Yukiyo wrote:

(Written feedback)
I want to always remember what I am as a learner and explore what kind of teacher I would enjoy being. I won't make my students do what I don't want to do or couldn't possibly do. And I'll try to find a friend outside my workplace who knows how to accept a teacher's anxiety and grumbling.

Asserting our culture

I started my career in a language classroom and never intended to be an academic. But I landed in the academy as a teacher educator. Since then I have felt pressure from some of my colleagues to be academic. Being academic, they seemed to think, meant being positivist. I did not feel comfortable with the idea, but was not able to pinpoint why for a long time. Perhaps it was because I was not a proper academic, I thought. I learned not to be intimidated over the years, but I was unable to talk back. It was through conversations with Yukiyo and other female teachers that I have come to see that my problem is not just my problem. It is a structural problem deeply rooted in the gender bias in education and science. In this chapter I have presented my understanding of the issue in two modes: paradigmatic/separate and narrative/connected. Yukiyo's story is not just an example to support a theoretical argument. It is as important as, if not more important than theories and it should be read on its own terms. I do not want it to be explained away by theories. So rather than saying anything more about it I shall conclude this chapter by asserting the culture which I think I share with Yukiyo and other female JSL teachers I have worked with.

Yes, we are story tellers. Yes, we are connected knowers. We may not be grammarians. We may not be very good at paradigmatic arguments. But we know teaching is caring. Is there anything more important than that? We may sometimes be silent, but that is part of our struggle for personal autonomy. And we can help each other in our struggle if we so wish. We may not write action research papers or give presentations on our practice, but we do reflect in action. We deserve celebration of our successes in our daily practice.

Asserting our culture can be an important step forward to our teacher autonomy.

Reflection/discussion questions

1. Which mode do you tend to use more: paradigmatic knowing or narrative knowing? And separate knowing or connected knowing? How are your

tendencies reflected in your way of working with your students and reflecting on your experience?
2. Do you ever experience difficulty in sharing your reflection with others? If yes, what makes it difficult? If no, can you think of how you could possibly cause such difficulty to others?
3. How does Yukiyo's story resonate with your experience?

Notes

1. According to a report issued by Cultural Agency of the Japanese Ministry of Education (Bunkacho Bunkabu Kokugoka, 1992), in 1991 72 per cent of the JSL teacher educators in a full-time university position in Japan were men, whereas 72 per cent of the total population of JSL teachers were women. The Cultural Agency no longer counts teachers and teacher educators by gender, and the current demography is unknown, but it is not likely that the figures are very different from the ones in 1991.
2. I am aware that separate and connected knowing can coexist in one person (Clinchy, 1996), but I will use the terms 'separate knower' and 'connected knower' to simplify my argument.
3. The figures are those for 1996. The Cultural Agency of the Japanese Ministry of Education stopped counting JSL teachers by gender after that year.

Postscript: Implications for Language Education

Richard C. Smith

Introduction

As editors, David Palfreyman and I began our invitation to contributors with the following statement of assumptions: "Learner autonomy has become an influential concept in language education in a variety of contexts in recent years, and 'culture' has often been mentioned as a significant variable in connection with its appropriateness and/or practicality." In order to encourage a move beyond the national/ethnic stereotyping of learners which has tended to characterize discussions in this area to date (see Introduction), we made a deliberate attempt to solicit diverse perspectives from a variety of contexts, encouraging contributions relating to "national, institutional, small group or other types of culture". As a starting point, we invited contributors to consider some or all of the following questions: "1. What might learner autonomy mean in the context of a particular culture?; 2. Should/Can learner autonomy be enhanced in that culture?; 3. If so, how?"

In this short postscript I hope to avoid imposing a false unity on the diversity of views contributed by chapter authors. Instead, I want to offer a further springboard for reflection and action by revisiting answers to our initial questions, with a particular focus on possible implications for language teachers and teacher educators. With this focus in mind, I shall consider, in turn, the availability of different "Meanings of autonomy", the implications of "Culture as resource" and "Culture as constraint", and new priorities in asserting "Autonomy as a value".

Meanings of autonomy

One of our initial questions to contributors was "What might learner autonomy mean in the context of a particular culture?" A variety of answers are offered in the preceding chapters, and a clear, though potentially discomforting implication is that autonomy is a multifaceted concept, susceptible to a variety of interpretations. Holec's (1981: 3) definition of learner autonomy as "the ability to take charge of one's own learning" (with which the Introduction to this book begins) retains its validity as a common reference point; however, there are different emphases available regarding what "ability to take charge" entails, and different views, also, of what an individual's "own" learning might mean when learning is viewed as inevitably occurring within the constraints and with the resources of particular sociocultural contexts.

With reference to this first point – that "ability to take charge" can be differentially interpreted – one implication for language educators and teacher educators seems to be that we should resist reduction to, for example, technical *or* psychological *or* political interpretations, instead remaining open to different possible sources of insight for practice (cf. Oxford's plea, in this volume). For purely practical purposes, teachers may need to be aware that different 'versions' of autonomy are in circulation, and learn to identify the biases within them. Such biases might include, for example, over-technical emphases on the power of self-access, distance learning and/or ICT alone to develop autonomy; the limitations of 'psychological' awareness-raising approaches which place responsibility on learners but which fail to acknowledge mechanisms of control *over* learners; and, perhaps, the way 'political' versions can underestimate learners' needs for authoritative information and guidance. Palfreyman's chapter shows that different interpretations of autonomy can circulate within the same 'organizational culture', and it seems that some versions can serve managerial more than learners' or teachers' interests. Indeed, as Holliday indicates most clearly, our own particular professional discourses of autonomy can blind us to actual instances of autonomous learning behaviour. It seems important, then, to keep an open mind and be aware of the strengths of different approaches but critical at the same time of attempts to reduce or co-opt learner autonomy to overly narrow interpretations of what "ability to take charge" entails.

In relation to the second point above – that the contents, processes and meaning of individuals' "own" learning will vary according to sociocultural context – this book offers a particularly rich source of insights for educators. From Riley's overview of differences in concepts of 'self' and 'personhood' across cultures to Toohey and Norton's in-depth investigation of individual struggles to access and make use of local social 'affordances', the overall message seems clear: that individuals' control over their own learning can only be developed in ways which are relevant to *them*, and always in relation to and under the influence of particular background and new cultures. I shall consider these issues from the point of view of practice in the following two sections before returning to the question of 'meanings' of autonomy in the final section.

Culture as resource

Our second and third questions in relation to diverse learning contexts were "Should/Can learner autonomy be enhanced?", and "If so, how?" Accounts in this collection reveal how differently learners can perceive learning for their own purposes in different contexts (cf. Benson, Chik and Lim, and Gao), and show also that the material and psychological resources they draw upon as well as the constraints they face are likely to vary according to setting. Such variations explain why there cannot be a 'one-size-fits-all' approach to developing autonomy across cultures, as is emphasized by several contributors. Learners' background cultures have often been seen as a hindrance to the development of autonomy, a view which has been associated with claims for some contexts that promoting autonomy is a form of Western cultural imperialism (see Introduction). However, the overall message which emerges from this collection is a more positive one – that promoting autonomy can be both viewed as appropriate and made feasible in a wide variety of settings, so long as what students already know and want is seen not as a hindrance but as a major resource.

It seems clear that both the appropriateness and the feasibility of promoting autonomy depend very largely on degree of 'fit' of the teacher's conceptions with those of students (cf. Holliday and Clemente for examples of *lack* of fit). One way for educators to avoid *in*appropriate imposition on students has already been suggested above, that is, being self-critical with regard to one's own professional preconceptions and becoming aware of different interpretations from those one has 'inherited' as a teacher. Holliday suggests this need most strongly as a means to avoid cultural imperialism, while Smith shows how, in practice, teachers can develop new conceptions *through* interventions which set out to investigate and utilize students' existing 'social autonomy'. In this connection, many of the research approaches which have been used by chapter authors to access learner perspectives could be adapted by teachers in their own practice. These include uses of narrative (Benson, Chik and Lim, and Aoki), interview (Gao, Toohey and Norton, Palfreyman, Clemente, Aoki), learner diaries (Toohey and Norton), ethnographic observation (Toohey and Norton, Smith, Fonseka), more structured observation (Vieira), learning logs (Schwienhorst), reflective writing (Smith, Vieira) and conversation groups (Aoki). These approaches to investigation can (as illustrated particularly in the accounts by Benson, Chik and Lim, Smith, Schwienhorst, Vieira and Aoki) serve at the same time as effective means for developing students' ability to reflect on and take greater metacognitive control of their learning.

Teachers might be encouraged to get to know better how their own students can or could learn for themselves, in their own 'spaces of freedom', by accounts such as those by Benson, Chik and Lim, Gao, and Toohey and Norton, which reveal that learners can find value in various resources that teachers themselves may be unaware of. As practitioner accounts in this collection also make clear, developing autonomy in ways which are meaningful to learners may, then, need to involve a dialectic between the investigation and use of existing resources and the development of access to appropriate new resources. Thus, Fonseka shows how, even in a 'resource-poor' environment, building on what *is* available (in this case, including learners' affective needs for enjoyment, and their love of songs and performance) can combine with new input and ideas of autonomy to productive effect. Using learners' ideas for classroom work (what 'fits' with their own priorities), and increasing their control over resource selection can be similarly productive (cf. Smith).

Even in the 'resource-rich' settings of self-access centres and computer-based learning which are often associated with the idea of autonomy, building on and enhancing the creativity students themselves bring might need to be seen as a key priority, and Schwienhorst shows both how learners can be creative within the constraints of a MOO environment and how new tools can be developed in the service of learners, not of the technology. Finally, a particularly successful strategy for developing 'individual' autonomy, as emphasized by authors in several settings (e.g. Smith, Fonseka, Schwienhorst), is collaboration among learners. Here, too, learners' 'background' culture – in this case relating, surely, to universal needs for meaningful relationships with others – can be seen as a usable resource, not a constraint.

Culture as constraint

Despite the above, there is a need to consider seriously constraints on the development and/or exercise of learner autonomy, specifically within educational settings, but also in wider social situations (cf. Toohey and Norton). As several contributors make clear (for example, Smith, Fonseka, Vieira), the promotion of learner autonomy is by no means a generally established goal in practice in their teaching contexts, and, paradoxically, when it does become established in name (or under names such as 'learner independence'), certain professional and institutional conceptions and practices connected with it can be seen to actually hinder its development. Indeed, whether autonomy 'should' and 'can' be promoted in a particular context may depend largely on the conception of autonomy and type of approach adopted (Holliday, Smith).

Interestingly, then, *professional* and *organizational* cultures emerge more strongly than 'national', 'ethnic' or *learner* cultures as significant constraints on the appropriateness and feasibility of promoting autonomy. Needs for critical self-awareness on the part of teachers have already been sufficiently emphasized above, in the light of the fact that teachers' 'ideological baggage' can get in the way of developing students' 'own' autonomy: impositions of power can continue under the cloak of developing learner autonomy, and here we need to be careful not only about culturism (Holliday) but also sexism and other '-isms' and the degree to which our own preferred ways of knowing can have a negative impact on some learners (Aoki). There may also be needs for teachers to develop a critical awareness of the way (discourses within) organizational cultures (Palfreyman) can limit our freedom to act for the benefit of students. There seem to be clear requirements for (teacher education for) 'teacher autonomy' in these respects, and both Vieira and Aoki offer constructive suggestions. Just as one resource for the development of learner autonomy has emerged as collaboration among learners (cf. 'Culture as resource' above), negotiation of meaning and collaboration among colleagues in our own institution and/or between different institutions emerge from both Vieira's and Aoki's accounts as particularly salient. Collaboration can enhance our own autonomy as teachers in the face of constraints, helping us to identify ways to utilise existing opportunities as well as construct new resources for learner development and our development as teachers.

Autonomy as a value

While there are undoubtedly dangers in the imposition on learners of 'culturist' conceptions and approaches connected with autonomy, denying its validity for learners from particular backgrounds may involve equally culturist assumptions (Benson, Chik and Lim; Holliday). Indeed, the voices of learners consulted in the writing of several chapters in this collection remind us that there *are* – from their points of view – serious needs for developing learner autonomy across cultures.

Finally, then, I would like to draw attention to the way a fuller and deeper picture of needs for learner autonomy can be seen to emerge from this collection's emphasis on cases of learning in sociocultural context. The three opening chapters show particularly clearly, it seems to me, the degree and extent to which developing an ability to take charge of learning can be significant from learners' own perspectives – and we should remind ourselves that learner voices are usually excluded from our professional discussions. Clearly, not all language learners in the world are involved or likely to be involved in literally 'crossing borders' in the way Chik and Lim, the Chinese students in Gao's account, and Eva in Toohey and Norton's all are or have been. However, such learners can provide us with deep insights into facets of learner autonomy which may have been neglected in the past (cf. Smith, 1996). Among these, I would stress the implication, firstly, that individual language learners, from 'East', 'West', 'North' or 'South', do have their own voices – have the ability to reflect on and express their own views about what and how they are learning, though these voices are often denied or only partially accessed. When the relatively free expression of these voices is encouraged, as frequently in this collection, we can learn at least the following:

1. Language learning (and the learning of teaching; cf. Aoki's chapter) involves the whole 'person', not just particular (e.g. cognitive) aspects of the person in separation from other (including affective) dimensions;
2. One reason for this is that language learning inevitably involves, indeed in many ways 'is' culture learning, particularly when people are (or are likely to be) 'immersed' in a new culture;
3 This involves transformations of identity which can be stressful as well as liberating; changes of perception regarding one's 'background' culture and newly experienced cultures; and actual changes in relationships with people in these cultures;

4. It is also clear that contexts, as well as identities, are in a state of flux – cultures are changing. New resources for language learning are becoming available in many contexts, within and outside institutions; increasingly, people may move from culture to culture over the course of their lives;

5. In a world of change, learners in various contexts can and do exercise agency and resourcefulness in making use of/creating resources for their own learning purposes, although access to such resources can also be denied;

6. Gaining further control over the above processes (that is, over transformations in emotional relation to language-and-culture learning, overall identity transformation, changing relationships to others and changing opportunities for learning) can be seen as deeply significant by the people concerned, in relation to their lives.

These insights lead me to end with a final suggestion, that in future more emphasis may need to be placed not only on what autonomy *is* for different learners in different settings but also on what it is *for* – that is, what aspects of language learning or more general learning we associate it with and why. Learners' accounts of what is significant for them might recall us to why we became educators in the first place, potentially implying fresh needs for us to see beyond the acquisition of language system and skills in our current conceptions equally of language learning and of learner autonomy. We might decide, for example, to recognize more than we have tended to do in the past the importance of language teaching *as education*, involving ideas of developing 'voice', agency and self-esteem in general, engaging 'the whole person' and – specifically in our field – guiding students across cultural boundaries, intellectually, imaginatively and affectively as well as literally. Within language education, autonomy deserves to be associated more consistently with these important areas, in particular, perhaps – given the contents of this collection and the historical context of its production (cf. Preface) – with the notion of cross-cultural understanding. In reasserting our values as language *educators*, maybe we can become better attuned to the interests and needs of learners – and better able to develop their autonomy in areas of deep significance to us *as well as* them.

References

Aase, L., Fenner, A.-B., Little, D. and Trebbi, T. (2000). *Writing as Cultural Competence: a Study of the Relationship between Mother Tongue and Foreign Language Learning within a Framework of Learner Autonomy*. CLCS Occasional Paper No. 56. Dublin: Trinity College, Centre for Language and Communication Studies.

Allen, N.J. (1985). The category of the person: a reading of Mauss' last essay. In M. Carrithers, S. Collins and S. Lukes (eds), *The Category of the Person*. Cambridge: Cambridge University Press.

Allwright, D. (1990). *Autonomy in Language Pedagogy*. CRILE Working Paper 6. Lancaster: University of Lancaster, Centre for Research in Education.

Amossy, R. (ed.) (1999). *Images de soi dans le discours: La construction de l'ethos*. Lausanne: Delachaux & Niestlé.

Anderson, C. (In process). The dominant discourse in British EFL: the methodological contradictions of a professional culture. Unpublished PhD thesis. Canterbury: Canterbury Christ Church College, Department of Language Studies.

Andrade, A.I. (2002). Reflexões sobre um percurso de didáctica curricular ou questões em volta de uma didáctica da sustentabilidade linguístico-educativa. Paper presented at Encontro da Sociedade Portuguesa de Didáctica da Língua e da Literatura, University of Coimbra, Coimbra.

Angelil-Carter, S. (1997). Second language acquisition of spoken and written English: acquiring the skeptron. *TESOL Quarterly* 31/2: 263–87.

Aoki, N. (2002a). Aspects of teacher autonomy: capacity, freedom, and responsibility. In P. Benson and S. Toogood (eds), *Learner Autonomy 7: Challenges to Research and Practice*. Dublin: Authentik.

Aoki, N. (2002b). Teachers' conversation with partial autobiographies. *Hong Kong Journal of Applied Linguistics* 7/2: 152–68.

Aoki, N. and Smith, R.C. (1999). Learner autonomy in cultural context: the case of Japan. In S. Cotterall and D. Crabbe (eds), *Learner Autonomy in Language Learning: Defining the Field and Effecting Change*. Frankfurt am Main: Lang.

Appel, C. and Mullen, T. (2000). Pedagogical considerations for a web-based tandem language learning environment. *Computers and Education* 34/3–4: 291–308.

Asad, T. (1979). Anthropology and the analysis of ideology. *Man (N.S.)* 14: 607–27.

Atkinson, D. (1997). A critical approach to critical thinking. *TESOL Quarterly* 3/1: 71–94.

Atkinson, D. (1999). TESOL and culture. *TESOL Quarterly* 33/4: 625–54.

Atkinson, D. and Ramanathan, V. (1995). Cultures of writing: an ethnographic comparison of L1 and L2 university writing/language programs. *TESOL Quarterly* 29/3: 539–68.

Au, S.Y. (1988). A critical appraisal of Gardner's socio-psychological theory of second-language (L2) learning. *Language Learning* 38: 75–100.

Auerbach, E.R. (1997). Family literacy. In V. Edwards and D. Corson (eds), *Literacy*. vol. 2, *Encyclopedia of Language and Education*. Dordrecht: Kluwer.

Bacon, S.M. and Finnemann, M.D. (1990). A study of the attitudes, motives, and strategies of university foreign language students and their disposition to authentic oral and written input. *Modern Language Journal* 74/4: 459–73.

Bailey, K.M., Curtis, A. and Nunan, D. (2001). *Pursuing Professional Development: the Self as Source*. Boston: Heinle & Heinle.

Bakhtin, M.M. (1981). *The Dialogic Imagination: Four Essays by M.M. Bakhtin*. Austin: University of Texas Press.

Bandura, A. (1997). *Self-efficacy: the Exercise of Control*. New York: Freeman.

Barfield, A., Ashwell, T., Carroll, M., Collins, K., Cowie, N., Critchley, M., Head, E., Nix, M., Obermeier, A. and Robertson, M.C. (2002). Exploring and defining teacher autonomy. In A.S. Mackenzie and E. McCafferty (eds), *On Developing Autonomy: Proceedings of the JALT College and University Educators' Conference, Shizuoka, Japan*. Tokyo: JALT.

Barnard, R. (2002). Student challenge for New Zealand. *Guardian Unlimited*, 21 February 2002. Accessed 4 June 2002 from: http://education.guardian.co.uk/tefl/story/0,5500,653895,00.html.

Baumann, G. (1996). *Contesting Culture*. Cambridge: Cambridge University Press.

Becker, H.S. (1998). *Tricks of the Trade*. Chicago: University of Chicago Press.

Bedell, D.A. and Oxford, R.L. (1996). Cross-cultural comparisons of language learning strategies in the People's Republic of China and other countries. In R. Oxford (ed.), *Language Learning Strategies around the World: Cross-cultural Perspectives*. Manoa: University of Hawaii Press.

Belenky, M.F., Clinchy, B.M., Goldberger, N.R. and Tarule, J.M. (1986). *Women's Ways of Knowing: the Development of Self, Voice, and Mind*. New York: Basic Books.

Benson, M.J. (1994). Academic listening in an ethnographic perspective. In J. Flowerdew (ed.), *Academic Listening*. Cambridge: Cambridge University Press.

Benson, P. (1995). A critical view of learner training. *Learning Learning* 2/2. Accessed 10 March 2003 from http://www.miyazaki-mu.ac.jp/~hnicoll/learnerdev/LLE/Phil22E.html

Benson, P. (1997). The philosophy and politics of learner autonomy. In P. Benson and P. Voller (eds), *Autonomy and Independence in Language Learning*. London: Longman.

Benson, P. (2000). Autonomy as a learners' and teachers' right. In B. Sinclair, I. McGrath and T. Lamb (eds), *Learner Autonomy, Teacher Autonomy: Future Directions*. Harlow: Longman.

Benson, P. (2001). *Teaching and Researching Autonomy in Language Learning*. Harlow: Longman.

Benson, P. (2002). Teachers' and learners' theories of autonomy. Paper presented at the 4th Symposium of the Scientific Commission on Learner Autonomy in Language Learning, 13th AILA World Congress of Applied Linguistics, Singapore, 16–21 December.

Benson, P. and Voller, P. (eds) (1997a). *Autonomy and Independence in Language Learning*. Harlow: Longman.

Benson, P. and Voller, P. (1997b). Introduction: autonomy and independence in language learning. In P. Benson and P. Voller (eds), *Autonomy and Independence in Language Learning*. Harlow: Longman.

Berg, B. and Östergren, B. (1979). Innovation processes in higher education. *Studies in Higher Education* 4: 261–8.

Berk, L.E. and Winsler, A. (1995). *Scaffolding Children's Learning: Vygotsky and Early Childhood Education*. Washington, DC: National Association for the Education of Young Children.

Bialystok, E. (1981). The role of conscious strategies in second language proficiency. *Modern Language Journal* 65/1: 24–35.

Billig, M. (1987). *Arguing and Thinking: a Rhetorical Approach to Social Psychology*. Cambridge: Cambridge University Press.

Block, D. (2002). Destabilized identities and cosmopolitanism across language and cultural borders: two case studies. *Hong Kong Journal of Applied Linguistics* 7/2: 1–19.

Block, D. and Cameron, D. (eds) (2002). *Globalization and Language Teaching*. London: Routledge.

Bloor, M. and Bloor, T. (1988). Syllabus negotiation: the basis of learner autonomy. In A. Brookes and P. Grundy (eds), *Individualization and Autonomy in Language Learning*. London: Modern English Publications/The British Council.

Boud, D. (1981). Moving towards autonomy. In D. Boud (ed.), *Developing Student Autonomy in Learning*. London: Kogan Page.

Bourdieu, P. (1977). The economics of linguistic exchanges. *Social Science Information* 16/6: 645–68.

Bourdieu, P. (1982). *Ce que parler veut dire: L'économie des échanges linguistiques*. Paris: Fayard.

Bourdieu, P. (1984). *Distinction: a Social Critique of the Judgement of Taste*. London: Routledge.

Bray, J., Lee, J., Smith, L. and Yorks, L. (2000). *Collaborative Inquiry in Practice: Action, Reflection, and Making Meaning*. Thousand Oaks: Sage.

Breen, M.P. (1984). Process syllabuses in language teaching. In C.J. Brumfit (ed.), *General English Syllabus Design*. Oxford: Pergamon/The British Council.

Breen, M.P. (1985). The social context for language learning: a neglected situation? *Studies in Second Language Acquisition* 7/2: 135–58.

Breen, M.P. (1987). Contemporary paradigms in syllabus design: Part II. *Language Teaching* 20/3: 157–74.

Breen, M.P. (ed.) (2001a). *Learner Contributions to Language Learning: New Directions in Research*. Harlow: Longman.

Breen, M.P. (2001b). Introduction: conceptualization, affect and action in context. In M.P. Breen (ed.), *Learner Contributions to Language Learning: New Directions in Research*. Harlow: Longman.

Breen, M.P. (2001c). Postscript: new directions for research on learner contributions. In M.P. Breen (ed.), *Learner Contributions to Language Learning: New Directions in Research*. Harlow: Longman.

Breen, M.P. and Littlejohn, A. (eds) (2000). *Classroom Decision-making: Negotiation and Process Syllabuses in Practice*. Cambridge: Cambridge University Press.

Breen, M.P. and Mann, S.J. (1997). Shooting arrows at the sun: perspectives on a pedagogy for autonomy. In P. Benson and P. Voller (eds), *Autonomy and Independence in Language Learning*. Harlow: Longman.

Broady, E. (1996). Learner attitudes towards self-direction. In E. Broady and M.-M. Kenning (eds), *Promoting Learner Autonomy in University Language Teaching*. London: CILT.

Brockett, R.G. and Hiemstra, R. (1991). *Self-Direction in Adult Learning: Perspectives on Theory, Research and Practice.* London: Routledge.

Brookes, A. and Grundy, P. (eds) (1988). *Individualization and Autonomy in Language Learning.* London: Modern English Publications/The British Council.

Brookfield, S. (1985). Self-directed learning: a critical review of research. In S. Brookfield (ed.), *Self-directed Learning: From Theory to Practice.* London: Jossey-Bass.

Brookfield, S. (1986). *Understanding and Facilitating Adult Learning.* San Francisco: Jossey-Bass.

Brookfield, S. (1993). Self-directed learning, political clarity, and the critical practice of adult education. *Adult Education Quarterly* 43/4: 227–42.

Brown, L.M. and Gilligan, C. (1992). *Meeting at the Crossroads: Women's Psychology and Girls' Development.* New York: Ballantine Books.

Bruner, J. (1979). From communication to language: a psychological perspective. In V. Lee (ed.), *Language Development.* New York: Wiley & Sons.

Bruner, J. (1986). *Actual Minds, Possible Worlds.* Cambridge, MA: Harvard University Press.

Buchan, D. (1972). *The Ballad and the Folk.* London: Routledge.

Budwig, N. (n.d.). *Language and the Construction of Self: Developmental Reflections.* Accessed 8 January 2003 from http://www.massey.ac.nz/~alock/nancy/nancy2.htm.

Bunkacho Bunkabu Kokugoka. (1992). *Heisei 3 Nendo Kokunai no Nihongo Kyouiku Kikan no Gaiyoo.* Tokyo: Bunkacho Bunkabu Kokugoka.

Bunkacho Bunkabu Kokugoka. (1998). *Heisei 8 Nendo Kokunai no Nihongo Kyouiku Kikan no Gaiyoo.* Tokyo: Bunkacho Bunkabu Kokugoka.

Burkitt, I. (1991). *Social Selves: Theories of the Social Formation of Personality.* London: Sage.

Butt, R., Raymond, D., McCue, G. and Yamagishi, L. (1992). Collaborative autobiography and the teacher's voice. In I.F. Goodson (ed.), *Studying Teachers' Lives.* London: Routledge.

Canagarajah, A.S. (1999). *Resisting Linguistic Imperialism in English Teaching.* Oxford: Oxford University Press.

Canagarajah, A.S. (2002a). Globalization, methods, and practice in periphery classrooms. In D. Block and D. Cameron (eds), *Globalization and Language Teaching.* London: Routledge.

Canagarajah, A.S. (2002b). Hidden sites of critical learning. Plenary paper presented at the 8th Annual Conference, TESOL Arabia, 'Critical Reflection and Practice', Abu Dhabi.

Canagarajah, A.S. (2003). Subversive identities, pedagogical safe houses, and critical learning. In B. Norton and K. Toohey (eds), *Critical Pedagogies and Language Learning.* Cambridge: Cambridge University Press.

Canário, R. (2002). Formação inicial de professores: que futuro(s)? – Síntese dos Relatórios de Avaliação dos cursos para o 3º ciclo e do Ensino Básico e Ensino Secundário. In N. Afonso and R. Canário (eds), *Estudos sobre a situação da formação inicial de professores.* Porto: Porto Editora.

Candlin, C. (1997). General editor's preface. In P. Benson and P. Voller (eds), *Autonomy and Independence in Language Learning.* Harlow: Longman.

Candy, P.C. (1991). *Self-direction for Lifelong Learning.* San Francisco: Jossey-Bass.

Canha, M. (2001). Investigação em didáctica e prática docente. Unpublished MA dissertation. Aveiro: University of Aveiro.

Carr, A.A., Jonassen, D.H., Litzinger, M.E. and Marra, R.M. (1998). Good ideas to foment educational revolution: the role of systemic change in advancing situated learning, constructivism, and feminist pedagogy. *Educational Technology* 38/1: 5–15.

Carr, W. (1995). *For Education: Towards Critical Educational Inquiry*. Buckingham: Open University Press.

Carrithers, M., Collins, S. and Lukes, S. (eds) (1985). *The Category of the Person*. Cambridge: Cambridge University Press.

Carson, J.G. and Longhini, A. (2002). Focusing on learning styles and strategies: a diary study in an immersion setting. *Language Learning Journal* 52/2: 401–38.

Carter, B.A. (2001). From awareness to counselling in learner autonomy. *AILA Review* 15: 26–33.

Carter, K. (1993). The place of story in the study of teaching and teacher education. *Educational Researcher* 22/1: 5–12, 18.

Chamot, A.U. (2001). The role of learning strategies in second language acquisition. In M.P. Breen (ed.), *Learner Contributions to Language Learning: New Directions in Research*. Harlow: Longman.

Chamot, A.U. and El-Dinary, P.B. (1999). Children's learner strategies in language immersion classrooms. *Modern Language Journal* 83/3: 319–38.

Chamot, A.U. and O'Malley, J.M. (1996). Implementing the Cognitive Academic Language Learning Approach (CALLA). In R. Oxford (ed.), *Language Learning Strategies around the World: Cross-cultural Perspectives*. Manoa: University of Hawaii Press.

Chamot, A.U., Barnhardt, S., El-Dinary, P. and Robbins, J. (1996). Methods for teaching learning strategies in the foreign language classroom. In R. Oxford (ed.), *Language Learning Strategies around the World: Cross-cultural Perspectives*. Manoa: University of Hawaii Press.

Champagne, M.-F., Clayton, T., Dimmitt, N., Laszewski, M., Savage, W., Shaw, J., Stroupe, R., Thein, M.M. and Walter, P. (2001). The assessment of learner autonomy and language learning. *AILA Review* 15: 45–55.

Chandler, D. (1983). *A History of Cambodia*. Boulder: Westview Press.

Chang C.F. (2000). The conflicting perceptions between British teachers and Taiwanese students connected with a study skills course. Unpublished MA dissertation. Canterbury: Canterbury Christ Church University College, Department of Language Studies.

Chick, J.K. (1996). Safe-talk: collusion in apartheid education. In H. Coleman (ed.), *Society and The Language Classroom*. Cambridge: Cambridge University Press.

Chin, C. (1999). The effects of three learning strategies on EFL vocabulary acquisition. *Korea TESOL Journal* 2/1: 1–12.

Chouliaraki, L. and Fairclough, N. (1999). *Discourse in Late Modernity: Rethinking Critical Discourse Analysis*. Edinburgh: Edinburgh University Press.

Clandinin, D.J. and Connelly, F.M. (2000). *Narrative Inquiry: Experience and Story in Qualitative Research*. San Francisco: Jossey-Bass.

Clark, A. (1998). Magic words: how language augments human computation. In P. Carruthers and J. Boucher (eds), *Language and Thought: Interdisciplinary Themes*. Cambridge: Cambridge University Press.

Clark, C.M. (ed.) (2001). *Talking Shop: Authentic Conversation and Teacher Learning*. New York: Teachers College Press.

Clark, R. and Ivanič, R. (1997). *The Politics of Writing*. London: Routledge.

Clément, R., Dörnyei, Z. and Noels, K.A. (1994). Motivation, self-confidence, and group cohesion in the foreign language classroom. *Language Learning* 44/3: 417–48.

Clemente, M. (2001). Teachers' attitudes within a self-directed language learning scheme. *System* 29: 45–67.

Clinchy, B. (1996). Connected and separate knowing: toward a marriage of two minds. In N. Goldberger, J. Tarule, B. Clinchy, and M. Belenky (eds), *Knowledge, Difference, and Power: Essays Inspired by Women's Ways of Knowing*. New York: Basic Books.

Cohen, A.D. (1998). *Strategies in Learning and Using a Second Language*. Harlow: Longman.

Coleman, H. (1987). Teaching spectacles and learning festivals. *ELT Journal* 41/2: 97–103.

Coleman, H. (ed.) (1996a). *Society and the Language Classroom*. Cambridge: Cambridge University Press.

Coleman, H. (1996b). Autonomy and ideology in the English language classroom. In H. Coleman, (ed.), *Society and the Language Classroom*. Cambridge: Cambridge University Press.

Cortazzi, M. and Jin, L. (1996). English teaching and learning in China. *Language Teaching* 29/1: 61–80.

Cortazzi, M. and Jin, L. (1998). The culture the learner brings: a bridge or a barrier? In M. Byram and M. Fleming (eds), *Language Learning in Intercultural Perspective*. Cambridge: Cambridge University Press.

Cortese, G. and Riley, P. (eds) (2002). *Domain-specific English: Textual Practices across Communities and Classrooms*. Bern: Lang.

Cotterall, S. (1995). Developing a course strategy for learner autonomy. *ELT Journal* 49/3: 219–27.

Cotterall, S. and Crabbe, D. (eds) (1999). *Learner Autonomy in Language Learning: Defining the Field and Effecting Change*. Frankfurt am Main: Lang.

Cowan, J. (1990). *Dance and the Body Politic in Greece*. Princeton: Princeton University Press.

Crabbe, D. (1999). Defining the field: introduction. In S. Cotterall and D. Crabbe (eds), *Learner Autonomy in Language Learning: Defining the Field and Effecting Change*. Frankfurt am Main: Lang.

Crewe, E. and Harrison, E. (1998). *Whose Development? an Ethnography of Aid*. London: Zed Books.

Crookes, G. and Schmidt, R. (1991). Motivation: reopening the research agenda. *Language Learning* 41/4: 469–512.

Csikszentmihalyi, I. (1991). *Flow: the Psychology of Optimal Experience*. New York: HarperCollins.

Dadour, E.S. and Robbins, J. (1996). University-level studies using strategy instruction to improve speaking ability in Egypt and Japan. In R. Oxford (ed.), *Language Learning Strategies around the World: Cross-cultural Perspectives*. Manoa: University of Hawaii Press.

Dakin, J. (1968). *Songs and Rhymes for the Teaching of English: Teacher's Book*. London: Longmans.

Dam, L. (1995). *Learner Autonomy 3: From Theory to Classroom Practice*. Dublin: Authentik.

Dam, L. (2000). Why focus on learning rather than teaching? From theory to practice. In D. Little, L. Dam and J. Timmer (eds), *Focus On Learning Rather Than Teaching: Why and How?* Dublin: Trinity College, Centre for Language and Communication Studies.

Dam, L. and Gabrielsen, G. (1988). Developing learner autonomy in a school context: a six year experiment beginning in the learners' first year of English. In H. Holec (ed.), *Autonomy and Self-directed Learning: Present Fields of Application.* Strasbourg: Council of Europe.

Deci, E.L. and Ryan, R.M. (1985). *Intrinsic Motivation and Self-determination in Human Behavior.* New York: Plenum.

Derné, S. (1994). Cultural conceptions of human motivation. In D. Crane (ed.), *The Sociology of Culture: Emerging Theoretical Perspectives.* Oxford: Blackwell.

De Silva, K.M. (1981). *A History of Sri Lanka.* London: Hurst.

Dickinson, L. (1987). *Self-instruction in Language Learning.* Cambridge: Cambridge University Press.

Dickinson, L. (1988). Learner training. In A. Brookes and P. Grundy (eds), *Individualization and Autonomy in Language Learning.* London: Modern English Publications/The British Council.

Dickinson, L. (1992). *Learner Autonomy 2: Learner Training for Language Learning.* Dublin: Authentik.

Dickinson, L. (1995). Autonomy and motivation: a literature review. *System* 23/2: 165–74.

Dickinson, L. (1996). Culture, autonomy and common-sense. In [L. Dickinson (ed.)], *Autonomy 2000: the Development of Independence in Language Learning. Conference Proceedings.* Bangkok: King Mongkut's Institute of Technology Thonburi.

Diouf, W., Sheckley, B.G. and Kehrhahn, M. (2000). Adult learning in a non-western context: the influence of culture in a Senegalese farming village. *Adult Education Quarterly* 51/1: 32–44.

Dobbin, F.R. (1994). Cultural models of organization: the social construction of rational organizing principles. In D. Crane (ed.), *The Sociology of Culture: Emerging Theoretical Perspectives.* Oxford: Blackwell.

Donato, R. (2000). Sociocultural contributions to understanding the foreign and second language classroom. In J.P. Lantolf (ed.), *Sociocultural Theory and Second Language Learning.* Oxford: Oxford University Press.

Donato, R. and McCormick, D. (1994). A sociocultural perspective on language learning strategies: the role of mediation. *Modern Language Journal* 78: 453–64.

Dore, R.P. and Sako, M. (1989). *How the Japanese Learn to Work.* London: Routledge.

Dörnyei, Z. (1994). Motivation and motivating in the foreign language classroom. *Modern Language Journal* 78/2: 273–84.

Dörnyei, Z. (2001). *Teaching and Researching Motivation.* Harlow: Longman.

Duranti, A. (1997). *Linguistic Anthropology.* Cambridge: Cambridge University Press.

Eck, A., Legenhausen, L. and Wolff, D. (1994). Der Einsatz der Telekommunikation in einem lernerorientierten Fremdsprachenunterricht. In W. Gienow and K. Hellwig (eds), *Interkulturelle Kommunikation und prozeßorientierte Medienpraxis im Fremdsprachenunterricht: Grundlagen, Realisierung, Wirksamkeit.* Seelze: Friedrich.

268   *References*

Edwards, R. (1991). The politics of meeting learner needs: power, subject, subjection. *Studies in the Education of Adults* 23/1: 85–97.

Ehrman, M.E. (1996). *Understanding Second Language Learning Difficulties.* Thousand Oaks: Sage.

Ehrman, M. and Oxford, R. (1989). Effects of sex differences, career choice, and psychological type on adult language learning choices. *Modern Language Journal* 73/1: 1–13.

Ellis, R. (1996). *The Study of Second Language Acquisition.* Oxford: Oxford University Press.

Ellis, R. (2001). The metaphorical constructions of second language learners. In M.P. Breen (ed.), *Learner Contributions to Language Learning: New Directions in Research.* Harlow: Longman.

Ellsworth, E. (1992). Why doesn't this feel empowering? Working through the repressive myths of critical pedagogy. In C. Like and J. Gore (eds), *Feminisms and Critical Pedagogy.* New York: Routledge.

Erickson, F. and Schultz, J. (1982). *The Counsellor as Gatekeeper.* New York: Academic Press.

Ericsson, A.K. and Simon, H.A. (1984). *Protocol Analysis: Verbal Reports as Data.* Cambridge, MA: MIT Press.

Esch, E. (1996). Promoting learner autonomy: criteria for the selection of appropriate methods. In R. Pemberton, E.S.L. Li, W.W.F. Or and H.D. Pierson (eds), *Taking Control: Autonomy in Language Learning.* Hong Kong: Hong Kong University Press.

Estrela, M.T., Esteves, M. and Rodrigues, A. (2002). *Síntese da investigação sobre formação inicial de professores em Portugal.* Porto: Porto Editora.

Fairclough, N. (1992). *Discourse and Social Change.* Cambridge: Polity Press.

Fairclough, N. (1995). *Critical Discourse Analysis: Papers in the Critical Study of Language.* Harlow: Longman.

Farmer, R. (1994). The limits of learner independence in Hong Kong. In D. Gardner and L. Miller (eds), *Directions in Self-access Language Learning.* Hong Kong: Hong Kong University Press.

Fernandez, J.W. (1986). *Persuasions and Performances: the Play of Tropes in Culture.* Bloomington: Indiana University Press.

Fishman, J. (1977). Language and ethnicity. In H. Giles (ed.), *Language, Ethnicity and Intergroup Relations.* London: Academic Press.

Fiske, J. (1989). *Understanding Popular Culture.* London: Routledge.

Flowerdew, L. (1998). A cultural perspective on group work. *ELT Journal* 52/4: 323–9.

Foley, W. (1997). *Anthropological Linguistics: an Introduction.* Oxford: Blackwell.

Fonseka, E.A.G. (1993–94). *English Through Singing, Years 1–6: Teacher's Handbook.* Bandarawela: Thilaka.

Fonseka, E.A.G. (1995). Oral poetry and Sri Lanka's diglossia-affected children. In J. Schuchalter (ed.), *Interdependence and Interaction.* Vaasa: University of Vaasa Press.

Fonseka, E.A.G. (1996). Children's songs in promoting learner autonomy. In [L. Dickinson (ed.)], *Autonomy 2000: the Development of Independence in Language Learning. Conference Proceedings.* Bangkok: King Mongkut's Institute of Technology Thonburi.

Fonseka, E.A.G. (1997). *English Children's Songs: Their Use in Promoting Oral Skills in Primary Schoolchildren in Sri Lanka*. Vaasa: University of Vaasa Press.

Fonseka, E.A.G. (2001). English language teaching in post-colonial Sri Lanka. *Silhouette (Journal of The General Sir John Kotelawala Defence Academy)* 2000–2001: 126–31.

Foucault, M. (1977). *Madness and Civilization: a History of Insanity in the Age of Reason*. London: Tavistock.

Foucault, M. (1991). *Discipline and Punish: the Birth of the Prison*. Harmondsworth: Penguin.

Frankl, V.E. (1997). *Man's Search for Meaning*. Revised and updated edition. New York: Washington Square Press.

Freire, P. (1972). *Pedagogy of the Oppressed*. Harmondsworth: Penguin.

Gao, X. (2002). A qualitative enquiry into Chinese students' learner strategy use after arrival in the UK. Unpublished MA dissertation. Coventry: University of Warwick, Centre for English Language Teacher Education.

Gardner, R.C. (1985). *Social Psychology and Second Language Learning: the Role of Attitudes and Motivation*. London: Arnold.

Gardner, R.C. and Lambert, W. (1972). *Attitudes and Motivation in Second Language Learning*. Rowley, MA: Newbury House.

Geertz, C. (1973). *The Interpretation of Cultures*. London: Fontana.

Giddens, A. (1991). *Modernity and Self-identity: Self and Society in the Late Modern Age*. Palo Alto: Stanford University Press.

Gilligan, C. (1986) Remapping the moral domain: new images of the self in relationship. In T.C. Heller, M. Sosna and D.E. Wellbery (eds), *Reconstructing Individualism: Autonomy, Individuality and the Self in Western Thought*. Palo Alto: Stanford University Press.

Giroux, H.A. (1983). *Theory and Resistance in Education: a Pedagogy for the Opposition*. South Hadley, MA: Bergin & Garvey.

Goffman, E. (1969). *The Presentation of Self in Everyday Life*. London: Allen Lane.

Goldstein, T. (1996). *Two Languages at Work: Bilingual Life on the Production Floor*. Berlin: Mouton.

Goodman, J. (1992). Feminist pedagogy as a foundation for reflective practice. In L. Valli (ed.), *Reflective Teacher Education: Cases and Critiques*. Albany, NY: State University of New York Press.

Goodwin, M.H. (1990). *He-said-she-said: Talk as Social Organization among Black Children*. Bloomington, IN: Indiana University Press.

Gore, J.M. (1993). *The Struggle for Pedagogies: Critical and Feminist Discourses as Regimes of Truth*. New York: Routledge.

Green, J.M. and Oxford, R.L. (1995). A closer look at learning strategies, L2 proficiency, and gender. *TESOL Quarterly* 29/2: 261–97.

Gremmo, M.-J., Holec, H. and Riley, P. (1985). Interactional structure: the role of the role. In P. Riley (ed.), *Discourse and Learning*. Harlow: Longman.

Grice, H.P. (1975). Logic and conversation. In P. Cole and J. Morgan (eds), *Syntax and Semantics 3: Speech Acts*. New York: Academic Press.

Gubrium, J.F. and Holstein, J.A. (1997). *The New Language of Qualitative Research*. New York: Oxford University Press.

Gumperz, J. (ed.) (1982). *Discourse Strategies*. Cambridge: Cambridge University Press.

Gutierrez, K. (1993). Biliteracy and the language-minority child. In B. Spodek and O. Saracho (eds), *Language and Literacy in Early Childhood Education*. New York: Teachers College Press.

Haarman, H. (1986). *Language in Ethnicity: a View of Basic Ecological Relations*. Berlin: Mouton.

Hall, J.K. (1993). The role of oral practices in the accomplishment of our everyday lives: the sociocultural dimension of interaction with implications for the learning of another language. *Applied Linguistics* 14/2: 145–65.

Hall, J.K. (1995). (Re)creating our worlds with words: a sociohistorical perspective of face-to-face interaction. *Applied Linguistics* 16/2: 206–32.

Hall, S. (1997). The work of representation. In S. Hall (ed.), *Representation: Cultural Representations and Signifying Practices*. London: Sage/Open University.

Handleman, D. (1982). Reflexivity in festival and other cultural events. In M. Douglas (ed.), *Essays in Sociological Perception*. London: Routledge.

Handy, C. (1993). *Understanding Organizations*. Oxford: Oxford University Press.

Hargreaves, D. (1975). *Interpersonal Relations and Education*. London: Routledge.

Harklau, L. (2000). From the 'good kids' to the 'worst': representations of English language learners across educational settings. *TESOL Quarterly* 34/1: 35–67.

Harmer, J. (2001). *The Practice of English Language Teaching*, 3rd edition. Harlow: Longman.

Hatch, E. (1992). *Discourse and Language Education*. Cambridge: Cambridge University Press.

Hayagoshi, H. (1996). British teachers' perceptions of Japanese students, in contrast with Japanese students' perceptions of their own needs and wants. Unpublished masters dissertation. Canterbury: Canterbury Christ Church University College, Department of Language Studies.

Helgesen, G. (1998). *Theory and Methodology*. Eurasia Political Culture Research Network. Accessed 20 January 2003 from http://130.225.203.37/EPCREN/discuss/msgReader$20.

Ho, J. and Crookall, D. (1995). Breaking with Chinese cultural traditions: learner autonomy in English language teaching. *System* 23/2: 235–43.

Hofstede, G. (1986). Cultural differences in teaching and learning. *International Journal of Intercultural Relations* 10: 301–20.

Hofstede, G. (1990). *Cultures and Organizations: Software of the Mind*. London: McGraw Hill.

Holec, H. (1979). *Autonomie et apprentissage des langues étrangères*. Strasbourg: Council of Europe.

Holec, H. (1980). Learner training: Meeting needs in self-directed learning. In H.B. Altman and C.V. James (eds), *Foreign Language Learning: Meeting Individual Needs*. Oxford: Pergamon.

Holec, H. (1981). *Autonomy and Foreign Language Learning*. Oxford: Pergamon.

Holec, H. (ed.). (1988). *Autonomy and Self-directed Learning: Present Fields of Application*. Strasbourg: Council of Europe.

Holliday, A.R. (1994). *Appropriate Methodology and Social Context*. Cambridge: Cambridge University Press.

Holliday, A.R. (1996a). Developing a sociological imagination: expanding ethnography in international English language education. *Applied Linguistics* 17/2: 234–55.

Holliday, A.R. (1996b). Cultural accommodation in an ESL curriculum project. Unpublished paper. Canterbury: Canterbury Christ Church University College, Department of Language Studies.

Holliday, A.R. (1997a). Six lessons: cultural continuity in communicative language teaching. *Language Teaching Research* 1/3: 212–38.

Holliday, A.R. (1997b). The politics of participation in international English language education. *System* 25/3: 409–23.

Holliday, A.R. (1999a). Small cultures. *Applied Linguistics* 20/2: 237–64.

Holliday, A.R. (1999b). Authenticity and autonomy: the struggle to relate education to people. In V. Crew, V. Berry and J. Hung (eds), *Exploring Diversity in the Language Curriculum*. Hong Kong: Hong Kong Institute of Education.

Holliday, A.R. (2001a). Achieving cultural continuity in curriculum innovation: dealing with dominant discourses. In D. Hall and A. Hewings (eds), *Innovation in English Language Teaching: a Reader*. London: Routledge/Macquarie University/The Open University.

Holliday, A.R. (2001b). Finding social autonomy. In P. Bodycott and V. Crew (eds), *Language and Cultural Immersion: Perspectives on Short Term Study and Residence Abroad*. Hong Kong: Hong Kong Institute of Education.

Holliday, A.R. (2002a). *Doing and Writing Qualitative Research*. London: Sage.

Holliday, A.R. (2002b). Japanese fragments: an exploration in cultural perception and duality. *Asia Pacific Journal of Language in Education* 5/1: 1–28.

Holliday, A.R. (forthcoming). *The Struggle to Teach English as an International Language*. Oxford: Oxford University Press.

Horwitz, E.K. (1999). Cultural and situational influences on foreign language learners' beliefs about language learning: a review of BALLI studies. *System* 27: 557–76.

Hsiao, T.-Y. (1995). A factor-analytic and regressional study of language learning strategies used by university students of Chinese, French, German, and Spanish. Unpublished doctoral dissertation. Austin: University of Texas at Austin.

Hsiao, T.-Y. and Oxford, R.L. (2002). Comparing theories of language learning strategies: a confirmatory factor analysis. *Modern Language Journal* 86/3: 368–83.

Huttunen, I. (1988). Towards learner autonomy in a school context. In H. Holec (ed.), *Autonomy and Self-directed Learning: Present Fields of Application*. Strasbourg: Council of Europe.

Huttunen, I. (1997). The main outcomes of the projects. In H. Holec and I. Huttunen (eds), *Learner Autonomy in Modern Languages: Research and Development*. Strasbourg: Council of Europe.

Hymes, D. (1974). *Foundations in Sociolinguistics: an Ethnographic Approach*. Philadelphia: University of Philadelphia Press.

Illich, I. (1979). *Deschooling Society*. Harmondsworth: Penguin.

Imbert, H. and Rixon, S. (1994). *Green Light*. London: Macmillan.

Jahoda, G. and Lewis, I.M. (eds) (1988). *Acquiring Culture: Cross-cultural Studies in Child Development*. London: Routledge.

Janesick, V.J. (1994). The dance of qualitative research design: metaphor, methodolatry, and meaning. In N.K. Denzin and Y.S. Lincoln (eds), *A Handbook of Qualitative Research*. Thousand Oaks: Sage.

Jay, G. and Graff, G. (1995). A critique of critical pedagogy. In M. Bérubé and C. Nelson (eds), *Higher Education under Fire: Politics, Economics and the Crisis of the Humanities*. New York: Routledge.

Jenkins, J. (2000). *The Phonology of English as an International Language: New Models, New Norms, New Goals*. Oxford: Oxford University Press.

Johnson, K.E. and Golombek, P.R. (eds) (2002). *Teachers' Narrative Inquiry as Professional Development*. New York: Cambridge University Press.

Jones, J.F. (1995). Self-access and culture: retreating from autonomy. *ELT Journal* 49/3: 228–34.

Jordan, G. and Weedon, C. (1995). The celebration of difference and the cultural politics of racism. In B. Adam and S. Allan (eds), *Theorizing Culture: an Interdisciplinary Critique after Postmodernism*. London: UCL Press.

Kağıtçıbaşı, Ç. (1988). Diversity of socialization in cross-cultural perspective: A model of change. In P.R. Dasen, J.W. Berry and N. Sartorius (eds), *Health and Cross-cultural Psychology: Toward Applications*. Newbury Park: Sage.

Karlsson, L., Kjisik, F. and Nordlund, J. (1997). *From Here to Autonomy: a Helsinki University Language Centre Autonomous Learning Project*. Helsinki: Yliopistopaino.

Karlsson, L., Kjisik, F. and Nordlund, J. (eds) (2001). *All Together Now: Papers from the 7th Nordic Conference and Workshop on Autonomous Language Learning, Helsinki, September 2000*. Helsinki: University of Helsinki Language Centre.

Kaylani, C. (1996). The influence of gender and motivation on EFL learning strategy use. In R. Oxford (ed.), *Language Learning Strategies around the World: Cross-cultural Perspectives*. Manoa: University of Hawaii Press.

Kelly, R. (1996). Language counselling for learner autonomy: the skilled helper in self-access language learning. In R. Pemberton, E.S.L. Li, W.W.F. Or and H.D. Pierson (eds), *Taking Control: Autonomy in Language Learning*. Hong Kong: Hong Kong University Press.

Kelly, G.A. (1955/1991). *The Psychology of Personal Constructs*, vol. 1. London: Routledge.

Kenny, B. (1993). For more autonomy. *System* 21/4: 431–42.

Kirshner, D. and Whitson, J. (1997). *Situated Cognition: Social, Semiotic and Psychological Perspectives*. Mahwah: Erlbaum.

Kirtikara, K. (1996). Autonomy rediscovered. In [L. Dickinson (ed.),] *Autonomy 2000: the Development of Independence in Language Learning. Conference Proceedings*. Bangkok: King Mongkut's Institute of Technology Thonburi.

Kneller, G.F. (1965). *Educational Anthropology: an Introduction*. New York: Wiley & Sons.

Knowles, J.G. and Cole, A.L., with Presswood, C.S. (1994). *Through Preservice Teachers' Eyes: Exploring Field Experiences through Narrative and Inquiry*. New York: Merrill.

Kojic-Sabo, I. and Lightbown, P. (1999). Students' approaches to vocabulary learning and their relationship to success. *Modern Language Journal* 99/2: 176–92.

Kramsch, C. (1993). *Context and Culture in Language Teaching*. Oxford: Oxford University Press.

Kramsch, C. (1998). *Language and Culture*. Oxford: Oxford University Press.

Kramsch, C. and Thorne, S.L. (2002). Foreign language learning as global communicative practice. In D. Block and D. Cameron (eds), *Globalization and Language Teaching*. London: Routledge.

Ku, P.N. (1995). Strategies associated with proficiency and predictors of strategy choice: a study of language learning strategies of EFL students at three educational levels in Taiwan. Unpublished doctoral dissertation. Bloomington: Indiana University.

Kubota, R. (1999). Japanese culture constructed by discourses: implications for applied linguistics research and ELT. *TESOL Quarterly* 33/1: 9–35.

Kubota, R. (2001). Discursive construction of the images of US classrooms. *TESOL Quarterly* 35/1: 9–37.

Kubota, R. (2002). (Un)ravelling racism in a nice field like TESOL. *TESOL Quarterly* 36/1: 84–92.

La Fontaine, J.S. (1985). Person and individual: some anthropological reflections. In M. Carrithers, S. Collins and S. Lukes (eds), *The Category of the Person*. Cambridge: Cambridge University Press.

Lai, J. (2001). Towards an analytic approach to assessing learner autonomy. *AILA Review* 15: 34–44.

Lakoff, G. and Johnson, M. (1980). *Metaphors We Live by*. Chicago: University of Chicago Press.

Lamb, T. (2000). Finding a voice: learner autonomy and teacher education in an urban context. In B. Sinclair, I. McGrath and T. Lamb (eds), *Learner Autonomy, Teacher Autonomy: Future Directions*. Harlow: Longman.

Lantolf, J.P. (ed.). (2000). *Sociocultural Theory and Second Language Learning*. Oxford: Oxford University Press.

Lantolf, J.P. and Appel, G. (1994). *Vygotskian Approaches to Second Language Research*. New York: Ablex.

Lantolf, J.P. and Pavlenko, A. (2001). (S)econd (L)anguage (A)ctivity theory: understanding second language learners as people. In M.P. Breen (ed.), *Learner Contributions to Language Learning: New Directions in Research*. Harlow: Longman.

Laufer, B. and Hulstijn, J. (2001). Incidental vocabulary acquisition in a second language: The construct of task-induced involvement. *Applied Linguistics* 21/1: 1–26.

Lave, J. and Wenger, E. (1991). *Situated Learning: Legitimate Peripheral Participation*. Cambridge: Cambridge University Press.

Lawson, M.J. and Hogben, D. (1996). The vocabulary learning strategies of foreign language students. *Language Learning* 46/1: 101–35.

Legutke, M. and Thomas, H. (1991). *Process and Experience in the Language Classroom*. Harlow: Longman.

Levine, A., Reves, T., and Leaver, B.L. (1996). Relationship between language learning strategies and Israeli versus Russian cultural-educational factors. In R. Oxford (ed.), *Language Learning Strategies around the World: Cross-cultural Perspectives*. Manoa: University of Hawaii Press.

Levine, G. (ed.), (1992). *Constructions of the Self*. New Brunswick: Rutgers University Press.

Levinson, S. (1983). *Pragmatics*. Cambridge: Cambridge University Press.

Lévi-Strauss, C. (1977). *L'Identité*. Paris: Quadrige PUF.

Lewis, B. (1982). *The Muslim Discovery of Europe*. London: Norton.

Lim, H.-Y. (2002). The interaction of motivation, perception and environment: one EFL learner's experience. *Hong Kong Journal of Applied Linguistics* 7/2: 91–106.

Little, D. (1991). *Learner Autonomy 1: Definitions, Issues, and Problems*. Dublin: Authentik.

Little, D. (1995). Learning as dialogue: the dependence of learner autonomy on teacher autonomy. *System* 23/2: 175–81.

Little, D. (1996a). Freedom to learn and compulsion to interact: promoting learner autonomy through the use of information systems and information technologies. In R. Pemberton, E.S.L. Li, W.W.F. Or and H.D. Pierson (eds), *Taking Control: Autonomy in Language Learning*. Hong Kong: Hong Kong University Press.

Little, D. (1996b). The politics of learner autonomy. *Learning Learning* 2/4: 7–10.

Little, D. (1997a). Autonomy and self-access in second language learning: some fundamental issues in theory and practice. In M. Müller-Verweyen (ed.), *Neues Lernen, selbstgesteuert, autonom: New Developments in Foreign Language Learning, Self-management, Autonomy*. Munich: Goethe-Institut.

Little, D. (1997b). Language awareness and the autonomous language learner. *Language Awareness* 6/2–3: 93–104.

Little, D. (1997c). The role of writing in second language learning: Some neo-Vygotskian reflections. In R. Kupetz (ed.), *Vom gelenkten zum freien Schreiben im Fremdsprachenunterricht: Freiräume sprachlichen Handelns*. Frankfurt am Main: Lang.

Little, D. (1999a). Learner autonomy is more than a Western cultural construct. In S. Cotterall and D. Crabbe (eds), *Learner Autonomy in Language Learning: Defining the Field and Effecting Change*. Frankfurt am Main: Lang.

Little, D. (1999b). Developing learner autonomy in the foreign language classroom: a social-interactive view of learning and three fundamental pedagogical principles. *Revista Canaria de Estudios Ingleses* 38: 77–88.

Little, D. (2001a). How independent can independent language learning really be? In J.A. Coleman, D. Ferney, D. Head and R. Rix (eds), *Language-learning Futures: Issues and Strategies for Modern Language Provision in Higher Education*. London: CILT.

Little, D. (2001b). Learner autonomy and the challenge of tandem language learning via the Internet. In A. Chambers and G. Davies (eds), *Information and Communications Technologies and Language Learning: a European Perspective*. Lisse: Swets & Zeltlinger.

Little, D. (2001c). We're all in it together: exploring the interdependence of teacher and learner autonomy. In L. Karlsson, F. Kjisik and J. Nordlund (eds), *All Together Now: Papers from the 7th Nordic Conference and Workshop on Autonomous Language Learning, Helsinki, September 2000*. Helsinki: University of Helsinki Language Centre.

Little, D. (2002). Learner autonomy and autonomous language learning: some theoretical perspectives and their practical implications. In P. Evangelisti and C. Argondizzo (eds), *L'apprendimento autonomo delle lingue straniere*. Catanzaro: Rubbettino.

Little, D. and Brammerts, H. (eds) (1996). *A Guide to Language Learning in Tandem via the Internet*. CLCS Occasional Paper No. 46. Dublin: Trinity College, Centre for Language and Communication Studies.

Little, D. and Dam, L. (1998). Learner autonomy: what and why? *Language Teacher Online* 22/10. Accessed 15 January 2003 from http://langue.hyper.chubu.ac.jp/jalt/pub/tlt/98/oct/littledam.html

Little, D., Dam, L. and Timmer, J. (eds) (2000). *Focus on Learning Rather than Teaching: Why and How?* Dublin: Trinity College, Centre for Language and Communication Studies.

Little, D., Ushioda, E., Appel, M. C., Moran, J., O'Rourke, B. and Schwienhorst, K. (1999). *Evaluating Tandem Language Learning by E-Mail: Report on a Bilateral Project*. CLCS Occasional Paper No. 55. Dublin: Trinity College, Centre for Language and Communication Studies.

Littlejohn, A. (1997). Self-access work and curriculum ideologies. In P. Benson and P. Voller (eds), *Autonomy and Independence in Language Learning*. Harlow: Longman.

Littlewood, W. (1996a). Autonomy in communication and learning in an Asian context. In [L. Dickinson (ed.)], *Autonomy 2000: the Development of Independence in Language Learning. Conference Proceedings*. Bangkok: King Mongkut's Institute of Technology Thonburi.

Littlewood, W. (1996b). 'Autonomy': An anatomy and a framework. *System* 24/4: 427–35.

Littlewood, W. (1999). Defining and developing autonomy in East Asian contexts. *Applied Linguistics* 20/1: 71–94.

Littlewood, W. (2000). Do Asian students really want to listen and obey? *ELT Journal* 54/1: 31–5.

Mauss, M. (1938). A category of the human mind: the notion of person; the notion of self. In M. Carrithers, S. Collins and S. Lukes (eds) (1985), *The Category of the Person*. Cambridge: Cambridge University Press.

McCarthy, M. (1991). *Discourse Analysis for Language Teachers*. Cambridge: Cambridge University Press.

McDonough, S.H. (1999). Learner Strategies. *Language Teaching* 32/1: 1–18.

McGrath, I. (2000). Teacher autonomy. In B. Sinclair, I. McGrath and T. Lamb (eds), *Learner Autonomy, Teacher Autonomy: Future Directions*. Harlow: Longman.

McGroarty, M. (1998). Constructive and constructivist challenges for applied linguistics. *Language Learning* 48: 591–622.

McKay, S. and Wong, S.-L. (1996). Multiple discourses, multiple identities: investment and agency in second-language learning among Chinese adolescent immigrant students. *Harvard Educational Review* 66/3: 577–608.

Mead, G.H. (1934). *Mind, Self and Society*. Chicago: Chicago University Press.

Mebo, P. (1995). Class size and student behaviour: a comparison of strategies employed in different size classes by students studying communication skills in the Kenyan State University. Unpublished PhD thesis. Leeds: University of Leeds, School of Education.

Miller, P. and Rose, N. (1990). Governing economic life. *Economy and Society* 19/1: 1–31.

Miller, P.J. (1988). Factories, monitorial schools and Jeremy Bentham: the origins of the 'management syndrome' in popular education. In A. Westoby (ed.), *Culture and Power in Educational Organisations: a Reader*. Buckingham: Open University Press.

Milton, K. (1996). *Environmentalism and Cultural Theory: Exploring the Role of Anthropology in Environmental Discourse*. London: Routledge.

Moreira, M.A. and Ferreira, P. (2002). Analysing learning tasks: materials for learner development. In F. Vieira, M.A. Moreira, I. Barbosa and M. Paiva (eds), *Pedagogy for Autonomy and English Learning: Proceedings of the Working Group – Pedagogy for Autonomy*. Braga: University of Minho.

Moreira, M.A., Vieira, F. and Marques, I. (1999). Pre-service teacher development through action research. *The Language Teacher* 23/12: 15–18, 36.

Morgan, G. (1986). *Images of Organization*. London: Sage.

Moulden, H. (1985). Extending self-directed learning of English in an engineering college. In P. Riley (ed.), *Discourse and Learning*. Harlow: Longman.

Mozzon-McPherson, M. (n.d.). *Language Advising*. Accessed 1 April 2003 at http://www.lang.ltsn.ac.uk/resources/goodpractice.aspx?resourceid=93.

Mühlhäusler, P. and Harré, R. (1990). *Pronouns and People: the Linguistic Construction of Social and Personal Identity*. Oxford: Blackwell.

Naiman, N., Frohlich, M., Stern, H.H. and Todesco, A. (1978). *The Good Language Learner*. Toronto: Ontario Institute for Studies in Education.

Nanamoli, B. (1991). *The Path of Purification*. Kandy: Buddhist Publication Society.

Noddings, N. (1984). *Caring: a Feminine Approach to Ethics and Moral Education*. Berkeley: University of California Press.

Noels, K., Pelletier, L. and Vallerand, R. (2000). Why are you learning a second language?: motivation orientations and self-determination theory. *Language Learning* 50/1: 57–85.

Norton, B. (1997). Language, identity, and the ownership of English. *TESOL Quarterly* 31/3: 409–30.

Norton, B. (2000). *Identity and Language Learning: Gender, Ethnicity and Educational Change*. Harlow: Longman.

Norton, B. (2001). Non-participation, imagined communities and the language classroom. In M.P. Breen (ed.), *Learner Contributions to Language Learning: New Directions in Research*. Harlow: Longman.

Norton, B. and Toohey, K. (2002). Identity and language learning. In R. Kaplan (ed.), *Oxford University Press Handbook of Applied Linguistics*. Oxford: Oxford University Press.

Norton Peirce, B. (1995). Social identity, investment, and language learning. *TESOL Quarterly* 29/1: 9–31.

Nunan, D. (1997a). Does learner strategy training make a difference? *Lenguas Modernas* 24: 123–42.

Nunan, D. (1997b). Designing and adapting materials to encourage learner autonomy. In P. Benson and P. Voller (eds), *Autonomy and Independence in Language Learning*. Harlow: Longman.

Nyikos, M. (1990). Sex-related differences in adult language learning: socialisation and memory factors. *Modern Language Journal* 74/3: 274–87.

Nyikos, M. and Oxford, R.L. (1993). A factor analytic study of language learning strategy use: interpretation from information-processing theory and social psychology. *Modern Language Journal* 77/1: 11–22.

Ochs, E. and Schieffelin, B. (1984). Language acquisition and socialization: three developmental stories and their implications. In R. Shweder and R. Levine (eds), *Culture Theory: Essays on Mind, Self and Emotion*. Cambridge: Cambridge University Press.

Ogbu, J. (1991). Immigrant and involuntary minorities in comparative perspective. In M. Gibson and J. Ogbu (eds), *Minority Status and Schooling: a Comparative Study of Immigrant and Involuntary Minorities*. New York: Garland.

O'Malley, J.M. and Chamot, A.U. (1990). *Learning Strategies in Second Language Acquisition*. Cambridge: Cambridge University Press.

O'Malley, J.M., Chamot, A.U., Stewner-Manzanares, G., Kupper, L. and Russo, R.P. (1985). Learning strategy applications with students of English as a second language. *TESOL Quarterly* 19/4: 557–84.

O'Rourke, B. and Schwienhorst, K. (2003). Talking text: Reflections on reflection in computer-mediated communication. In D. Little, J. Ridley and E. Ushioda (eds), *Learner Autonomy in the Foreign Language Classroom: Learner, Teacher, Curriculum and Assessment*. Dublin: Authentik.

Oxford, R. (1990). *Language Learning Strategies: What Every Teacher Should Know*. Boston: Heinle & Heinle.

Oxford, R.L. (1994). Language learning strategies: An update. *ERIC Digest* ED376707. Accessed 27 June 2002 from http://www.ed.gov/databases/ERIC_Digests/ed376707.html.

Oxford, R.L. (1995). Alternative routes to L2 learner motivation. Unpublished manuscript. Tuscaloosa: University of Alabama.

Oxford, R. (ed.) (1996a) *Language Learning Strategies around the World: Cross-Cultural Perspectives*. Manoa: University of Hawaii Press.

Oxford, R.L. (1996b). When emotion meets (meta)cognition in language learning histories. *International Journal of Educational Research* 23/7: 581–94.

Oxford, R.L. (2001). "The bleached bones of a story": Learners' constructions of language teachers. In M.P. Breen (ed.), *Learner Contributions to Language Learning: New Directions in Research*. Harlow: Longman.

Oxford, R.L. and Anderson, N.J. (1995). A crosscultural view of learning styles. *Language Teaching* 28: 201–15.

Oxford, R.L. and Burry-Stock, J.A. (1995). Assessing the use of language learning strategies worldwide with the ESL/EFL version of the strategy inventory for language learning (SILL). *System* 23/1: 1–23.

Oxford, R.L. and Crookall, D. (1989). Research on language learning strategies: methods, findings, and instructional issues. *Modern Language Journal* 73/4: 404–19.

Oxford, R.L. and Ehrman, M.E. (1995). Adults' language learning strategies in an intensive foreign language program in the United States. *System* 23: 359–86.

Oxford, R.L. and Leaver, B.L. (1996). A synthesis of strategy instruction for language learners. In R. Oxford (ed.), *Language Learning Strategies around the World: Cross-cultural Perspectives*. Manoa: University of Hawaii Press.

Oxford, R.L. and Nyikos, M. (1989). Variables affecting choice of language learning strategies by university students. *Modern Language Journal* 73/3: 291–300.

Oxford, R.L. and Shearin, J. (1994). Expanding the theoretical framework of language learning motivation. *Modern Language Journal* 78/1: 12–28.

Oxford, R.L., Park-Oh, Y.Y., Ito, S. and Sumrall, M. (1993). Learning a language by satellite television: What influences student achievement? *System* 21/1: 31–48.

Packer, M. (1993). Away from internalization. In E. Forman, N. Minick and C.A. Stone (eds), *Contexts for Learning: Sociocultural Dynamics in Children's Development*. New York: Oxford University Press.

Palfreyman, D. (1999). The technologization of learning. *Newsletter of the AILA Scientific Commission on Learner Autonomy in Language Learning* 5. Accessed 28 February 2003 from http://www.vuw.ac.nz/lals/LALLnews/news1999.html#contributions.

Palfreyman, D. (2001). The socio-cultural construction of learner autonomy and learner independence in a tertiary EFL institution. Unpublished PhD thesis. Canterbury: Canterbury Christ Church University College, Department of Language Studies.

Papa, M. and Iantorno, G. (1979). *Famous British and American Songs and Their Cultural Background*. London: Longman.

Papert, S. (1991). Situating constructionism. In I. Harel and S. Papert (eds), *Constructionism*. Norwood: Ablex.

Pavlenko, A. and Lantolf, J.P. (2000). Second language learning as participation and the (re)construction of selves. In J.P. Lantolf (ed.), *Sociocultural Theory and Second Language Learning*. Oxford: Oxford University Press.

Pemberton, R., Li, E.S.L., Or, W.W.F. and Pierson, H.D. (1996). (eds) *Taking Control: Autonomy in Language Learning.* Hong Kong: Hong Kong University Press.

Pemberton, R., Toogood, S., Ho, S. and Lam, J. (2001). Approaches to advising for self-directed language learning. *AILA Review* 15: 16–25.

Pennycook, A. (1994). *The Cultural Politics of English as an International Language.* Harlow: Longman.

Pennycook, A. (1997). Cultural alternatives and autonomy. In P. Benson and P. Voller (eds), *Autonomy and Independence in Language Learning.* London: Longman.

Pennycook, A. (1998). *English and the Discourses of Colonialism.* London: Routledge

Pennycook, A. (2001). *Critical Applied Linguistics: a Critical Introduction.* Mahwah: Erlbaum.

Pereira, A., Almeida, S. Costa, S. and Ferraz, L. (2001). Actividades para aprender a aprender. In F. Vieira (ed.), *Cadernos 2. GT-PA.* Braga: University of Minho.

Peters, T.J. and Waterman, R.H. (1986). *In Search of Excellence: Lessons from America's Best-Run Companies.* New York: Harper & Row.

Phillipson, R. (1992). *Linguistic Imperialism.* Oxford: Oxford University Press.

Pierson, H.D. (1996) Learner culture and learner autonomy in the Hong Kong Chinese context. In R. Pemberton, E.S.L. Li, W.W.F. Or and H.D. Pierson (eds), *Taking Control: Autonomy in Language Learning.* Hong Kong: Hong Kong University Press.

Pintrich, P.R. and Schunk, D.H. (1996). *Motivation in Education: Theory, Research, and Applications.* Englewood Cliffs: Merrill.

Pollard, A. and Filer, A. (1999). Learning, Policy and Pupil Career. In M. Hammersley (ed.), *Researching School Experience.* London: Falmer Press.

Prabhu, N.S. (1987). *Second Language Pedagogy.* Oxford: Oxford University Press.

Press, M.-C. (1996). Ethnicity and the autonomous language learner: different beliefs and strategies? In E. Broady and M.-M. Kenning (eds), *Promoting Learner Autonomy in University Language Teaching.* London: CILT.

Pressley, M. and Woloshyn, V. (1995). *Cognitive Strategy Instruction that Really Improves Children's Academic Performance.* Cambridge, MA: Brookline Books.

Pugsley, J. (1988). Autonomy and individualization in language learning: institutional implications. In A. Brookes and P. Grundy (eds), *Individualization and Autonomy in Language Learning.* London: Modern English Publications/The British Council.

Ram, K. (2002). Stranded between the 'posts': sensory experience and immigrant female subjectivity. In C. Barron, N. Bruce and D. Nunan (eds), *Knowledge and Discourse: Towards an Ecology of Language.* Harlow: Longman.

Rampton, B. (1995). Politics and change in research in applied linguistics. *Applied Linguistics* 16/2: 233–56.

Reid, J. (ed.) (1998). *Understanding Learning Styles in the Second Language Classroom.* Upper Saddle River: Prentice Hall.

Ribbins, P.M., Jarvis, C.B., Best, R.E. and Oddy, D.M. (1988). Meanings and contexts: the problem of interpretation in the study of a school. In A. Westoby (ed.), *Culture and Power in Educational Organisations: a Reader.* Buckingham: Open University Press.

Richards, J.C. and Lockhart, C. (1994). *Reflective Teaching in Second Language Classrooms.* Cambridge: Cambridge University Press.

Richert, A.E. (1992). Voice and power in teaching and learning to teach. In L. Valli (ed.), *Reflective Teacher Education*. Albany: State University of New York Press.

Ridley, J. (1997). *Reflection and Strategies in Foreign Language Learning: a Study of Four University Level Ab Initio Learners of German*. Frankfurt am Main: Lang.

Riley, P. (1988). The ethnography of autonomy. In A. Brookes and P. Grundy (eds), *Individualization and Autonomy in Language Learning*. London: Modern English Publications/The British Council.

Riley, P. (1994). Aspects of learner discourse: why listening to learners is so important. In E. Esch (ed.), *Self-access and the Adult Language Learner*. London: CILT.

Riley, P. (1997). The guru and the conjurer: aspects of counselling for self-access. In P. Benson and P. Voller (eds), *Autonomy and Independence in Language Learning*. London: Longman.

Riley, P. (1999). On the social construction of 'the learner'. In S. Cotterall and D. Crabbe (eds), *Learner Autonomy in Language Learning: Defining the Field and Effecting Change*. Frankfurt am Main: Lang.

Riley, P. (2002). Epistemic communities: the social knowledge system, discourse and identity. In G. Cortese and P. Riley (eds), *Domain-specific English: Textual Practices across Communities and Classrooms*. Bern: Lang.

Rivers, W. (2001). Autonomy at all costs: an ethnography of metacognitive self-assessment and self-management among experienced language learners. *Modern Language Journal* 85/2: 279–90.

Roberts, J. (1998). *Language Teacher Education*. London: Arnold.

Roberts, C., Byram, M., Barro, A., Jordan, S. and Street, B. (2001). *Language Learners as Ethnographers*. Clevedon: Multilingual Matters.

Robertson, H.-J. (1992). Teacher development and gender equity. In A. Hargreaves and M.G. Fullan (eds), *Understanding Teacher Development*. London: Cassell.

Roebuck, R. (2000). Subjects speak out: how learners position themselves in a psycholinguistic task. In J.P. Lantolf (ed.), *Sociocultural Theory and Second Language Learning*. Oxford: Oxford University Press.

Rogoff, B. (1994). Developing understanding of the idea of communities of learners. *Mind, Culture and Activity* 1/4: 209–29.

Rogoff, B. (1996). *Apprenticeship in Thinking*. Oxford: Oxford University Press.

Rogoff, B. and Lave, J. (eds) (1984). *Everyday Cognition: Its Development in Social Context*. Cambridge, MA: Harvard University Press.

Rose, N. (1996). Identity, genealogy, history. In S. Hall and P. Du Gay (eds), *Questions of Cultural Identity*. London: Sage.

Rubin, J. (1981). Study of cognitive processes in second language learning. *Applied Linguistics* 2/2: 117–31.

Rubin, J. (1987). Learner strategies: theoretical assumptions, research history and typology. In A. Wenden and J. Rubin (eds), *Learner Strategies in Language Learning*. Hemel Hempstead: Prentice Hall International.

Ruddick, S. (1996). Reason's 'femininity': a case for connected knowing. In N. Goldberger, J. Tarule, B. Clinchy and M. Belenky (eds), *Knowledge, Difference, and Power: Essays Inspired by Women's Ways of Knowing*. New York: Basic Books.

Ryan, G.W. and Bernard, H.R. (2000). Data management and analysis methods. In N.K. Denzin and Y.S. Lincoln (eds), *Handbook of Qualitative Research*. Thousand Oaks: Sage.

Said, E. (1978). *Orientalism*. New York: Pantheon Books.

Salaman, G. (1997). Culturing production. In P. Du Gay (ed.), *Production of Cultures/Cultures of Production*. London: Sage.

Sarangi, S. (1995). Culture. In J. Verschueren, J.O. Östman and J. Blomaert (eds), *Handbook of Pragmatics*. Amsterdam: Benjamins.

Schmidt, R. (1990). The role of consciousness in second language learning. *Applied Linguistics* 11/2: 129–58.

Schmidt, R., Boraie, D. and Kassabgy, O. (1996). Foreign language motivation: internal structure and external connections. In R. Oxford (ed.), *Language Learning Motivation: Pathways to the New Century*. Manoa: University of Hawaii Press.

Schmitt, N. (1997). Vocabulary learning strategies. In N. Schmitt and M. McCarthy (eds), *Vocabulary: Description, Acquisition and Pedagogy*. Cambridge: Cambridge University Press.

Schön, D.A. (1983). *The Reflective Practitioner: How Professionals Think in Action*. New York: Basic Books.

Schön, D.A. (1987). *Educating the Reflective Practitioner: Toward a New Design for Teaching and Learning in the Professions*. San Francisco: Jossey-Bass.

Schön, D.A. (1991). Concluding comments. In D.A. Schön (ed.), *The Reflective Turn: Case Studies in and on Educational Practice*. New York: Teachers College Press.

Schwienhorst, K. (1998). The 'third place': virtual reality applications for second language learning. *ReCALL* 10/1: 118–26.

Schwienhorst, K. (1999). Teacher autonomy in MOOs: supporting language teaching in collaborative virtual environments. *Journal of Information Technology for Teacher Education* 8/2: 199–214.

Schwienhorst, K. (2000). Virtual reality and learner autonomy in second language acquisition. Unpublished PhD thesis. Dublin: Trinity College Dublin.

Schwienhorst, K. (2002a). The state of VR: a meta-analysis of virtual reality tools in second language acquisition. *Computer-Assisted Language Learning* 15/3: 221–39.

Schwienhorst, K. (2002b). Why virtual, why environments? Implementing virtual reality concepts in computer-assisted language learning. *Simulation and Gaming* 33/2: 196–209.

Scollon, R. and Scollon, S.W. (1995). *Intercultural Communication: a Discourse Approach*. Oxford: Blackwell.

Serrano-Sampedro, I. (1997). An experience in helping teachers develop self-directed learning in the classroom. In H. Holec and I. Huttunen (eds), *Learner Autonomy in Modern Languages: Research and Development*. Strasbourg: Council of Europe.

Shamim, F. (1996). In or out of the action zone: location as a feature of interaction in large ESL classes in Pakistan. In K.M. Bailey and D. Nunan (eds), *Voices from the Language Classroom*. Cambridge: Cambridge University Press.

Shaw, J. (2002). Team-teaching as negotiating autonomy and shared understandings of what we are doing. Paper presented at the 4th Symposium of the Scientific Commission On Learner Autonomy in Language Learning, 13th AILA World Congress of Applied Linguistics, Singapore, 16–21 December.

Short, J., Williams, E. and Christie, B. (1976). *The Social Psychology of Telecommunications*. London: Wiley.

Shweder, R. and Levine, R. (eds). *Culture Theory: Essays on Mind, Self and Emotion*. Cambridge: Cambridge University Press.

Sinclair, B. (1997). Learner autonomy: the cross-cultural question. *IATEFL Issues* 139: 12–13.

Sinclair, B. (2000). Learner autonomy: the next phase. In B. Sinclair, I. McGrath and T. Lamb (eds), *Learner Autonomy, Teacher Autonomy: Future Directions*. Harlow: Longman.

Sinclair, B., McGrath, I. and Lamb, T. (eds) (2000). *Learner Autonomy, Teacher Autonomy: Future Directions*. Harlow: Longman.

Smith, R.C. (1994). Some thoughts on the formation of the JALT Learner Development N-SIG. *Learning Learning* 1/1. Accessed 7 March 2003 from http://www. miyazaki-mu.ac.jp/~hnicoll/learnerdev/LLE/Richard11E.html

Smith, R.C. (1996). Learning Japanese, from learners' points of view: affective and social factors in independent learning. Accessed 1 April 2003 from http://www. warwick.ac.uk/~elsdr/Independent_learning.pdf.

Smith, R.C. (1997). From Asian views of autonomy to revised views of Asia: Beyond Autonomy 2000. *Newsletter of the AILA Scientific Commission on Learner Autonomy in Language Learning* 3. Accessed 7 March 2003 from http://www.vuw. ac.nz/lals/LALLnews/news1997.html#asia.

Smith, R.C. (2000). Starting with ourselves: teacher–learner autonomy in language learning. In B. Sinclair, I. McGrath and T. Lamb (eds), *Learner Autonomy, Teacher Autonomy: Future Directions*. Harlow: Longman.

Smith, R.C. (2001). Group work for autonomy in Asia: insights from teacher-research. *AILA Review* 15: 70–81.

Smith, R.C. and Barfield, A. (2001). Interconnections: Learner autonomy, teacher autonomy. *Learning Learning* 8/1. Accessed 10 March 2003 from http://www. miyazaki-mu.ac.jp/~hnicoll/learnerdev/LLE/8.1/smithE.html

Smyth, J. (1997). Teaching and social policy: images of teaching for democratic change. In B.J. Biddle, T.L. Good and I.F. Goodson (eds), *International Handbook of Teachers and Teaching*. Dordrecht: Kluwer.

Spack, R. (1997). The rhetorical construction of multilingual students. *TESOL Quarterly* 31/4: 765–74.

Sperber, D. (1982). *On Anthropological Knowledge*. Cambridge: Cambridge University Press.

Sri Lanka Ministry of Education. (1984). *English for Me*. Colombo: Sri Lanka Government Press.

Stein, P. (1998). Reconfiguring the past and the present: performing literacy histories in a Johannesburg classroom. *TESOL Quarterly* 32/3: 517–28.

Stevens, W. (1972). Idea of order at Key West. In H. Stevens (ed.), *The Palm at the End of the Mind: Selected Poems and a Play by Wallace Stevens*. New York: Vintage.

Stokes, M. (1994). Turkish arabesk and the city: urban popular culture as spatial practice. In A.S. Ahmed and H. Donnan (eds), *Islam, Globalisation and Postmodernity*. London: Routledge.

Sullivan, P. (2000). Playfulness as mediation in communicative language teaching in a Vietnamese classroom. In J.P. Lantolf (ed.), *Sociocultural Theory and Second Language Learning*. Oxford: Oxford University Press.

Swales, J. (1990). *Genre Analysis*. Cambridge: Cambridge University Press.

Swidler, A. (1986). Culture in action: symbols and strategies. *American Sociological Review* 51: 273–86.

Takahashi, E. (1998). Language development in social interaction: a longitudinal study of a Japanese FLES program from a Vygotskyan approach. *Foreign Language Annals* 31/3: 392–406.

Tharp, R.G. and Gallimore, R. (1988). *Rousing Minds to Life: Teaching, Learning, and Schooling in Social Context.* Cambridge: Cambridge University Press.

Thavenius, C. (1999). Teacher autonomy for learner autonomy. In S. Cotterall and D. Crabbe (eds), *Learner Autonomy in Language Learning: Defining the Field and Effecting Change.* Frankfurt am Main: Lang.

Thomsen, H. (2000). Learners' favoured activities in the autonomous classroom. In D. Little, L. Dam, and J. Timmer (eds), *Focus on Learning Rather Than Teaching: Why and How?* Dublin: Trinity College, Centre for Language and Communication Studies.

Thomsen, H. and Gabrielsen, G. (1991). *New Classroom Practices in Foreign Language Teaching: Co-operative Teaching-Learning.* Copenhagen: Danmarks Lærerhøjskole.

Tom, A. (1985). Inquiring into inquiry oriented teacher education. *Journal of Teacher Education* 36/5: 35–44.

Tong, W.M. (2002). 'Filial piety': A barrier or a resource? A qualitative case study of English classroom culture in Hong Kong secondary schools. Unpublished PhD thesis. Canterbury: Canterbury Christ Church University College, Department of Language Studies.

Toohey, K. (1996). Learning English as a second language in kindergarten: A community of practice perspective. *The Canadian Modern Language Review* 52/4: 549–76.

Toohey, K. (1998). "Breaking them up, taking them away": ESL students in grade one. *TESOL Quarterly* 32/1: 61–84.

Toohey, K. (2000). *Learning English at School: Identity, Social Relations and Classroom Practice.* Clevedon: Multilingual Matters.

Toohey, K. (2001). Disputes in child L2 learning. *TESOL Quarterly* 35/2: 257–78.

Trappes-Lomax, H. and McGrath, I. (eds) (1999). *Theory in Language Teacher Education.* Harlow: Longman.

Tremblay, P. and Gardner, R. (1995). Expanding the motivation construct in language learning. *Modern Language Journal* 79: 505–20.

Triandis, H.C. (1995). *Individualism and Collectivism.* Boulder: Westview Press.

Tudor, I. (1997). *Learner-centredness as Language Education.* Cambridge: Cambridge University Press.

Usher, R. and Edwards, R. (1994). *Postmodernism and Education: Different Voices, Different Worlds.* London: Routledge.

Ushioda, E. (1996). *Learner Autonomy 5: the Role of Motivation.* Dublin: Authentik.

Ushioda, E. (2000). Tandem language learning via e-mail: From motivation to autonomy. *ReCALL* 12/2: 121–8.

van Lier, L. (1996). *Interaction in the Language Curriculum: Awareness, Autonomy, and Authenticity.* Harlow: Longman.

van Lier, L. (2000). From input to affordance: social-interactive learning from an ecological perspective. In J.P. Lantolf (ed.), *Sociocultural Theory and Second Language Learning.* Oxford: Oxford University Press.

van Manen, M. (1990). *Researching Lived Experience: Human Science for an Action Sensitive Pedagogy.* London: State University of New York Press.

Vieira, F. (1997). Teacher development for learner autonomy: Ideas from an in-service teacher training project. *ELT News* (The British Council and Teachers of English in Austria) 33: 61–7.

Vieira, F. (1998). *Pedagogia para a autonomia na aula de língua estrangeira.* Braga: University of Minho.

Vieira, F. (1999a). Pedagogy for autonomy: teacher development and pedagogical experimentation – an in-service teacher training project. In S. Cotterall and D. Crabbe (eds), *Learner Autonomy in Language Learning: Defining the Field and Effecting Change*. Frankfurt am Main: Lang.

Vieira, F. (ed.) (1999b). *Cadernos 1. GT-PA*. Braga: University of Minho.

Vieira, F. (2000). Teacher development towards a pedagogy for autonomy in the foreign language classroom. In R. Ribé (ed.), *Developing Learner Autonomy in Foreign Language Learning*. Barcelona: University of Barcelona.

Vieira, F. (ed.) (2001a). *Cadernos 2. GT-PA*. Braga: University of Minho.

Vieira, F. (2001b). Planificar e avaliar actividades centradas na competência de aprendizagem. In F. Vieira (ed.), *Cadernos 2. GT-PA*. Braga: University of Minho.

Vieira, F. (2001c). Pedagogia para a autonomia – o papel do professor na construção do saber e na renovação das práticas. *Revista Inovação* 14/1–2: 169–90.

Vieira, F. (2002). Learner autonomy and teacher development: an introduction to GT-PA as a learning community. In F. Vieira, M.A. Moreira, I. Barbosa and M. Paiva (eds), *Pedagogy for Autonomy and English Learning: Proceedings of the Working Group – Pedagogy for Autonomy*. Braga: University of Minho.

Vieira, F., Moreira, M.A., Barbosa, I. and Paiva, M. (eds). (2002). *Pedagogy for Autonomy and English Learning: Proceedings of the Working Group – Pedagogy for Autonomy*. Braga: University of Minho.

Voller, P, (1997). Does the teacher have a role in autonomous language learning? In P. Benson and P. Voller (eds), *Autonomy and Independence in Language Learning*. London: Longman.

Vygotsky, L.S. (1978). *Mind in Society: the Development of Higher Psychological Processes*. Cambridge, MA: Harvard University Press.

Vygotsky, L. (1979). Consciousness as a problem of psychology of behavior. *Soviet Psychology* 17: 29–30.

Waite, S. (1994). Low-resourced self-access with EAP in the developing world: the great enabler? *ELT Journal* 48/3: 233–42.

Wallace, M.J. (1991). *Training Foreign Language Teachers: a Reflective Approach*. Cambridge: Cambridge University Press.

Wallace, M.J. (1998). *Action Research for Language Teachers*. Cambridge: Cambridge University Press.

Ward, S.A. (1980). *Dippidito: Teacher's Book*. London: Longman.

Watkins, D.A. (1996). Learning theories and approaches to research: a cross-cultural perspective. In D.A. Watkins and J.B. Biggs (eds), *The Chinese Learner: Cultural, Psychological and Contextual Influences*. Hong Kong: Comparative Education Research Centre, University of Hong Kong/Australian Council of Educational Research.

Watkins, D.A. and Biggs, J.B. (eds). (1996). *The Chinese Learner: Cultural, Psychological and Contextual Influences*. Hong Kong: Comparative Education Research Center, University of Hong Kong/Australian Council of Educational Research.

Weber, M (1921/1978). *Economy and Society*. Berkeley: University of California Press.

Weedon, C. (1996). *Feminist Practice and Poststructuralist Theory*. Oxford: Blackwell.

Wenden, A. (1986). What do second language learners know about their language learning? A second look at retrospective accounts. *Applied Linguistics* 7/2: 186–205.

Wenden, A. (1991). *Learner Strategies for Learner Autonomy*. Englewood Cliffs: Prentice Hall.

284 *References*

Wenden, A. (2002). Learner development in language learning. *Applied Linguistics* 23/1: 32–55.

Wenden, A. and Rubin, J. (1987). *Learner Strategies in Language Learning*. Hemel Hempstead: Prentice-Hall International.

Wenger, E. (1998). *Communities of Practice: Learning, Meaning and Identity*. Cambridge: Cambridge University Press.

Wenger, E., McDermott, R. and Snyder, W.M. (2002). *Cultivating Communities of Practice*. Cambridge, MA: Harvard Business School Press.

Wharton, G. (2000). Language learning strategy use of bilingual foreign language learners in Singapore. *Language Learning* 50/2: 203–43.

Widdowson, H.G. (1987). The roles of teacher and learner. *ELT Journal* 41/2: 83–8.

Widdowson, H.G. (1990). *Aspects of Language Teaching*. Oxford: Oxford University Press.

Wigfield, A., Eccles, J.S., and Rodriguez, D. (1998). The development of children's motivation in school contexts. In A. Iran-Nejad (ed.), *Review of Research in Education*. Washington, DC: American Educational Research Association.

Willett, J. (1995). Becoming first graders in an L2: an ethnographic study of language socialization. *TESOL Quarterly* 29/3: 473–504.

Willis, P. (1977). *Learning to Labour*. London: Saxon House.

Wong Fillmore, L. (1979). Individual differences in second language acquisition. In C. Fillmore, D. Kempler, and W. Wang (eds), *Individual Differences in Language Ability and Language Behavior*. New York: Academic Press.

Wright, S. (ed.) (1994). *Anthropology of Organizations*. London: Routledge.

Wright, T. (1987). *Roles of Teachers and Learners*. Oxford: Oxford University Press.

Yang, N.-D. (1992). Second language learners' beliefs about language learning and their use of learning strategies: a study of college students of English in Taiwan. Unpublished doctoral dissertation. Austin: University of Texas at Austin.

Yang, N.-D. (1999). The relationship between EFL learner's beliefs and learning strategy use. *System* 27/4: 515–35.

Young, D.J. (ed.) (1998). *Affect in L2 Learning: a Practical Guide to Dealing with Learner Anxieties*. Englewood Cliffs: Prentice Hall.

Zeichner, K. and Tabachnick, R. (1991). Reflections on reflective teaching. In R. Tabachnick and K. Zeichner (eds), *Issues and Practices in Inquiry-oriented Teacher Education*. London: Falmer Press.

Zeichner, K.M. (1994). Research on teacher thinking and different views of reflective practice in teaching and teacher education. In I. Carlgren, G. Handal and S. Vaage (eds), *Teachers' Minds and Actions: Research on Teachers' Thinking and Practice*. London: Falmer Press.

Zimmerman, B.J. and Martinez-Pons, M. (1988). Construct validation of a strategy model of self-regulated learning. *Journal of Educational Psychology* 80: 284–90.

Zimmerman, B.J. and Martinez-Pons, M. (1990). Student differences in self-regulated learning: relating grade, sex, and giftedness to self-efficacy and strategy use. *Journal of Educational Psychology* 82: 51–9.

Zumthor, P. (1990). *Oral Poetry: an Introduction*. Minneapolis: University of Minnesota Press.

Index

NB: **bold** page numbers indicate chapter or section headings.